The Ethiopian.

CW01091590

The Peoples of Africa

General Editor: Parker Shipton

This series is about the African peoples from their origins to the present day. Drawing on archaeological, historical and anthropological evidence, each volume looks at a particular group's culture, society and history.

Approaches will vary according to the subject and the nature of evidence. Volumes concerned mainly with culturally discrete peoples will be complemented by accounts which focus primarily on the historical period, on African nations and contemporary peoples. The overall aim of the series is to offer a comprehensive and up-to-date picture of the African peoples, in books which are at once scholarly and accessible.

Already published

The Shona and their Neighbours*
David Beach

The Berbers*
Michael Brett and Elizabeth Fentress

The Peoples of the Middle Niger*
Rod McIntosh

The Ethiopians: A History*
Richard Pankhurst

The Egyptians*
Barbara Watterson

In preparation

The Swahili
Mark Horton and John Middleton

The Peoples of Kenya
John Middleton

*Indicates title commissioned under the general editorship of Dr David Phillipson of Gonville and Caius College, Cambridge

The Ethiopians

A History

Richard Pankhurst

The right of Richard Pankhurst to be identified as author of this work has been asserted in accordance with the Copyright, Designs and Patents Act 1988.

First published 1998
First published in paperback 2001

2 4 6 8 10 9 7 5 3 1

Blackwell Publishers Ltd
108 Cowley Road
Oxford OX4 1JF
UK

Blackwell Publishers Inc.
350 Main Street
Malden, Massachusetts 02148
USA

British Library Cataloguing in Publication Data

A CIP catalogue record for this book is available from the British Library.

Library of Congress Cataloging-in-Publication Data

Pankhurst, Richard.
  The Ethiopians : a history / Richard Pankhurst.
    p. cm. — (The peoples of Africa)
  Includes bibliographical references and index.
  ISBN 0-631-18468-6 (hdbk) 0-631-22493-9 (pbk)
  1. Ethiopia—History. 2. Ethnology—Ethiopia. I. Title. II. Series.
  DT381 .P39 2000
  963—dc21
                                     98-009224

Typeset in 11 on 12½ pt Sabon
By Best-set Typesetter Ltd, Hong Kong
Printed in Great Britain by MPG Books Ltd, Bodmin, Cornwall

This book is printed on acid-free paper

For Henok Alula

Contents

Plates

Maps

Series Editor's Preface

The Peoples of Africa series has been designed to provide reliable and up-to-date accounts of what is known about the development and antecedents of the diverse populations in that continent, and about their relations with others near or far. It is hoped that the series will enjoy a wide readership in many parts of the world, including Africa itself.

This series has counterparts relating to other continents, and it may be appropriate to discuss here aspects specific to a series dealing with Africa. Africa is a continent of contrasts – not only in its physical environments and in the life-styles and economies of its peoples, but also in the extent to which writing has influenced its development and recorded its past. Parts of Egypt have one of the longest histories of literacy in the world; on the other hand, some interior regions – notably in south-central Africa – remained wholly unrecorded in writing up to a hundred years ago. The historical significance of this contrast has been both varied and far-reaching.

The books in this series variously combine perspectives of archaeology, anthropology and history. It will be obvious that someone studying the past of a non-literate people will adopt techniques very different from those that are at the disposal of historians who can base their work on written sources. The relevance of archaeology is by no means restricted to non-literate contexts, but it is clearly a pre-eminent means of illustrating even the comparatively recent past in those parts of Africa where writing was not employed. It may be less obvious to those not familiar with Africa that non-literate peoples were by no means ignorant of their past, traditional knowledge about which was often preserved and orally transmitted through several generations, albeit not infrequently subject to change – conscious or unconscious – in the light of contemporary circumstances. Further clues about the non-literate African past can be obtained from studying the distributions and interrelationships of modern languages. Each of these approaches presents its own problems, and has its own potential to illustrate particular aspects of the past.

Each volume in the series is a specialist's attempt to condense, and to order, a large and diverse body of scholarship on a way of life. The series describes both changes and continuities, relating historic processes occurring at all levels of scale, from the domestic to the intercontinental. The changing definitions and self-definitions of peoples, in the light of new communications and sensitive ethnic and national politics, pose difficult problems for theory and description. More often than not it is debatable where, and when, one population ends and another begins. Situating African societies flexibly in time and space, and taking account of continual movements, anomalies, and complexities in their cultures, these volumes attempt to convey some sense of the continent's great variety, to dispel myths about its essential character or its plight, and to introduce fresh and thoughtful perspectives on its role in human history.

Dr David Phillipson
PARKER SHIPTON

Table of Dates

Prehistoric Period (discoveries)
Austrapithecus teeth and bones	4.4 million years
Lucy, or Berkenesh, skeleton	3.2 million years
Man-made tools	2.5 million years
Possible arrival of wheat and barley	8,000 BC

Period of the Pharoahs
Puntite myrrh in Egypt	*c.*3546–3190 BC
Puntite slave in Egypt	*c.*3100–2965 BC
Egyptian fleet sent to Punt	*c.*2985–2946 BC
Hatshepsut's expedition to Punt	*c.*1501–1479 BC
Ramses III's expedition to Punt	*c.*1198–1167 BC

Pre-Aksumite Period
Beginning of contacts across Red Sea	*c.*2000–1000 BC?
King Solomon	*c.*974–932 BC
Founding of Yéha	*c.*700–500 BC
Ptolemaic expeditions	*c.*305–221 BC

Aksumite Period
Rise of Aksumite civilization	*c.*300 BC
Founding of Aksum	*c.*100 BC–100 AD
First minting of coins	*c.*270 AD
Ezana's Christian conversion	*c.*330 AD
Kaléb's expedition to Arabia	*c.*525 AD
Arrival of first Muslims	*c.*615 AD
Decline of Akum	*c.*800–1000

Medieval Period

Zagwé dynasty	*c.*1137–1270 AD
'Solomonic restoration'	*c.*1270
Amda Seyon	1312–42
Yeshaq	1412–27
Zar'a Ya'qob	1433–68
Ba'eda Maryam	1468–78
Lebna Dengel	1508–40
Ahmad (Gragn)'s first campaign	1527
Portuguese intervention	1541
Ahmad (Gragn)'s death	1543
Galawdéwos	1540–59
Sarsa Dengel	1563–97
Susneyos	1606–32

Gondar Period

Founding of city as capital	1636
Fasiladas	1632–67
Iyasu I	1681–1706
Bakaffa	1721–30
Iyasu II	1730–55

Modern Period

Téwodros II	1855–68
Maqdala battle	1868
Menilek (king of Shawa)	1865–89
Yohannes IV	1871–89
Gundat and Gura battles	1875, 1876
Dogali battle	1887
Matamma battle	1889
Menilek II (emperor)	1889–1913
Wechalé treaty	1889
Adwa battle	1896
Lej Iyasu	1913–16
Zawditu	1916–30
Haile Sellassie's coronation	1930
Italian Fascist invasion	1935–6
Liberation from Italian rule	1940–1
Abortive coup d'état	1960
Revolution	1974
Victory of EPRDF	1990

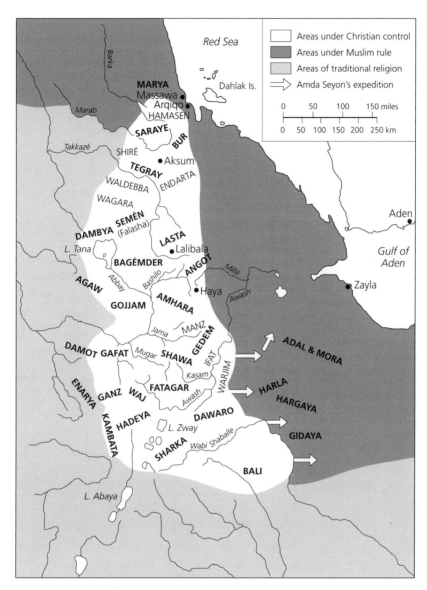

Map 1   *The Ethiopian Christian Empire at the time of Amda Seyon
(1314–1344).*

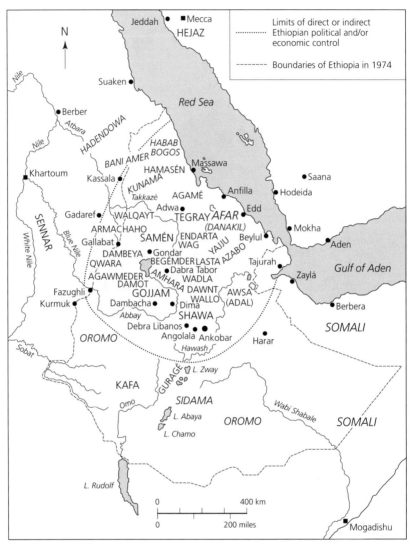

Map 2   *Ethiopia in the first half of the nineteenth century.*

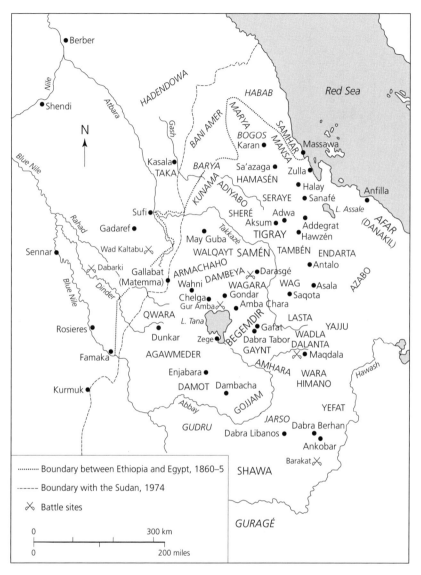

Map 3   Ethiopia at the time of Emperor Téwodros II (1855–1868).

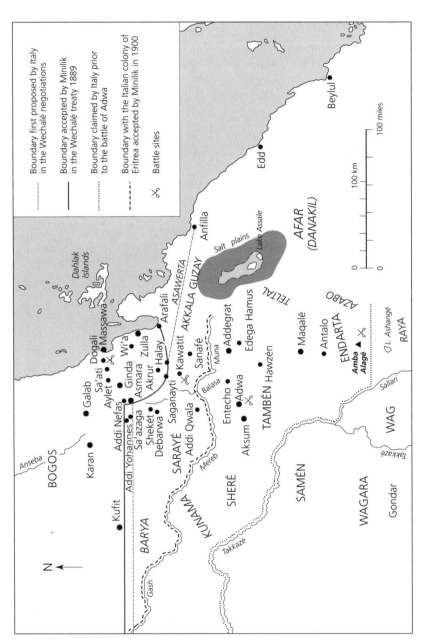

Map 4 Frontier changes with the Italians, 1889–1900.

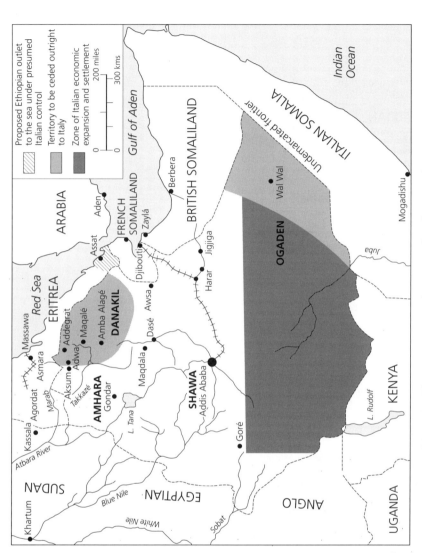

Map 5 *The Hoare–Laval proposals of December 1935.*

Proposed Ethiopian outlet to the sea under presumed Italian control

Territory to be ceded outright to Italy

Zone of Italian economic expansion and settlement

0   200 miles

0   300 kms

Indian Ocean

ITALIAN SOMALIA

Undemarcated frontier

Mogadishu

Gulf of Aden

BRITISH SOMALILAND

Berbera

Wal Wal

OGADEN

Juba

ARABIA

Aden

FRENCH SOMALILAND

Zaylá

Jigjiga

Harar

Djibouti

Awsa

Assat

Red Sea

ERITREA

Massawa

Asmara

Addegrat

Maqalé

Amba Alagé

DANAKIL

Dasé

Adwa

Aksum

Marab

Takkazé

Maqdala

AMHARA

Gondar

L. Tana

SHAWA

Addis Ababa

L. Rudolf

KENYA

Agordat

Kassala

Khartum

SUDAN

Atbara River

Blue Nile

EGYPTIAN

White Nile

Sobat

Goré

ANGLO

UGANDA

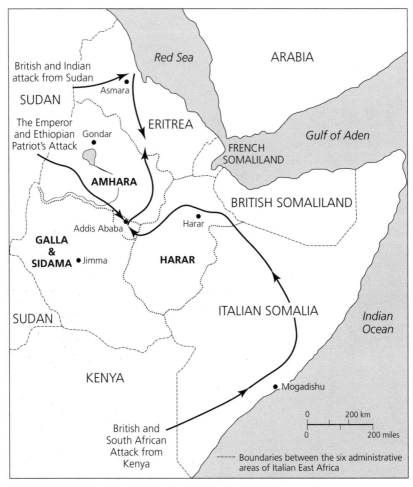

Map 6   *The Ethiopian Liberation Campaign, 1941.*

1

Prehistory and Geography

Cradle of Humanity

Recent research in paleoanthropology has given rise to the belief that the Ethiopian section of the African Rift Valley was the original home of humanity. An African location for the beginnings of human existence accords well with the speculations of Charles Darwin. Writing, it will be recalled, at a time when as yet very little fossil evidence was available, he declared it probable that Africa was 'formerly inhabited by extinct apes allied to the gorilla and chimpanzee', that these were 'man's nearest allies', and that it was 'more probable that our early progenitors lived on the African continent than elsewhere'.

Paleoanthropology in Ethiopia is still in its infancy. It began, for practical purposes, with the discovery in 1963 of the remarkably extensive prehistoric stone tool 'factory' at Melka-Konturé, 55 miles south of Addis Ababa. Since that time, however, paleoanthropological researches in the country have made immense, and very remarkable, strides.

The most important evidence for the belief that the Ethiopian Rift Valley was the first home of humanity was a spectacular discovery, which took place at Hadar, in the Afar region of the middle Awash Valley, in 1974. This was the finding by an American-French team, led by Donald Johanson, of Chicago University, of the remains of the oldest known hominid, i.e. erect-walking human ancestor. Known to scientists by the Hadar classification AL 288-1, and believed to be 3.2 million years old, the bones constitute a little over half the skeleton of a fully-grown woman now generally known internationally, after the

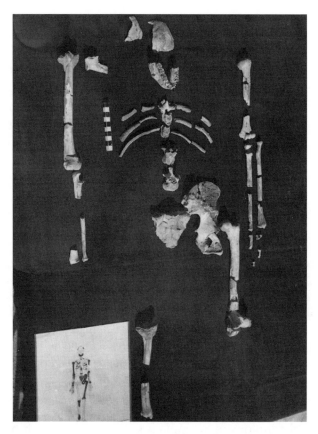

Plate 1   Lucy, or Denkenesh: bones of the first known hominid, discovered in the Awash area of south-east Ethiopia. Photo: Ethiopian Ministry of Culture.

Beatles' song, as Lucy, but spoken of in Ethiopia as Denqenesh or Berqenash. Paleoanthropologists, however, call her *Australopithecus afarensis*. The first of these words, it will be recalled, means 'Southern Ape', while the second alludes to the Afar area, where the discovery was made.

Lucy's skeleton is carefully preserved in Addis Ababa, where an exact plaster cast is also on permanent display in the National Museum. She stood no more than three and a half feet off the ground, and probably weighed only sixty pounds. She had a tiny brain, like an ape, but walked erect. Her pelvis and leg bones were, on the other hand, almost identical to those of modern humans.

Her V-shaped jaw was likewise similar to that of our own species, and differed markedly from the box-like parallel tooth formation found on apes. Generally classified as a hominid, because she walked erect, she seems, however, as Johanson declared, to have been 'a transitional one', with 'ongoing riddles' about many of her features. Her discovery was of immense scientific significance, the more so as her skeleton seemed to indicate that humanity, contrary to earlier belief, began to walk before it evolved enlarged brains.[1]

Subsequent research, carried out by Johanson and his team at Hadar in 1976–7, was scarcely less memorable. It resulted in the discovery of man-made stone tools, dating back around 2.5 million years. These tools were at that time the oldest known anywhere in the world. These were much older than for example Mary Leakey's justly famous finds of stone tools in the Olduvai Gorge, Tanzania, which are relatively recent, being only 1.8 million years old.

A no less important discovery was made at Aramis, in the Afar area 45 miles south of Hadar, in December 1992. The work was carried out by a joint American–Japanese–Ethiopian team of paleoanthropologists, led by Professor Timothy White, of the University of California at Berkeley, Dr Gen Suwa of Tokyo University, and Dr Berhane Asfaw, of the Ethiopian Government's Paleoanthropology Laboratory in Addis Ababa. Working in a 4.4 million year-old sediment they found fifty-odd fragments of teeth, arm bones, and parts of the skull and jaw, of seventeen to twenty individuals, constituting an entirely new species of primates. These were given the scientific name *Australopithecus*, or Southern Ape, *ramidus*, a word which in the local Afar language means Root, or Ancestry.

These prehistoric inhabitants of what is now eastern Ethiopia, though significantly larger than Lucy, were much smaller than modern humans. Little over four feet high, they probably weighed no more than 65 pounds. Scholars at the time of writing have not found any hip or leg bones to establish beyond all doubt that members of this newly discovered species walked upright, but their arms seem to have been far too small for swinging, like monkeys, through the trees. Though otherwise ape-like, the forward opening for the spine at the base of their skulls, and their

[1] Johanson and Edey, 1981, p. 357.

teeth, which are much smaller than those of apes, are reminiscent of the hominids of later times. The bones of *Australopithecus ramidus* were in fact so perfectly positioned between those of humans and apes that the species has been said to constitute Darwin's 'missing link', and have led Timothy White to observe, 'Darwin was right: humans evolved from the African ape'. Statements suggesting the existence of a single 'missing link', however, deserve qualification. The evolution of humanity was probably a gradual transition, as a result of which some fossils will display certain more 'ape-like' features, while others will have features more resembling our own, more 'advanced' species.

Paleoanthropologists speculate that if members of the *Australopithecus ramidus* species walked erect, as seems most likely, they could well have made use of simple tools, as this would have been easier if these hominids were not moving on their knuckles. They could likewise have developed an enlarged brain, which would probably have evolved as a result of the use of tools. Walking on two legs would also have given them an advantage over their predecessors, in being able to carry in their arms both infants and food. Scientists speculate further that these early beings probably still slept for safety in trees, but in the daytime were equally at home on the ground. Their habitat, it is believed, was a thickly wooded plain, inhabited by monkeys, saber-toothed cats, antelopes, hyenas, wild pigs, bears, bats and sundry rodents. It is further believed that members of the species were predominantly vegetarians, but may also have scavenged meat, and perhaps banded together to hunt small animals. Though walking upright like humans the mental abilities of the species may not have been very different from that of apes. It is thought that they may have used stone tools, but more probably temporary tools fashioned of sticks and branches.

Subsequent investigations, carried out by American and Ethiopian paleoanthropologists in the Gona Valley, south-west of Hadar, between 1992 and 1994, led to the discovery of several thousand stone tools thought to be between 2.6 and 2.5 million years old. These are assumed to be the oldest such tools thus far found. Similar finds, dating from roughly the same time, were also made in the Omo Valley of southern Ethiopia.

The earliest stone tools thus far dated are thought to have been produced, it will be noticed, over half a millennium after the time of Lucy, and almost two millennia after that of Ethiopia's supposed 'missing link'. One reason for this may be that research in the region is still at an early stage, and that the dating of stone tools, which have as far as is known changed little over the centuries, can, unlike that of human fossils, be carried out only through the analysis of the geological strata in which they are found. It is, however, anticipated by paleoanthropologists that earlier hoards of stone tools may yet be uncovered.

Archaeological research in recent years has revealed the existence in Ethiopia of many Later Stone Age paintings, and a few bas reliefs, some of the older dating back perhaps to around 10,000 BC. Rock paintings have been found at numerous sites in Harargé, Gamu Gofa, Tegray, as well as further north in Eritrea. Most of these pictures are devoted to the representation of animals, and pastoral activity. Human themes are also found. Some depict the milking of cattle, others the use of bows and arrows, spears and shields. Animals painted include both humped and humpless cattle, as well as goats, elephants, and lions.

Archaeological investigation of early foodstuffs in Ethiopia is still in its early stages. Some authors have argued that grass seeds, including both sorghum and the cereal *tef* (*Eragrostis tef*), are native to Ethiopia, but others assume that they were imported, mainly from the Middle East. Desmond Clark has postulated that wheat and barley may have come down the Nile to the Ethiopian region from Egypt towards the end of the Pleistocene period, i.e. prior to 10,000 years ago, or at least in the second or third millennium BC. Others have argued that these crops may have been introduced into the region by the Egyptian expeditions to the Land of Punt, described in the following chapter. The definitive prehistoric context of these plants, as of sorghum, finger-millet, and many others, has still to be finally established. Uncertainty also exists about the prehistory of the false banana (*Musa ensete*), which has apparently long been a staple crop of south-west Ethiopia. Its cultivation, some believe, may date back to Pleistocene times.

Research on Ethiopian prehistory is still, it should be emphasized, too recent to allow of more than tentative conclusions. Investigations in the next few decades may well bring about significant changes in our view of the region's past. Enough is, however, already known to establish that the Afar area was one of the earliest, if not, sometimes claimed, in fact the oldest home of humanity. It is no less apparent that Ethiopia enjoys an historic position in the development of cereal cultivation, and that the country is the site of numerous cave paintings, which provide invaluable, but still insufficiently analysed, glimpses of pastoral, hunting, and other activity of the past.

The Geographical Setting

The Ethiopian region, the subject of this book, lies on the eastern side of Africa. Situated almost centrally between the Tropic of Cancer and the Equator, the region constitutes in a sense the heart of the Horn of Africa, and covers an area of well over a million square kilometres. The region, one of the largest on the African continent, thus covers an area as great as France and Spain combined.

The region, which is largely mountainous, but embraces the Blue Nile and its tributaries, as well as a major stretch of the African Rift Valley, is one of immense geographical, and other, contrasts. High mountains, which in the Samén area tower more than 4,600 metres above sea level, give way to flat lowlands, with the Afar, or Dankali, depression sinking below it.

Temperature is no less varied. It ranges from the icy cold of the high mountains, with frost, and in places even snow, through the temperate highlands – the site of most of Ethiopia's historic settlements – to the torrid lowlands. The neighbouring Red Sea and Gulf of Aden ports, upon which the area is dependent for much of its foreign trade, are reputedly among the hottest places in the world.

Differences in rainfall are no less considerable. Torrential downpours in the highlands contrast with limited precipitation in the parched, almost waterless lowlands. Such variations led to considerable differences in vegetation: tropical jungles in the west, fertile plateaux, suitable for cereal cultivation, in the central highlands, and scrublands, verging on deserts, on the eastern and southern periphery.

These climatic differences led in turn to major differences in human activity and life-style. The world's three principal types of traditional economic activity – agriculture, pastoralism, and hunting – were all represented in the region – as were handicraft workers. The great northern and central highlands were inhabited by subsistence farmers, who were unique in Africa south of the

Sahara in that they practised plough cultivation. The southern highlands were occupied, on the other hand, by peasants cultivating the local plant *musa ensete*, or false banana, and various root crops.

The highlands, as a whole, were major centres of plant domestication and crop diversity, where the cereal *teff* (*Eragrostis teff*), the oil-seed *nug* (*Guizotia abyssinica*) and perhaps finger-millet, or *Eleusine corocana*, locally known as *dagusa*, were first domesticated. Other indigenous plants included the narcotic *chat* (*Catha edulis*), and, it may be argued, also coffee. Several cereals, and legumes, imported from the Middle East underwent genetic variation in Ethiopia, where they exist today as endemic, or unique, forms, which would seem to suggest a very long period of cultivation, and adaptation.

The lowlands, which were no less extensive than the highlands, were, by contrast, occupied by pastoralists, with large herds of cattle in the better watered areas, and the redoubtable camel in those of lower precipitation. Forest land, and lands bordering rivers and lakes, were again different in that they were the abode of hunters of monkeys, hippopotami, crocodiles, and other animals, the eating of whose flesh was rejected by the peoples of other areas. The arid coastal plains represented yet another economic and cultural area, in which the inhabitants included fishermen and sailers of dhows.

Linguistic and Religious Diversity

The mountainous character of much of the region, with its innumerable ravines, rivers and flash-torrents, rendered communications within the country difficult, and, during the rainy season, virtually impossible. This resulted in the perpetuation of many different ethnic, linguistic, and religious groups, which, though often significantly interacting, were over the millennia never fully assimilated. These varied peoples, whose precise geographical location in not a few cases changed considerably, as well as expanding or contracting, over the centuries, belonged to four main linguistic groups, currently known as Semitic, Cushitic, and, outside the focus of this book, the Omotic and Nilo-Saharan.

The Semitic languages are currently located mainly in the north and centre of the present-day Ethiopian state. They are represented there by the ancient ecclesiastical language, Geʿez, and three currently spoken tongues: Tegrenya, in most of the north; Tegray, in a strip of territory near the Red Sea coast, and Amharic, more widely, in the centre, and north-west, of the country. Semitic languages, however, also exist in pockets to the south and east. A group of Guragé languages are thus found in the south, and Adaré, also known as Harari, and Argobba, both in the south-east. The former is unusual in being traditionally spoken only within a single settlement – the walled city of Harar.

The Cushitic languages predominate today in the south of the country. They consist of the widely diffused Oromifa, earlier referred to as Galla or Afan Oromo; Sidamo, Hadeya, Kambata, and Darasa, all spoken in closely circumscribed areas in the south-west; and Somali, in an extensive area to the south-east. Cushitic languages, however, also exist in the north, where there are pockets of Agaw, Béja, Qemant and Saho, as well as Afar, or Dankali, which occupies a wide area in the north-east.

The Omotic languages are clustered in the south-west. They include Wolayta, earlier more often called Walamo, besides Gamu-Gofa, Kullo-Konta, Zayza-Zargula, Kafa-Mocha, Gemerra, and Maji, all to the west, and Ari, to the east.

The Nilo-Saharan languages are found on Ethiopia's western periphery. They include Kunama in the far north, Gumuz and Berta, and further south, Anuak and Nuer, the diffusion of which stretches far over into Sudan, as well as Surma, Me'en, and Masango.

The religious pattern, in which all three of the world's great monolithic religions are represented, was also varied.

The highlands and lowlands were characterized by a great religious divide. The northern and central highlands were thus inhabited largely by Ethiopian Orthodox Christians, for the most part peasants, whose governors and imperial rulers were traditionally also of that faith.

The lowlands, particularly to the east, including the ports, and the great commercial centre of Harar, were by contrast populated by Muslims. The latter were also of paramount importance as travelling or resident merchants and craftsmen, even in otherwise Christian areas or towns.

Falashas, members of a small Judaic group, also known as Béta Esra'él, were scattered in the north, and north-west, of the country. They served largely as craftsmen, mainly blacksmiths, weavers, and potters, but also as builders. These occupations, entirely irrespective of their practioners' religious affiliation, were traditionally mainly held in low repute.

Numerically far more important than the latter were the adherents of local animist religions, which preponderated in an extensive, but gradually contracting, area of the south and west. Most such faiths doubtless predated the coming of the monotheistic religions, but were in many instances unable to withstand the superior power of the adherents of these religions.

The religious scene was, however, far more complex than the above words may suggest. Voluntary, or forcible, conversion from one faith to another over the centuries was not infrequent; dynastic and other marriages in many cases transcended religious divisions; and, perhaps even more importantly, the beliefs and practices of the various religions in many areas significantly influenced each other.

Foreign Contacts

Despite its immense internal difficulties of communication, the Ethiopian region, because of its geographical position relatively near the Red Sea, and Gulf of Aden coast, enjoyed significantly close economic and cultural contacts with many other parts of the world. Not a few such contacts dated back to ancient or medieval times.

The region's relations with Egypt and the Nile Valley began as early as the time of the Pharaohs, who despatched numerous expeditions down the Red Sea in quest of myrrh, and other local products. Many centuries later, after the coming of Christianity to Ethiopia in the early fourth century, Coptic Egypt was the land from which Ethiopian Christendom obtained most of its patriarchs. Contacts between the two countries also owed much to a frequent exchange of embassies, primed largely by Egyptian fears that the rulers of Ethiopia might interfere with the flow of the Nile, then considered so important for the welfare of Egypt. Ethiopia was subsequently deeply affected by Egypt's modernization, and expansion into Sudan, which, in the nineteenth century, almost inevitably brought the two countries into deadly military conflict.

Contacts with parts of inner Africa, most notably Meroe, were also of considerable antiquity. One of Ethiopia's principal import-export trade routes likewise later ran westwards to Sudan, and, through it, to Egypt and the Mediterranean world. Relations, as is customary among neighbours, were, however, not always cordial, and on occasion led to war. This happened in ancient and medieval times, as well as in the nineteenth century.

Economic, religious, and cultural contacts across the Red Sea, and Gulf of Aden, were particularly important. Much of the Ethiopian region's sea-borne import-export trade for centuries passed to or from Arabia, and was based on such Arab ports as Aden or Jeddah. Many Yamanis moreover settled in the Ethiopian region, where numerous Arab merchants did business. Not a few Ethiopian Muslims travelled on pilgrimage to Mecca, and even larger numbers of Christians and Animists were taken across the sea as slaves.

Relations with ancient Israel, Palestine, and the Judaic world were also significant. They found early expression in the legendary account of the Ethiopian Queen of Sheba's visit to King Solomon, as well as, it may be argued, in notable Judaic influences in Ethiopian Christianity. Christian Ethiopia long afterwards established a presence in the Holy Land, to which many Ethiopian Christians over the centuries travelled on pilgrimage.

Ties with Armenia, which, like Ethiopia, had been converted to Christianity in ancient times, were also memorable. Christians from the two countries, both firmly wedded to the Monophysite creed, often met, and doubtless exchanged views, in Jerusalem. Numerous Armenians likewise made their way to Ethiopia, where several gained prominence as traders or envoys in the service of Ethiopian rulers, and later, in the nineteenth and twentieth centuries, worked as craftsmen, and merchants, of all kinds.

Contacts with the Mediterranean region were also long-established. Hellenistic traders were prominent throughout the Red Sea area in ancient times. Greek was used on many Aksumite coins and inscriptions, and at least one ancient ruler of Ethiopia was reportedly familiar with that language. Christian Ethiopia, in medieval times, later developed contacts with Rome, whither many Ethiopian ecclesiastics made their way, and where the Pope afforded them a hospice. Travellers from Venice, and other parts of the Italian peninsula, found their way to Ethiopia, some of them as traders or adventurers, and in a few cases as artists. Greek traders, and builders, were also active in Ethiopia in later years.

Links between the Ethiopian region and the Indian sub-continent, particularly the Gujarat area, also dated back to ancient times, when Indian traders first made their appearance in the Red Sea area. Indian cottons, silks, and spices were long in great demand in Ethiopia, whence India obtained both ivory and gold. The Ethiopian state despatched embassies to the Mogul Empire. Indian craftsmen on several memorable occasions served as builders of Ethiopian palaces, and even churches, and were later also important as traders, many of them based in Bombay. Slaves from Ethiopia were for many centuries taken to the sub-continent, where some succeeded in establishing ruling dynasties.

The Ethiopian region also for a time had significant relations with the Ottoman Empire. In the late sixteenth century this polity established itself on the Red Sea coast, whence it on several occasions sought forcibly to penetrate the Christian interior. Relations were later stabilized, and Constantinople, in the late nineteenth and early twentieth centuries, became a useful point of contact between Ethiopia and the outside world.

Two-way contacts with Western Europe began in medieval times. They owed much to the desire of Ethiopian Christian rulers to obtain firearms, and other military matériel, from supposedly friendly European monarchs sharing their faith. The coming of a Portuguese diplomatic mission to Ethiopia, and subsequent Portuguese military intervention, both in the sixteenth century, were followed by unsuccessful attempts by Portuguese and Spanish Jesuits to convert the country to Roman Catholicism.

Travellers from the other European countries, Britain, France, Germany, and Italy, appeared on the Ethiopian scene a century or so after the Portuguese. Far from numerous until the early nineteenth century, their numbers later rapidly increased, in the era of the Scramble for Africa. This culminated, for Ethiopia, in the country's resounding victory over the Italians, at the battle of Adwa in 1896, and was followed by the establishment, in the Ethiopian capital, Addis Ababa, of Italian, French, British, Russian, German, Belgian, United States, and Ottoman legations. By the latter years of the century reforming emperors of Ethiopia were beginning to utilize European, and other foreign, skills for the modernization of their age-old realm.

The country's external relations owed much, throughout this time, to technological developments in the outside world, among them the opening of the Suez Canal, and to the advent of the steam-boat, and later the aeroplane, the radio, and the machine-gun. Ethiopia's entry into the League of Nations, in 1923, was followed, a decade or so later, by fascist Italy's unprovoked aggression, and, after Mussolini's entry into the European war, by the country's liberation, with British aid. Ethiopia, a founder member of the United Nations, thereafter played a major role in African diplomacy, much of which was centred on Addis Ababa, as well as, more generally, in the unfolding of international relations – and, more fearfully, superpower politics.

2

Punt, Pharaohs and Ptolemies, the Aksumite Kingdom, and the Coming of Christianity

The region later to be known as Ethiopia lay on the African side of the Red Sea, since antiquity a major commercial route linking Egypt and the Mediterranean area with India and the East. The Ethiopian region was, however, also important in its own right. It yielded such valuable commodities as gold, ivory and myrrh, not to mention slaves, and was the site of one of the two branches of the Nile, upon whose water, and silt, the people of Egypt depended for their very existence. For these, and other reasons, the region was known to the outside world almost since the dawn of history.

The Land of Punt and the Pharaohs

Ethiopia's first recorded contacts were with the Egyptians of the Pharaohs. In their inscriptions they refer to the southern Red Sea coast, with which they had commercial relations since time immemorial, as the Land of Punt. The term has been identified with territory on both the Arabian and African coasts. Consideration of the articles which the Egyptians obtained from Punt, notably gold and ivory, suggests, however, that these were primarily of African origin. The gold probably emanated from the Ethiopian interior, perhaps the Beni, or Bela, Shangul area of later times; the ivory came from elephants which abounded on the coast as well as in the interior of Africa. This leads us to suppose that the term Punt probably applied more to African than to Arabian territory.

An indication as to where on the African coast Punt was located can likewise be deduced from the long distance between Egypt and the southern Red Sea, the slow speed of ancient sailing, and the navigators' need to utilize 'trade winds', which blew in any direction for only a few months a year. Consideration of these factors suggests that the Egyptians would have traded with the nearest area from which tropical supplies could be obtained. This would most likely have been along the present Sudanese or Eritrean coasts, rather than those further south, such as those of Somalia or Kenya.[1]

The drama of Egyptian contacts with the Land of Punt was recorded extensively by the Pharaohs. Their accounts of expeditions to the territory are, however, one-sided. They depict such journeys as entirely their own heroic achievement, without in any way admitting that these were part, as closer scrutiny shows, of a two-way process, involving trade, and no doubt statecraft, on both sides.

Egyptian inscriptions are nevertheless invaluable in providing our earliest glimpses of the southern Red Sea area, which was later to constitute the Ethiopian coast. They reveal that Pharaohs of the First or Second Dynasties (3546–3190 BC) were in possession of myrrh, one of the most prized products obtained from Punt, possibly the eastern Tegray area of modern times. Egyptian inscriptions also record that during the Fourth Dynasty (3100–2965 BC) a son of Cheops, the builder of the Great Pyramid, was in possession of a Puntite slave.[2]

Supplies from Punt probably first reached Egypt overland. King Sahure (2958–2946 BC) of the Fifth Dynasty, however, later despatched a naval fleet, which returned with myrrh, gold and costly wood. King Pepy II (2738–2644 BC) of the Sixth Dynasty subsequently noted that he had a Tenq, or small-boned slave, from Punt.[3]

Pharaonic expeditions to Punt increased after the founding of the Egyptian Red Sea port of Wadi Gasus, north of Koseir, during the reign of King Mentuhotep IV (2242–2212 BC) of the Eleventh Dynasty. Egyptian familiarity with Punt also found expression, during the Twelfth Dynasty, in a popular tale of a mariner, a kind of early Sinbad the Sailor, ship-wrecked in Puntite waters.[4]

[1]   Kitchin, 1971, pp. 184–207.
[2]   Breasted, 1905, p. 127.
[3]   Breasted, 1962, I, p. 70.
[4]   Vychill, 1957, pp. 183–4.

Contact with Punt was subsequently facilitated by the cutting, on orders from King Sesostris III (2099–2061 BC), almost four thousand years before the Suez Canal, of a waterway between the Nile and the Red Sea.[5]

The New Egyptian Kingdom, founded around 1600 BC, witnessed many direct sailings from Egypt to Punt. By far the best known expedition to the latter region was despatched by Queen Hatshepsut (1501–1479 BC), whose achievements are recorded in inscriptions and pictorial reliefs on the walls of her famous temple of Dair el-Bahri at Thebes in southern Egypt.[6] 'As beautiful in execution as they are important in content' they constitute veritable archives in stone, and provide by far the most detailed source for the study of Puntite foreign trade ever produced. This expedition was, however, far from unique. The modern Swedish historian Säve-Söderberg observes that 'many, or even perhaps most' of the Pharaohs despatched fleets to Punt, though almost every ruler tried to claim that he was the first to do so.[7]

Though the Egyptian inscriptions are almost exclusively concerned with Pharaonic activities there are indications that the Puntites, within half a century of Hapshetsut's great expedition, were themselves undertaking commercial voyages to Egypt. Testimony of this is found in an Egyptian official's tomb at Thebes, dating from the reign of King Amenhotep II (1447–1420 BC). It contains a relief depicting the arrival of two chiefs of Punt, bringing articles from their country, including gold, incense, ebony trees, ostrich feathers and eggs, skins, antelopes(?) and oxen. There are also pictures of two Puntite vessels, which, though much smaller than those of the Pharaohs, were evidently seaworthy. Another tomb of the period depicts the arrival of other goods from Punt, among them fragrant gum, skins, and two wild animals, the happier in that they brought their skins on their backs.[8]

One of the last recorded Pharaonic expeditions to Punt was despatched by Ramses III (1198–1167 BC) of the Twentieth Dynasty. An inscription of his reign describes Egyptian vessels returning with Puntite products, among them many 'strange

---

[5] Breasted, 1905, pp. 183–4.
[6] Naville, 1894.
[7] Säve-Söderberg, 1946, p. 29.
[8] Davies, 1935, pp. 46–9; Davies, 1940, p. 136.

articles', 'plentiful myrrh', and a number of Puntites who brought it.[9]

Contacts between the Ethiopian region and ancient Israel seem also to have taken place during the reign of King Solomon (*c.*974–932 BC). This finds expression in biblical references to King Solomon's trade with the Land of Ophir. Ships of King Hiram of Tyre, sailed there in quest of gold, incense trees, and precious stones.

The story, which is reminiscent of Queen Hatshepsut's expedition to the Land of Punt half a millennium earlier, is told in the *Book of Kings*, I, 9:28. It recalls that Hiram's ships, made at Eloth, on the northern Red Sea coast, 'came to Ophir, and fetched from thence gold, four hundred and twenty talents, and brought it to king Solomon'. The journey is referred to in almost identical terms in the *Books of Chronicles*, II, 8:18. Ophir, to judge from the biblical context, as well as by the articles obtained therefrom, was probably on the African coast, not improbably the very gold and incense producing area which the Egyptians had earlier referred to as the Land of Punt.

The Elephant Country and the Ptolemies

Ancient ties between the Ethiopian region and Egypt were reborn in the early fourth century BC under the Egyptian Ptolemies. The *raison d'être* for this contact was now essentially strategic. The Seleucid dynasty of Babylon, the main enemies of the Ptolemies, was then using Indian elephants, aptly termed the 'tanks' of the ancient world, and the rulers of Egypt 'could not remain inferior in this respect'.[10]

Interest in the elephant-inhabited Red Sea area south of Egypt was manifested by the first Ptolemy, Soter (305–285 BC). He despatched an expedition along the African coast, and entrusted it to a captian called Philos, who wrote a book entitled *Aethiopica*, unfortunately long since lost.[11]

The capture of elephants along the African Red Sea coast was

---

[9] Breasted, 1962, IV, p. 203.
[10] Rostovtzeff, 1941, III, p. 1232.
[11] Sergew Hable Sellassie, 1972, p. 47.

later organized by Ptolemy II, Philadelphus (280–246 BC). He was 'passionately fond of the hunting of elephants, and gave great rewards to those who succeeded in capturing against all odds the most valiant of beasts, expending on this hobby great sums of money'. He 'not only collected great herds of war-elephants, but also brought to the knowledge of the Greeks other kinds of animals, which had never been seen and were objects of amazement'.[12] To promote his acquisition of elephants he tried to persuade the local hunters to renounce the killing of these animals, so that he could obtain them alive. He made the hunters 'many beautiful promises', but did so in vain, for the men replied that they 'would not change their way of life for all his kingdom'. Undeterred by this response he gave orders for the building of special boats, called *elephantegoi*, or 'elephant-carriers'. They were designed to transport the huge creatures from the Red Sea coast, and on the return journey were used to provision the hunters with grain and other supplies from Egypt. Hunting was so successful that special elephant parks were established, notably at Thebes and Memphis.[13]

Elephant exploitation was intensified during the reign of Ptolemy III, Eurgetes I (246–221 BC). He was so 'passionately fond' of hunting these animals that he sent one of his friends to 'spy out the land', and make 'a thorough investigation' of the nations lying along the coast.[14] One of many harbours visited at this time was Adulis, or Adulé, which was soon to become the principal port of the Aksumite realm. Evidence of a Ptolemaic presence at that port was found in a Greek inscription, erected there, in the name of 'Ptolemy, son of Ptolemy and Queen Arsinoe, twin gods'.[15]

These Ptolemaic adventures, which doubtless involved extensive elephant hunting far into the Ethiopian interior, were, however, short-lived. The Egyptians soon came to the conclusion that the difficulties of capturing and transporting elephants did not justify the effort and expense. The international use of these animals in war died out in the second century BC.

---

[12]   Diodorus, III, p. 36.
[13]   Photius, 1959–74, VII, p. 135.
[14]   Diodorus, III, p. 18.
[15]   McCrindle, 1897, pp. 57–8.

The Greeks, the 'Blameless Ethiopians' and the Bible

Contacts first with the land of Punt, and later with Ophir and the elephant-hunting lands, did much to shape the ancient world's image of Ethiopia. The Greeks, who first gave the country its name, i.e. the Land of Burnt Faces, regarded it with awe, both as a far-off realm, and as one inhabited by remarkable people. In the ninth century BC Homer in the *Odyssey* described the Ethiopians as *eschatoi andron*, i.e. 'the most distant of men'. He states that they lived 'at earth's two verges, in sunset lands and lands of the rising sun'. Later, in the fifth century BC, Herodotus likewise observed that the Ethiopians inhabited 'the ends of the earth'. His near contemporary, Aeschylus, agreed in *Prometheus Bound* that theirs was a 'land far off, a nation of black men', who lived 'hard by the fountain of the sun where is the river Aethiops'.[16]

The Ethiopians were regarded by the Greeks as the best people in the world. Homer speaks of them in the *Iliad* as the 'blameless Ethiopians'. He claims that they were visited by Zeus, the king of the gods, by the goddess Iris, who travelled to their country to participate in their sacrificial rites, and by Poseidon, the sea god, who 'lingered delighted' at their feasts. This theme was taken up, in the first century BC, by Diodorus of Sicily, who asserted that the gods Hercules and Bacchus were both 'awed by the piety' of the Ethiopians, whose sacrifices, he claims, were the most acceptable to the gods.[17]

Ethiopia, and the Ethiopians, were likewise frequently mentioned in the Bible. The *Book of Amos* thus links the Ethiopians, almost cryptically, with the Israelites, when it cites God as asking the latter, 'Are you not as the children of the Ethiopians unto me?' The *Book of Zephaniah* and the *Book of Isaiah* both follow the ancient Greeks in declaring that the country was a far off place, as suggested by the phrase 'beyond the rivers of Ethiopia'. Reference to the country is also found in *Genesis*, which speaks of a River Giyon, which 'compasseth the whole of Ethiopia', while the *Book of Numbers* relates that Moses 'married an Ethiopian woman'.

Perhaps the most important biblical reference to Ethiopia, and

[16] Greene, 1959, I, p. 340.
[17] For a consideration of these and other images of Ethiopia see Levine, 1974, pp. 1–6.

the one to which Ethiopians over the centuries paid the greatest emphasis, was, however, in *Psalm 68*, 31. It prophesied: 'Ethiopia shall soon stretch out her hands unto God.'

The Queen of Sheba Legend

The Bible also provided the basis for perhaps Ethiopia's most important legend: that of the Queen of Sheba's visit to King Solomon. The Ethiopian version, which went much further than the biblical, asserted that the queen had a son by Solomon, that this child, Menilek, later travelled to Jerusalem to see his father, brought back the Ark of the Covenant, and founded a dynasty which reigned in Ethiopia for close on three thousand years.

This legend is inextricably bound up with the ancient Ethiopian city of Aksum, as was noted in the early sixteenth century by the Portuguese traveller Francisco Alvares, the first foreign traveller to describe the settlement. He claimed that this 'very good town' was 'the city, chamber and abode' of the Queen who took camels 'laden with gold' to King Solomon when he was building the temple in Jerusalem.[18]

The identification of the Queen of Sheba with Ethiopia goes back at least to the early Christian era, albeit a full millennium after the time in which she lived. Josephus in his *Jewish Antiquities*, of the first century AD, refers to her as a 'Queen of Egypt and Ethiopia.'[19] Half a millennium later, however, the Egyptian traveller Kosmos Indikopleustes believed that she came from the 'country of the Himyarites', i.e. South Arabia.[20] The Ethiopian identification was nevertheless reasserted three centuries later in the Coptic *History of the Patriarchs of Alexandria*, which spoke of Ethiopia as the 'kingdom of Saba from which the Queen of the South came to Solomon, the Son of David the King'. Many Ethiopians to this day assume that Aksum was the Queen of Sheba's capital, and the repository of the biblical Ark of the Covenant. Several of the city's antiquities, as we shall see, are moreover popularly identified with the ancient queen.

[18] Beckingham and Huntingford, 1961, I, p. 27.
[19] For a discussion of the ideas of Josephus on this subject see Ullendorff, 1968, p. 27.
[20] McCrindle, 1897, pp. 51–2.

Pre-Aksumite Civilization: Yéha

The northern Ethiopian region appears, by around the second millennium BC, to have been in close contact with neighbouring peoples, most notably those of the Nubian lowlands to the west and the Tihama coast of Southern Arabia to the east.

These relations, which archaeologists have begun to study only in recent years, were of considerable cultural importance, and led *inter alia* to the emergence of a number of Afro-Asiatic languages, including a form of proto-Geʻez. Some authorities believe that wheat, barley, and the plough were introduced from Egypt, and some types of pottery from Sudan. Others hold that the idea of a priest-king was borrowed from South Arabia.

Current research, based on both archaeology and linguistic analysis, tends, however, to reject the old view that the civilization of the Ethiopian region resulted primarily from South Arabian settlement. Scholars are now arguing, with increasing conviction, that developments in the region were on the contrary largely generated within the area itself. It is, however, recognized that there were close contacts across the Red Sea, and that this narrow strip of water, so far from acting as a barrier, served to bring together the peoples on either side of it.

The millennium prior to the birth of Christ witnessed the rise in what is now northern Ethiopia of an important civilisation. Closely connected with that of the Sabaeans of South Arabia, it seems to have originally used the same Semitic language, employed the same script, and worshipped the same gods, primarily the disk of the sun and the crescent moon.

Dramatic testimony to the importance of this civilisation can be seen to this day at Yéha, 20 miles north of Aksum, and probably one of Ethiopia's earliest capitals. It dates to at least the middle of the first millennium BC, or, some believe, to as early as the eighth century.

Yéha is the site of an impressive stone temple reminiscent of buildings in Yaman. It consists of a huge oblong hall, no less than twenty metres long, fifteen wide, and ten high. Its solid walls, devoid of windows, are built of smoothly polished stone blocks, most of them more than a metre long, neatly placed one above or beside another, without any mortar. The roof and west wall are both missing, but several square niches in the remaining eastern wall indicate that the structure's eastern wing at least was once partitioned, probably with large wooden, beams, which have long since disappeared. There are indications that it also had a probably subterranean chamber or vault.

The temple, like many other antiquities of northern Ethiopia, was first mentioned by Alvares in the early sixteenth century. He describes it as 'a very large and handsome tower, both for its height and the good workmanship of its walls'. It had 'the look of a regal building, all of well-hewn stone', and was surrounded by 'good houses', with 'good walls and flat roofs above, like the residences of great lords'.[21]

The 'good houses', walls and terraces have long since disappeared, but other remains of the old town can still be seen. Several rows of ibex heads, doubtless taken from the temple, have been built into the façade of the neighbouring church of Abba Asfé, founded by a monk of that name. He was, as we shall see, one of the Nine Saints of the late fifth or early sixth century. The ibex was a sacred animal in ancient South Arabia, and identified with the moon god Ilmuqah. Its presence, and the church's location immediately beside the temple, are vivid examples of how Christian places of worship in Ethiopia, as elsewhere, were often placed on sites held sacred by adherents of earlier faiths. Several long stone blocks each some ten centimetres wide bearing inscriptions in Sabaean, almost certainly also taken there from the original temple, are likewise preserved in the church's *iqa-bét*, or store-house. Archaeological investigation has unearthed various interesting remains, including pottery, some decorated with representations of ibexes, and bronze seals, apparently for branding cattle.[22]

Yéha, though perhaps the most important, was but one of many early settlements in northern Ethiopia. Almost a hundred Sabaean, or pre-Aksumite, sites have thus been identified by archaeologists, and more are being discovered in each season's fieldwork. Some of the best known remains are perhaps those at Hawelti and Melazo, both south-east of Aksum, and Qohaytu and Matara, on the way to the Red Sea coast.[23]

[21] Beckingham and Huntingford, 1961, I, p. 141.
[22] Anfray (n.d.), pp. 18–28.
[23] For a recent archaeological discussion see R. Fattovitch, 'Remarks on the Pre-Aksumite Period in Northern Ethiopia', *Journal of Ethiopian Studies*, 23 (1990), pp. 1–33.

Aksum: Foreign Trade

The founding of the Aksumite state, and civilization, which may have taken place as early as 300 BC, was an important development in Ethiopian history. The Aksumites assumed control over the economically important region between the highlands and the coast, including places, such as Yéha, previously under Sabaean influence.

The early development of the city of Aksum is generally believed to have taken place around the first century AD, or somewhat earlier. Traditional Ethiopian king lists, though by no means necessarily reliable, mention an Aksumite ruler, called Bazén, believed to have begun to reign eight years before the birth of Christ.

Aksum doubtless owed its origin to its geographical location, in fertile, well-watered land, which allowed the development of extensive agriculture, and in particular the cultivation of cereals. Grain was apparently considered so important that the Aksumites placed on their coins representations of twin ears of wheat or barley, which appear to have been chosen as the city's official symbol. Dams, wells and a reservoir were also gradually established in the area.

The city was likewise well placed, in that the surrounding country, as far as the coast, was inhabited by vast herds of elephants. These animals, which had attracted the attention of the Ptolemies only a few centuries earlier, were highly prized for their ivory, which constituted a major Aksumite export. The Byzantine traveller Nonnosus reported around 531 AD that at Aue, a settlement half way to the coast, he had seen 'a large group of elephants, about five thousand in number . . . roaming over a large plain'.

Aksum also had the advantage of being situated within relatively easy access of lands yielding two important minerals: gold and salt. The city was thus within reach of the Blue Nile basin, and thence of the gold-producing lowlands of Beni, or Bela, Shangul, on the present Sudan frontier. Aksum was similarly less than a hundred miles from the Afar, or Dankali, depression, the source of rock salt, a valuable commodity in demand throughout the entire Ethiopian region.

Aksum was also situated only 100 miles from the Red Sea

coast, and hence enjoyed good communications with the outside world. Land routes from the city likewise ran north-westwards to Egypt and the Mediterranean, eastwards to the Gulf of Aden ports, westwards to Nubia, in its day an important civilisation, south-westwards, as we shall see, to the gold-producing areas, and southwards to the Ethiopian interior, much of which the Aksumites gradually brought under their control.

Aksum's sea-borne foreign trade, which is currently by far the best documented aspect of the country's economic life, was largely handled by the port of Adulis, fifteen days' journey from the capital, and one of the region's principal trading stations. This commerce was first described in the *Periplus of the Erythraean Sea*, a trade or shipping manual drawn up by an unknown Greek-speaking Egyptian sailor, merchant or customs official, probably around the first century AD. This dating has, however, long been a subject of almost irreconcilable controversy.

Articles shipped from the port, according to this text, consisted primarily of ivory, tortoise-shell and rhinoceros-horn, and a little obsidian. The latter, obtained at the coast east of Adulis, was a black volcanic stone, highly prized in the ancient world for the making of jewellery and votive offerings. Three other Aksumite exports were mentioned at about the same time by the Roman author Pliny (d. AD 79): hippopotamus-hides, slaves and apes.[24] Five of the above seven exports, ivory, rhinoceros-horn, hippopotamus-hides, slaves and apes, originated in the Ethiopian interior, while two, obsidian and tortoise shell, came from nearby Red Sea waters. Much of the export trade passed by way of the town of Coloe (The Qohayto of modern times), which the *Periplus* describes as 'the first market for ivory', and other commercial centres still only partially identified archaeologically.

The imports of Adulis, which were destined largely for Aksum, came mainly from Egypt, India and Arabia. The *Periplus* gives a long list of such imports. They included large quantities of cloth and clothing, among them Egyptian textiles, robes from Arsinoe in Egypt, dyed cloaks of many colours, fringed mantles, and cheap unlined coats. Other imports comprised glassware, much of it from Thebes, brass, used for making jewellery and coins, copper sheets, employed in the production of cutlery and jewellery, and iron, in that of spears, both for fighting and the hunting of el-

---

[24]   Pliny, 1947–56, I, p. 34.

ephants and other wild beasts. Many ready-made weapons, tools, and luxury goods were also imported. Such articles included axes, adzes and swords, large round copper drinking cups, Syrian and Italian wine, but 'not much', small quantities of olive oil, gold and silver plate for the king, and a small number of foreign coins for use in trade. Most imports mentioned in the *Periplus* came from Egypt, or the Mediterranean area, with both of which the author of the *Periplus* was particularly familiar. Imports from India were, however, also considerable, and included various kinds of cotton cloth, coats of skin, raw iron, and coloured lac.[25]

Adulis, a port of distinction with large and elegant buildings and at least one church, was briefly examined, early in the twentieth century, by the Italian archaeologist Roberto Paribeni, but would doubtless repay further investigation.[26]

Religion, Language and Writing

The Aksumites, prior to the coming of Christianity, had a pantheon of gods, derived from South Arabia, which they equated in their inscriptions with the gods of the ancient Greeks. The principal early Aksumite deities thus comprised Astar, who corresponded to Zeus, the Greek king of the gods; Mahrem, the equivalent of Ares, the Greek god of war; and Baher, who was equated with Poseidon, the Greek god of the sea. Aksum, as we shall see, later adopted Christianity, which became the official state religion in the early fourth century, after which the old gods were forgotten.[27]

The language spoken in Aksum was probably Geʿez, also referred to in Europe as Ethiopic, or something closely related to it. Geʿez, a Semitic tongue, belongs to the same family as Hebrew, Arabic, and half a dozen Ethiopian Semitic languages spoken to this day. Geʿez was at first written in Sabaean or South Arabian letters, seen on the earliest Aksumite inscriptions. Some ran, like writing in most Semitic languages, from right to left. Others, however, were written in the *boustrophedon*, or 'ploughwise' manner, in which the first line ran from right to left,

[25] On the trade of Adulis see Huntingford, 1980, pp. 20–3.
[26] Paribeni, 1907, pp. 438–572.
[27] Munro-Hay, 1991, pp. 186–202.

the second from left to right, the third from right to left, and so on. Sabaean writing was consonantal, and, like many Semitic tongues, made little or no use of vowels.

Aksumite writing around the early fourth century underwent two major changes, which may have resulted from the spread at around that time of Christianity, and the translation into Geʿez of the Bible, mainly from Greek. One change, which perhaps resulted from the wish to make Biblical texts more intelligible to the newly literate, was a modification of the lettering system. The consonantal characters hitherto in use were modified, in most cases by the addition of small marks or signs, to express vowel sounds. The old alphabet, based exclusively on consonantal symbols, was thus replaced by a syllabary of modified consonants, each with seven vowel combinations, to express seven different sounds: *lä, lu, li, la, lé, le, lo*, etc. A similar emergence of consonantal writing, it is interesting to note, occurred in India at about the same time.

The other development, which took place at Aksum at about the same time, perhaps under the influence of the Greek, was a change in the direction of writing. Boustrophedic writing was abandoned, and the direction of other writing reversed, so that Geʿez, like Greek, was thereafter written exclusively from left to right. Numerals, based on Greek letters, were also introduced, and the shapes of several Sabaean characters substantially modified, in some cases even turned sideways.

Geʿez, though mainly restricted to Aksum and its environs, was not unknown further afield. Aksumite script was used by Aksumite garrisons in South Arabia and appeared on Aksumite coins which circulated far beyond the confines of Aksumite power. Bibles and other Christian manuscripts from Aksum were likewise taken by Ethiopians on pilgrimage to Jerusalem and other religious centres, where they would doubtless have been seen by Christian clerics from other lands. One possible consequence was that the Armenian alphabet, invented at the beginning of the fifth century by the Armenian scholar Vardapet Mesrop Mashtotz, contains over half a dozen letters perhaps copied from the Ethiopic. Mashtotz could well have come across Aksumite writings in the Holy Land, and would doubtless have been interested in them as emanating from a fellow Christian land.[28]

---

[28]   Olderogge, 1974, I, pp. 195–203.

Many Aksumites must have been literate, not only in Ge'ez, but also in Greek, which was used on many of their coins and inscriptions. Familiarity with the latter language is confirmed by the *Periplus*, which states that the ruler of Aksum, whom he refers to as Zoskales, i.e. Za Hakele, was 'high-minded and skilled in Greek letters'.

Currency, Barter and 'Silent Trade'

Aksum in its heyday struck its own currency, and was the only African country outside the Roman Empire to do so. This was an indication of the importance of Aksumite trade, and doubtless contributed greatly to its expansion.

Production of money is believed to have started around AD 270, during the reign of King Endubis, and seems to have continued until at least the early seventh century. Coins were struck in gold, silver and bronze. They were identical in size, weight and value to the money of Rome and Byzantium, which would suggest that they were designed for foreign trade. This view is reinforced by the fact that the first Aksumite coins, and later the high denominations in gold, bore legends in Greek, then the principal commercial language of the eastern Mediterranean and Red Sea area. Later money, however, carried inscriptions in the local language, Ge'ez, which would seem to indicate that this currency was conceived primarily for circulation within the Aksumite realm itself.

Aksumite currency is of immense historical interest. It bore the names, effigies, and, in some cases, the descent of over twenty different kings, whose clothing, crowns and other decorations are often carefully depicted. An intriguing feature of the coins is that almost all bear the monarch's effigy on both the obverse and the reverse. The former often depicts the king with a crown, the latter with a head-cloth. Some commentators have argued that this apparent preoccupation with the ruler, rather than with any state insignia, suggests that the monarch was regarded as the supreme ruler, more important than the state itself. This conclusion is interesting in the light of subsequent Ethiopian history, for the monarchs of later times tended, as we shall see, to be considered, theoretically, all-powerful, and endowed with almost unlimited authority.

The earliest Aksum coins carried representations of the sun's disk and the moon's crescent, the symbols of ancient South Arabia. They were, however, abandoned in the early fourth century, and replaced, it is believed around AD 330, by the Cross of Christ. The change took place during the reign of the Aksumite King Ezana. He issued two sets of coins. The supposedly earliest bore representations of the sun and moon, while those apparently issued later carried the Cross. Aksum, it is interesting to note, was the first state in the world to use the Cross on its currency. Not a few coins also carried Christian slogans, such as 'By the Grace of God', 'Christ be with Us', and 'Mercy and Peace'.[29]

The coins of Aksum, though small and often scarcely legible without the aid of a magnifying glass, are in many instances beautifully struck. Some silver pieces are remarkable in that they bear gilt crowns or crosses. Production of coins appears to have been considerable. Many are found to this day by farmers, and their sharp-eyed children, after each year's rainy season.

Despite the minting of coins, the Aksumites also made extensive use of barter, notably in their trade with the gold-producing lands of the west or south-west, and doubtless also with the salt plains of the east. The prevalent form of exchange was described by the early sixth century Greek-speaking author Kosmos. He records, in his *Christian Topography*, that the King of Aksum sent officers to the gold-producing area every other year. They were accompanied by up to five hundred private merchants, who took advantage of the security these expeditions afforded to travel with them, but traded privately on their own account. Vividly describing the way in which these expeditions, and accompanying traders, did business, Kosmos writes:

> They take along with them to the mining district oxen, lumps of salt, and iron, and when they reach its neighbourhood they make a halt at a certain spot and form an encampment, which they fence round with a great hedge of thorns. Within this they live, and having slaughtered the oxen, cut them in pieces, and lay the pieces on the top of the thorns, along with the lumps of salt and iron. Then come the natives bringing gold in nuggets like peas . . . , and lay one or two or more of these on what pleases them – the pieces of flesh or the salt or the iron, and then they retire to some distance off. Then the owner of the meat approaches, and if he is satisfied he takes the gold away, and upon seeing this its owner comes and

[29]   On these coins see Munro-Hay and Juel-Jensen, 1995.

takes the flesh or the salt or the iron. If, however, he is not satisfied, he leaves the gold, when the native seeing that he has not taken it, comes and either puts down more gold, or takes up what he has laid down, and goes away. Such is the mode in which business is transacted with the people of that country because the language is different and interpreters are hardly to be found.

'The time they stay in that country', Kosmos continues, 'is five days more or less, according as the natives more or less readily come forward to buy up all their wares. On the journey homeward they all agree to travel well-armed, since some of the tribes through whose country they may pass might threaten to attack them from a desire to rob them of their gold. The space of six months is taken up with this trading expedition, including both the going and the returning. In going they march very slowly, chiefly because of the cattle, but in returning they quicken their pace lest on the way they should be overtaken by winter and its rains'.[30]

The gold trade was, it may be presumed, of no small importance to the development of Aksum. A large quantity of the rare metal was exported, but much was also used in the considerable minting of coins, as well as, no doubt, in the manufacture of jewellery.

Obelisks, Inscriptions, Palaces and Tombs

Aksum is famous for its obelisks, or monolithic stele. Cut out of hard granite, the majority are rudely fashioned stones, scarcely more than man height, but others are immense, beautifully carved, tapering monuments, which towered high into the sky. Three of the finest represent multi-storied houses, with a ground-floor door, complete with door and door handle, and above them row after row of windows.[31]

The biggest of these three stelae, now fallen and broken into several pieces, is the largest block of stone fashioned by humanity anywhere in the world. Exceeding 33 metres in height, and measuring two by three metres at the base, it was a remarkably impressive piece of workmanship, representing a twelve storey palace.

[30]　McCrindle, 1897, pp. 52–4.
[31]　For a detailed account of these obelisks see Munro-Hay, 1991, pp. 124–43, 266–8.

Plate 2   Aksum: the famous early fourth-century obelisk during the annual celebration for St Mary of Seyon, in November. Photo: Alula Pankhurst.

Scholars argue that it may have fallen while in the process of being erected.

The second largest obelisk, 25 metres high, was taken to Rome, in 1937, during the Italian fascist occupation, on the orders of Mussolini. He had it erected in front of the Ministry of Italian Africa, now the headquarters of the Food and Agriculture Organisation (FAO), to celebrate the fifteenth anniversary of his seizure of power in Italy. This stele has still not yet been returned.

The third largest obelisk which never fell down, is 24 metres high. The first foreigner to describe it, the British traveller Henry Salt, exclaimed, in 1805, 'My attention was for a long time riveted on this beautiful and extraordinary monument'. On seeing it again five years later, he confessed, 'it made nearly as forcible an impression upon my mind as at the first moment I beheld it'. Having by then inspected many Egyptian, Greek and Roman antiquities, he declared that comparison with them 'seemed to justify' him in considering it 'the most admirable and perfect monument of its kind'.

There are indications on several obelisks that some metal device, possibly we may imagine gilt, was once attached to the tops of them, probably to symbolize the religion of the ancient Aksumites. In pre-Christian times this symbol would probably have been a representation of the sun and moon, as carved for example on a much smaller standing obelisk at Matara. This symbol in Christian times may well have been replaced, as in the case of the Aksumite coins, by the Cross of Christ. Archaeological investigations in 1996, however, revealed a broken round metallic plaque, of exactly the size to fit onto one of the obelisks, and with holes evidently made to attach it to some other object. This disk bore a representation of a face, which gives rise to the supposition that some stelae may have borne the effigy of the ruler or other personage in whose memory they were erected.

Several large unfinished stelae can be seen lying in the vicinity of the two above obelisks at Aksum.

A smaller fallen Aksum obelisk, little more than eight metres long, is also of special historical interest. It is sculpted to display a column, with two long leaves which hold a box-like object formed by a rectangle surmounted by a triangle. This device, as evident from its position at the top of the stele, was presumably considered of special importance. Some writers have asked whether it might perchance have represented the Ark of the Covenant.

These and other Aksumite obelisks were quarried from a high rocky stretch of land at Wuchate Golo, some three miles west of the city, where several excavation sites and partially detached blocks of stone can still be discerned. Not far away, at Gobedra, the figure of a lioness is beautifully carved on a large fallen rock.

Obelisks were doubtless transported to their final place of erection by vast numbers of labourers, probably using sledges or rollers, or perhaps, as some historians have speculated, elephants. Though remarkably skilled in sculpting, transporting and erecting these immense blocks of stone, and in supporting them with smaller boulders, the Aksumites planted only about one-twelfth of the stele in the ground. The result was that over the centuries or millennia the majority fell, or were, more probably, knocked down by local or foreign enemies.[32]

Aksum is also renowned for its stone inscriptions.[33] The most numerous, and by far the most notable, to be seen in or around the town to this day, were erected in the fourth century by King Ezana. They report his military victories over enemies and 'rebels' in various parts of the country. Ezana is believed, as we have seen, to have struck his first coins with a representation of the sun and moon, and later ones with the Cross. A not dissimilar development is seen in his inscriptions: The earlier pay homage to Sabaean or Aksumite gods, while a later one bears a Cross, and refers to the apparently Christian Lord of Heaven.

One of the most interesting of Ezana's inscriptions recalls the Egyptian Rosetta Stone, in that it contains virtually identical texts in different languages: Greek, Ge'ez and Sabaean. His inscription tells of a rebellion by the Béja people west of Aksum, and the ensuing struggle, in dramatic detail. Ezana, we are told, responded by despatching his two brothers, Saizana and Adefan, against the rebels, who were duly captured, and brought to Aksum, together with 3,112 head of cattle, 6,224 sheep, and many beasts of burden. During the journey, which took four months, the brothers gave the rebels meat and wheat to eat, and beer, wine and water to drink. Six rebel chiefs, with 4,400 followers, were allotted 22,000 loaves of bread a day. On reaching Aksum the rebels were fed and clothed, after which they were given land at a place called Matlia, where each of the chiefs was accorded supplies, including 25,140 head of cattle, presumably for himself and his followers. This was the first recorded case of state-sponsored resettlement in Ethiopian history, but not the last.

Aksum in its day was the site also of many fine buildings of stone masonry. Their walls consisted of field stones set in mortar, often with finely dressed stone blocks at the corners or as stringer courses to add stability. The second storey floors and roofs were probably made of long wooden beams, and the windows and doors were framed in wood, with projecting beams. The latter, which were particularly characteristic of Aksumite building technique, are now generally referred to as 'monkey heads'. They are a recurrent feature of Ethiopian architecture, also represented in

[32] Barradas, 1996, p. 118–26.
[33] Munro-Hay, 1991, pp. 71–3, 214–15, 244–5.

stone, without any functional purpose, on the above-mentioned three largest Aksum obelisks. They are seen again, a thousand years later, on several of the famous rock-hewn churches of Lalibala, as well as many earlier and later structures.

Some Aksumite buildings were of considerable size. Kosmos in the sixth century described the 'four-towered palace' of the king, surmounted by 'four brazen figures' of unicorns. The ruins of several such palaces are reconded. One, known as Ta'arkha Maryam, which was destroyed during the Italian fascist occupation of 1936–41, measured 120 metres by 80, and covered an area six times as large as a contemporary palace in Hadramawt, and far more extensive than many European medieval royal edifices. The remains of another remarkably extensive palace, at Dungur, just west of Aksum, is popularly, but almost certainly incorrectly, associated with the Queen of Sheba.

The Aksumites were masters of stone work, which they carried out with great skill. The stones used in constructing their finer buildings were measured with care, and generally fitted together with precision. In at least two places in the city stones have been found with regularly spaced notches, presumably cut to assist the masons when measuring blocks of stone.

The rulers of Aksum likewise built a number of impressive royal tombs. Invariably excavated underground, they were fashioned from skilfully worked blocks of squarely cut granite. Some of the most important tombs were built, apparently, for Aksumite monarchs, in the immediate vicinity of the largest obelisks. Several, investigated by archaeologists in recent times, can be seen to this day, in some instances with stones held together with ancient iron clasps. One of these tombs is constructed not only of stone, but also of locally baked clay, and is accordingly referred to as the 'tomb of the brick arches'.

Two other fine stone tombs, built, according to tradition, for King Kaléb and his son King Gabra Masqal, in the early sixth century, lie on a spur of land which affords a dramatic view of the sharply pointed Adwa mountains to the north-east. Kaléb was one of Aksum's most important rulers, who launched a major expedition to South Arabia, in 525 AD, thus bringing part of that peninsula under temporary Aksumite rule.

The tombs attributed to Kaléb and Gabra Masqal were so well crafted that the British traveller Theodore Bent in the late nineteenth century exclaimed that they were 'built with a regularity which if found in Greece would at once make one assign them to a good period'. Both tombs are approached by broad stone steps, which lead to a vestibule connected to several sizeable chambers. One contains three large stone sarcophagi. There is every reason to believe that archaeological investigation currently underway in and around Aksum will lead to the discovery of further tombs.[34]

Though known above all for their excellently fashioned stone-work, Aksumite masons also made not insignifucant use of clay bricks. The houses of the common people were, it must be assumed, of much simpler stone, or wood, construction. Aksumite craftsmen, and jewellers, were also adept at metalwork, including the difficult process of inlaying gold into bronze. They also worked with considerable skill in glass, ivory, and ceramics.

Relations with Arabia and Meroe

The Aksumite realm, which perhaps began as a small ivory trading centre, rapidly expanded eastwards, westwards, and southwards, to emerge as the most powerful state between the Eastern Roman Empire and Persia.

The Aksumites, who had for several centuries enjoyed close contacts with south-west Arabia, first intervened there militarily around the beginning of the third century AD, and remained in occupation of the area until the second quarter of the sixth century. During this time the Aksumites produced coins for use in the Arabian territories they occupied, and Aksumite kings proudly referred to themselves in their inscriptions as rulers also of parts of the peninsula.

Not long after this Dhu Nuwas, a ruler of Himyar, who had been converted to Judaism, ousted the then Aksumite governor, and carried out a massacre of Christians at the local trading centre of Nagran. The Byzantine Emperor Justin I wrote to King Kaléb, urging him to intervene. The Aksumite monarch duly did so, around 517. Dhu Nuwas was killed in battle, after which Abraha, an Aksumite general, rebelled, and declared himself an independent king of Himyar. King Kaléb of Aksum made two attempts to depose him, but without success. Abraha proclaimed himself

---

[34] On Aksumite tombs see Munro-Hay, 1991, pp. 168, 255–7.

master of both Himyar and Saba, and built a notable cathedral at Sanaa as a centre of Christian pilgrimage.

Aksumite power meanwhile was also felt in the west, where Ezana conquered the neighbouring kingdom of Meroe around 325 AD.[35] This, if the conquest was in fact as total as some historians believe, left the Aksumite realm with no rival in the African interior, and enabled the Aksumites to expand their influence freely into the lands to the west and south, which were increasingly brought into the economic, political and religious orbit of Aksum.

Aksum thus emerged as a great commercial emporium and a major centre of political power. In the early sixth century the Byzantine envoy Nonnosus described it as a 'very big city', and 'practically the capital of all Ethiopia'. Kosmos at about the same testified that the city traded widely with countries as far apart as Egypt, Arabia, Persia, India and Ceylon.

Sheba's 'Heritage', and the Coming of Christianity

Aksum, though apparently founded almost a millennium after the time of the Queen of Sheba, is popularly much associated with her. Local tradition claims that an extensive ruined stone structure at Dungur, discovered only in the mid-twentieth century, was her palace; that a nearby sizeable fallen obelisk marks her grave; and that a large reservoir, near the city centre, was her bath. Testimony to Sheba's 'heritage' is also found in the name of Aksum's great church, St Mary of Seyon, the Ethiopian form of the word Zion. It is so-called because it is allegedly the repository of the Biblical Ark of the Covenant, brought by the queen's son and heir Menilek.

The Ethiopian Church claims that Christianity first reached Aksum during the time of the Apostles, and that 'many' at that time 'believed'. The faith did not, however, become the state religion until the early fourth century. It was then that King Ezana began, as we have seen, issuing coins bearing the Cross of Christ; and also issued a stone inscription which made mention of the Christian Lord of Heaven.

One very plausible, and apparently contemporary, account of

[35]   See Munro-Hay, 1991, p. 54.

how Christianity came to Aksum was written by the Byzantine ecclesiastical historian Rufinus. He states that Meropius, a Christian merchant, or as he calls him, 'a philosopher of Tyre', on the Syrian coast, made a voyage to India, and took with him two young boys whom he was educating, the elder by name Frumentius, the younger Aedesius. On the return journey the ship on which they were travelling put in for water on the Red Sea coast of Africa, but was seized as a reprisal against the Eastern Roman Empire, which had broken an earlier treaty. In the fracas Meropius and his companions were killed, but the two boys survived, and were later found studying, in all probability the Bible, under a tree. They were later taken to the king, who made Frumentius his secretary and treasurer, and Aedesius his cupbearer. Not long after this the monarch died, leaving his wife with an infant son as his heir. He had given the two boys permission to leave his country, but the bereaved queen, with tears in her eyes, begged them to stay, and help her govern the kingdom. She had, she said, no more faithful subjects in all the land. The two youngsters had little option but to consent. Frumentius meanwhile had sought out such foreign merchants as were Christians, and helped them establish churches and other Christian places of worship in and around Aksum.

When the young heir to the throne came of age Aedesius returned to Tyre, while Frumentius travelled to Alexandria, then the major centre of eastern Christianity. There he informed the great Patriarch Athanasius of the work he had accomplished for Christianity, and begged the latter to appoint a bishop. Athanasius, after some thought, replied, 'What other man can we find than you, who has already carried out such works?' He accordingly appointed Frumentius the country's first Christian bishop. 'These facts', Rufinus claims, 'I know, not from vulgar report, but from the mouth of Aedesius himself'.[36]

The royal heir mentioned in the above text was, it is believed, Ezana, the monarch known, as we have seen, for his coins bearing the Cross. Frumentius, for his part, duly returned to Ethiopia, where he is adopted the ecclesiastical name of Abba Salama, or Father of Peace, the appellation by which he is traditionally known in the country.

The coming of Christianity was a major turning point in

---

[36] Rufinus, 1849, p. 478–80.

Aksumite, and indeed Ethiopian, history. The advent of the new religion reinforced Aksum's ties with the Roman Empire, in which Emperor Constantine had then but recently established the faith. The latter's famous motto, *In hoc signo vinces*, i.e. 'By this Sign [the Cross] You will Conquer', found a close parallel in an early Aksumite coin, on which Ezana proclaimed 'By this Cross He will Conquer'.[37] Aksumite Christianity differed from Roman, however, in that the latter began as the religion of the dispossessed, and was only later accepted by Constantine, whereas Aksumite Christianity was imposed, like other major changes in subsequent Ethiopian history, by the highest in the land.

Frumentius's historic journey to Alexandria was significant in shaping the character of Aksumite Christianity. As a result of his travels, Aksum, and later Ethiopia as a whole, became closely linked to Coptic Egypt, and it was from Alexandria that the country was to obtain its patriarchs, for over the next fifteen hundred years.

Judging from subsequent evidence it may be supposed that Aksumite Christianity, like that of Ethiopia in later times, also enjoyed close ties with Jerusalem and Judaism. This can be traced to as early as the sixth century when King Kaléb is supposed to have despatched his crown to Jerusalem. His links with both Christianity and Judaism are likewise apparent from the fact that he had two sons, one called Gabra Krestos, literally Slave of Christ; the other named Israel. The former is known for his fine tomb, adjacent, as we have seen, to that of his father, while the other struck currency bearing his name, Israel.

Aksum's conversion to Christianity had far-reaching consequences. It made the country part of the Christian world, in which much of Ethiopia has remained to this day. Christianity over the centuries had an immense influence on the country, moulding its social life, no less than its spiritual and moral values, and had a profound influence on its culture, literature, poetry, and art. After the establishment of Christianity men and women from Aksum began making their way to Jerusalem on pilgrimage, and Ethiopians indeed continue to do so to the present.

A no less important development was the coming, towards the end of the fifth century, of the Nine Saints, a group of Greek-speaking missionaries, mainly, if not, entirely from Syria, then

---

[37]   Munro-Hay, 1991, p. 81.

referred to in Ethiopia as Rom, i.e. Rome, or the Eastern Roman Empire. One of them, Abba Asfé, founder of a monastery at Yéha, has already been referred to, while another, Abba Aragawi, will be mentioned shortly.[38] These holy men all established monasteries in the north of the country, several in the vicinity of Aksum, and played an important part in introducing the monastic system, and a Christian educational system, into Ethiopia.[39]

The Nine Saints were probably also involved in translating, or re-translating the Bible, mainly from the Greek, into Geʿez. The Ethiopian Bible differs from the western in that it includes the Apocrypha. This was important in biblical history, for the *Book of Enoch*, the *Book of Jubilees*, and the *Ascension of Isaiah*, were unknown except through their Ethiopic versions, which first came to the attention of European biblical scholars only in the late eighteenth century.

Christianity in the Aksumite period continued to make steady progress, so much so that Kosmos observed around 525 that 'everywhere' in the country there were 'churches of the Christians, and bishops, martyrs, monks and recluses, where the Gospel of Christ is proclaimed'.[40]

The first important church at Aksum is believed to date from the time of the city's conversion to Christianity in the early fourth century. Dedicated to Saint Mary, it was known, as we have seen, as the Church of St Mary of Seyon. A good account of the building, as it existed in the early sixteenth century, was written by Alvares. He states that it was a 'very large' and 'very noble' structure, with five naves of 'good width and great length', and 'seven chapels, all with their backs to the east and their altars well placed'. The ceiling and walls were 'covered with paintings', and the floor 'well worked with handsome cut stone'.

This fine building was shortly afterwards destroyed as a result of the famous Adal Muslim invasion led by Imam Ahmad ibn Ibrahim, later nicknamed Ahmad Grañ, or in Amharic the Left-

---

[38]   The Nine Saints comprised Abba Aléf, founder of the monastery of Behza; Abba Sehma, that of Sedenya; Abba Aragawi, of Dabra Damo; Abba Asfé, of Yéha; Abba Garima, of Madara; Abba Panteléwon, of a monastery called him, just outside Aksum; Abba Liqanos, of Dabra Kuanasel; Abba Guba, of Madara; and Abba Yemʿata, of a monastery in Garʿalta.

[39]   Ullendorff, 1968, p. 52.

[40]   McCrindle, 1897, p. 120.

handed. On the site of this church a new building was later constructed. Also dedicated to St Mary, it was erected in 1665 by Emperor Fasiladas, the founder of the first great castle of Gondar, and was restored by his grandson Emperor Iyasu I. This noble structure, which contains numerous fine paintings, including one of the Nine Saints, has a flat roof and crenellated walls, reminiscent of Gondarine architecture. Like many other Ethiopian places of worship it also fulfils the role of a museum. Its entrance thus houses two cannon captured long afterwards by Emperor Yohannes IV in the course of victories over Egyptian invaders in 1875–6. The nearby church store, a modern building situated in a small courtyard behind the church, is reputedly the resting place of the Ark of the Covenant, and contains a wealth of church property. This includes the crowns of a succession of emperors and church functionaries, numerous processional and hand crosses, many valuable illuminated manuscripts, and other treasures.

In front of the church are a collection of worked stones: the remains of the chairs of twelve judges, according to tradition, once attached to the Aksumite court. Towering above all these antiquities is the modern Church of Mary of Seyon, a large circular domed building erected long afterwards during the reign of Emperor Haile Sellassie, with a disproportionally tall adjacent bell-tower. The modern church, the site today of most of Aksum's great religious services, differs from its predecessor in being open to women.

The conversion of Aksum was followed by the founding of numerous monasteries. One of the earliest, and undoubedly finest, was that of Dabra Damo, believed to date from the time of King Gabra Masqal. It was founded by one of the Nine Saints, Abuna, or Abba, Aragawi, who was supposedly carried to its almost inaccessible summit by an amiable serpent, and is so depicted in innumerable church paintings. Today visitors can ascend only with the help of a rope provided by the no less friendly monks. Access, as in other Ethiopian monasteries, is barred to women, and even to female cattle, sheep, and chickens.

The method of wall construction at Dabra Damo repeats that depicted on the three principal obelisks of Aksum. There is the same alternate recession and projection of the walls, the same horizontal timbers built in at intervals, with beams ending in 'monkey heads' slotted into them. The windows and door frames likewise reproduce those of Aksum, and the monastery's twin doors are also of distinctively Aksumite style. The building has a pleasantly decorative appearance. It is produced by vertical planes of light and shade imparted by the alternate recession and projection of the walls, and enhanced by horizontal bands of ornament formed by the built-in timbers. This is emphasized by the deep bands of shadow cast by the projecting courses designed to throw off rain water.

Muhammad and the Advent of Islam

Aksum played an important, and honourable, role in the early history of Islam. This went back to the youth of the Prophet Muhammad, who as an infant was nursed by an Ethiopian woman, Baraka 'Umm Ayman. As a posthumous child he was later brought up by his maternal grandfather, Abdal Muttalib, who reportedly visited Aksum frequently on business.

The Prophet's association with Aksum is further indicated in the *hadith*, or Arab traditions about his life. They recall that at the beginning of his teaching Muhammad's followers came under bitter persecution in Arabia. The Prophet, it is said, then pointed across the Red Sea towards Abyssinia, and, strangely echoing the ancient Greek idea of the 'blameless Ethiopians', declared, 'Yonder lieth lies a country where no one is wronged: a land of righteousness. Depart thither; and remain there until it pleases the Lord to open your way'. In 615 AD a group of Muslims therefore made their way to Aksum, where they received hospitable treatment. They included Muhammad's son-in-law and future successor 'Uthman ibn 'Affan, the Prophet's daughter Ruqayya, and former maid Baraka, and two of his future wives, Umm Habiba and Umm Salma. The refugees soon exceeded a hundred.

An embassy from Arabia was later despatched to Aksum, with many costly presents, to request the refugees' return. The ambassadors were received by the then Aksumite king, whom the Arabs refer to as Ashama ibn Abjar, and is believed to have been the Aksumite ruler Armah. He reportedly listened to them, and then to the leader of the refugees, Muhammad's cousin Jafar ibn Ali Talib. Having heard what both sides had to say the monarch turned, it is said, to the Arab envoys, and declared, in a famous riposte, 'If you were to offer me a mountain of gold, I would not give up these people who have taken refuge with me'.

At the end of their persecution the refugees duly returned to Arabia. One of the women, Umm Habiba, was later betrothed to the Prophet, on which occasion King Armah provided a dowry. From her and another wife, Umm Salma, who had also found refuge at Aksum, Muhammad is said to have learnt of the beauty of its Church of St Mary of Seyon. Arab tradition holds that he was on one occasion shown an icon of the Holy Virgin – which doubtless originated in Aksum, and was so impressed with it that he shielded it with his hand, thus protecting it from a ban he had issued against the figurative representation of human images. The Prophet is said to have been much gratified by the kindness afforded by King Armah to his disciples. On learning of the monarch's death he supposedly prayed for the Aksumite ruler's soul, and subsequently told his followers to 'leave the Abyssinians in peace', thus exempting them from the *Jihad*, or Holy War.[41]

One of the Prophet's earliest converts was Bilal ibn Rabah, a freed slave of Abyssinian origin, born in Mecca. Because of his fine voice he became Muhammad's first *muadhdhin*, who called the faithful to prayer, and was described by Muhammad as 'the first fruit of Abyssinia'. Early contacts between Islam and Aksum also found expression in the use in the *Quran* of a number of Ge'ez words.[42]

The Decline of Aksum and the Rise of the Zagwe

Despite the Prophet's admiration for the Ethiopians, and his close ties with King Armah, the rise of Islam was in the long run detrimental to Aksum, which began to decline at around this time.

The actual reasons for the fall of Aksum are obscure. Some scholars have sought to see them in the economic field; others

<hr/>

[41] For detailed accounts of the flight of the early Muslim refugees to Aksum see inter alia Muir, 1878 and Watt, 1953.
[42] Jeffery, 1938.

in the political, or military. It has thus been postulated that an increase in the Aksumite population led to over-cropping of the land, and consequent soil degradation, as well as to defor-estation, resulting in soil erosion. Others have argued that Aksumite agriculture collapsed on account of climatic changes, followed by recurrent drought and famine. Proponents of a politico-military explanation hold, on the other hand, that the Aksumite state was seriously weakened by attacks from the Béja tribes to the west, and/or by difficulties, and rebellion, in south Arabia.[43]

Be all this as it may, there can be no denying that the rise of the new Islamic religion led to an Arab renaissance, which posed a major challenge to the city. The Arabs before long made them-selves the masters of the Red Sea, and its islands, including some immediately off the African coast. This brought an end to Aksum's hitherto commercial paramountcy in the region.

Aksumite power, for this and other reasons, including local rebellions, and perhaps land degradation, seems to have began to decline around the seventh century. The production of coins ceased around that time, and the city fell on increasingly hard times.

Ethiopian tradition holds that Aksumite power was later seriously challenged, around the ninth century, by a rebel queen, variously termed Judit, Gudit, or Esato, i.e. 'fire'. Said to have been either 'Pagan' or 'Jewish', in other words non-Christian, she is believed to have captured Aksum, and to have hurled down many of its historic obelisks. The legend of this legendary queen, who came, some think, from the country west or south-west of Aksum, finds support in two near contemporary documents. The first is in an interesting account by the late tenth century Arab geographer Ibn Hawqal who observes:

> The country of *Habasha* has been ruled by a woman for many years; she has killed the king of the *Habasha* who was called the *Hadani* [*Hasé* or *Asé*, i.e. Emperor]. Until today she rules with complete independence in her own country and the frontier areas of the territory of the *Hadani*, in the southern part of [the country of] the *Habasha*.

[43] For a recent assessment of Aksum chronology see Munro-Hay, 1990, pp. 47–53.

The second reference to a woman rebel is found in an eleventh-century Coptic work, the *History of the Patriarchs of Alexandria*. Referring to the Aksumite king, it observes:

> A woman, a queen of the Bani al-Hamwiyah had revolted against him and against his country. She took captive from it many people and burned many cities and drove him from place to place.[44]

The difficulties then apparently encountered by the Aksumite state are also illustrated in another passage in the same work. It tells of an Ethiopian ruler writing pathetically to his contemporary, King George of Nubia, to explain the problem of obtaining a bishop from Egypt: 'I have mentioned this to you . . . in fear that the Christian religion might pass away and cease among us. Six patriarchs [of Alexandria] have sat on the throne and have not paid attention to our lands, which are abandoned without a shepherd. Our bishops and priests are dead and our churches are ruined.'

Power, as we shall see, was subsequently usurped, in the early twelfth century, by a new dynasty, the Zagwé, which was based in the more southerly province of Lasta. The rise of this dynasty was a turning point in Ethiopian history, for it led to a major southward shift in the centre of political power. Several further shifts were to occur in ensuing centuries.

Medieval Coronation Ceremonies

Though Aksum ceased to be the political capital of the realm in the early twelfth century it continued to be the country's religious or spiritual capital. Its on-going importance can be seen from the fact that several medieval Ethiopian emperors – perhaps all who could in fact do so – travelled to Aksum for their coronation ceremonies. The first ruler recorded as doing so was the great fifteenth century centralizing Emperor Zar'a Ya'qob. Travelling to Aksum from Shawa he entered the city walls, after which he is reported by his chronicle to have thrown gold around to all and sundry. On the

---

[44] Quoted in Sergew Hable Sellassie, 1972, pp. 229–30.

coronation day itself he sat on a stone throne dating back from Aksumite times, and on other occasions seated himself on an ancient stone chair, flanked by those of the twelve Aksumite judges.[45] This stone furniture, as already noted, can be seen to this day.

Another ruler crowned at Aksum was the sixteenth-century emperor, Sarsa Dengel, who travelled there from the north-west of the country in 1580. The ceremonial rites, according to his chronicle, were carried out in the traditional manner. He was thus received by the city's clergy bearing a large golden cross, silver censers and twelve colourful silk umbrellas. The local priests and heads of nearby covenants sung hymns, and chanted, 'Be blessed, O King of Israel!' In front of them stood a group of Aksumite women holding a long cord as if to bar his way. Their leaders, two old women, had taken up positions, to the right and left of the path. On seeing the emperor they shouted at him arrogantly, 'Who are you, of what family, and of what descent?' Referring to the biblical kings of Israel and their claimed Ethiopian descendant, King Menilek, son of Solomon and the Queen of Sheba, he replied, 'I am the son of David, son of Solomon, son of Ebna Hakim', i.e. Menilek.

The women then questioned him again, no less insistantly, as to his identity, whereupon he spoke of his descent from more recent Ethiopian rulers, declaring, 'I am the son of Zar'a Ya'qob, son of Ba'eda Maryam, son of Na'od'. The women then once more inquired as to his identity and origin, whereupon he lifted his sword, and declared, 'I am Malak Sagad [i.e. Sarsa Dengel], son of King Wanag Sagad, son of Admas Sagad'. So saying, he cut the rope held by the girls, whereupon the women cried out, 'Truly, truly, you are the son of Seyon [Zion], the son of David, son of Solomon!'. The city's priests thereupon began chanting on the one side, and the women applauding on the other. Drums were beaten, and cannons and muskets fired, making a sound which the chronicler likens to that of thunder.[46]

Such coronation drama of late sixteenth century Aksum shows that the city, fifteen hundred years after its foundation, still retained much of its historic importance. With the rise of the city of Gondar, in the seventeenth century, Aksum, however, ceased to be

[45]   Perruchon, 1893, pp. 40–51.
[46]   Conti Rossini, 1907, pp. 89–91.

a place of coronation. It nevertheless remained the country's principal religious centre. This caused the late nineteenth-century British traveller Bent to describe it, in the title of a classic work, as *The Sacred City of the Ethiopians.*

3

The Zagwé Dynasty, Lalibala Churches, and the Solomonic 'Restoration'

The decline of Aksum was followed in the early twelfth century, by a southward shift in the balance of political power, from Tegray to Lasta, an area then largely inhabited by Agaw-speakers. There a chief called Marara, or Mara, founded a new dynasty known as the Zagwé. Its capital was at Adafa, not far from the present town of Lalibala, in the mountains of Lasta.

An Obscure and Poorly Documented Period

The Zagwé period, which extended from about 1137 to 1270 AD, is one of the most obscure in Ethiopian history, for it left remarkably few records. Archaeology, so rich for the Aksumite period, has precious little to contribute for that of the Zagwés. Unlike their Aksumite predecessors, they did not mint coins, or produce inscriptions, and, living much further from the coast, made far less use of imported, datable, articles. No known foreign traveller moreover described the country at this time. If the dynasty produced chronicles, they are apparently no longer extant. Subsequent writings on the Zagwés tend to be hostile, for their successors chose to refer to them as usurpers. Three members of the dynasty, Yemrahana Krestos, Lalibala, and Na'akweto La'ab, were, however, renowned as notable builders of churches, and, paradoxically enough, most members of the dynasty were canonized by the Ethiopian Church.

Traditional Ethiopian accounts of the Zagwé consist of legendary *gadl*, or largely imaginary, eulogized, lives of the principal canonized rulers. These works are summarized in the Ethiopian

Synaxarium, or collected lives of the saints. Several brief, by no means necessarily accurate, lists of Zagwé kings are also extant. Both sources apparently date from long after Zagwé times.

Some contemporary light on the period is, however, shed by two foreign sources: the already cited Coptic *History of the Patriarchs of Alexandria*, and the writings of the late twelfth and early thirteenth-century Armenian author Abu Salih.

Yemrahana Krestos, Harbé, and the Proposed Emancipation of the Church from Egypt

Despite the charge that they had usurped power from the Aksumite rulers there can be no denying that the Zagwé inherited, continued, and developed, their predecessors' Christian traditions, then well over five hundred years old. Several Zagwé rulers thus took a keen interest in the propagation of Christianity, and will ever be remembered as great church-builders.

Zagwé support for the Church appears to have started early in the dynasty's history. Tradition holds that Marara's grandson, Yemrahana Krestos, was the first great Zagwé church-builder. He is said to have erected one of the finest cave churches of Lasta, which to this day bears his name. This structure, only 42 feet long, is situated in a cave 12 miles NNE of Lalibala, and is *built* (not excavated, as the case with the subsequent, more famous Lalibala churches).

The church of Yemrahana Krestos, though erected a millennium after the Aksum obelisks, and five hundred years after Dabra Damo, is in characteristic Aksumite style. The walls, which resemble those of Dabra Damo, are made of horizontal beams set into a stone structure, which protrudes and recesses alternately, in typical Aksumite manner. Doors and windows are framed with wooded beams, with 'monkey-heads' reminiscent of those on the principal Aksum obelisks. The interior has well built arches, an elaborate nave ceiling, a dome over the sanctuary, and a wealth of carved and painted detail.

The reign of Yemrahana Krestos coincided with the capture of Jerusalem in 1189 by the Egyptian ruler Salah ad-Din, popularly known in the west as Saladin. Though a Muslim he was favourable to the Christians of Ethiopia, to whom he granted the Chapel of the Invention of the Cross in the Church of the Holy Sepulchre, in Jerusalem, and a station in the Grotto of the Nativity in nearby Bethlehem.

Yemrahana Krestos was succeeded by his cousin Harbé, a would-be reformer, who seems to have wished to emancipate Ethiopia from its age-old dependence on Coptic Egypt. This dated back to the time of Frumentius, who had been, as we have seen, ordained by Patriarch Athanasius of Alexandria. It had subsequently become customary for the Ethiopians to obtain their Metropolitans, or the heads of their church, from Egypt.

To break the country's subordination on Egypt, Harbé sought to increase the number of Coptic bishops to seven, which would have enabled him to have them ordain additional bishops in Ethiopia, and thereby gain independence of the Egyptian Church. The story of this attempted move is told in the *History of the Patriarchs*, which states that an Ethiopian monarch, whose name is not specified, summoned the country's Coptic bishop, Abba Mika'él, and requested him to consecrate further bishops. The prelate, however, refused, declaring that this could only be done by the Patriarch in Alexandria. The Ethiopian ruler thereupon despatched letters to both the Patriarch and the secular ruler of Egypt, telling them of his desire for more bishops. The ruler was at first sympathetic, and ordered the Patriarch to comply with the Ethiopian request. The prelate, however, warned him that if the number of bishops was increased the Ethiopians would be able to consecrate an Archbishop, after which they could appoint patriarchs for themselves, and develop 'enmity and hostility' towards their Muslim neighbours.

The Patriarch accordingly wrote to the Ethiopian monarch, commanding him to desist from his attempt to ordain more bishops. The messengers taking this message duly returned to Egypt, where they reported that fire had 'descended from heaven' upon the Ethiopian king's palace, that rain had not fallen, and that the country had experienced a great famine and pestilence. These were the first such calamities for which historical mention exists. The ruler was reportedly so terrified that he abandoned his plans to increase the number of bishops, and wrote to the Patriarch, begging forgiveness, whereupon God, it is claimed, 'removed His wrath' from the Ethiopians. Rain fell again, the fields were sown, commodity prices became cheap, and the epidemic came to an end.

A slightly different version of this story appears in the Ethiopian

Synaxarium. It claims that the Egyptian ruler at first agreed to the Ethiopian request, but that it was his nobles who came to him, saying that if the bishops became numerous the Ethiopians would 'wax bold', appoint as many bishops as they pleased, and become independent. The king, realizing the danger to his position, then told the Patriarch, to curse the Ethiopian ruler, after which the latter's palace caught fire, drought, famine and plague broke out, and 'great tribulation came upon the people'. When, however, he repented, 'God removed the famine and the plague', and 'the people rejoiced with great joy'.

Harbé's projected reform, according to both versions of the story, was thus frustrated by supernatural intervention. The Ethiopian Church's emancipation from Egypt was not in fact destined to be achieved for over seven hundred years.

Lalibala and his Monolithic Churches

Harbé was succeeded by his brother Lalibala. The best known of the Zagwé rulers he is renowned as a great builder, or, more exactly, excavator, of rock-hewn churches.

Lalibala's life is enshrined in legend. It is traditionally claimed that he was surrounded, shortly after his birth, by a cloud of bees, whereupon his mother, seized by the spirit of prophecy, cried out, 'The bees know that this child will become king!' He was accordingly named Lalibala, which means, 'The bee recognizes his sovereignty'.

King Lalibala, and no doubt other members of his dynasty, are said to have also asserted their legitimacy by reference to biblical writ. They are reported to have identified themselves with Moses, who, according to the *Book of Numbers* 12: 1, had 'married an Ethiopian woman'. Abu Salih, probably reflecting a contemporary local tradition, claimed in the early thirteenth century that the Zagwé ruler was 'of the family of Moses and Aaron, on account of the coming of Moses into Abyssinia', and that Moses had 'married the king's daughter'.

Lalibala, who, like some of his predecessors, had his capital at Adafa, later turned his attention to a nearby site, where the volcanic land lent itself to the excavation of rock-hewn churches. The locality was renamed Roha, after Al-Roha, the Arabic name for

Edessa, the holy city of Syrian Christendom. There he reputedly built a group of rock-hewn churches, for which he was canonized. They were so remarkable that after his death the place was renamed Lalibala in his honour.

Great as was Lalibala's reported contribution to the excavation of rock-hewn churches, it should be emphasized that neither he nor his dynasty was the initiator of them. Monolithic churches, some in the vicinity of Aksum, would seem to date back long before the Zagwé, perhaps to within a century or two of the coming of Christianity. Over a hundred such churches have been described in Tegray alone.[1] Rock-hewn churches can moreover be seen all over the Ethiopian region, from east of Karan, in Eritrea, to the vicinity of Goba, in Balé, a thousand miles to the south.

The rock churches of Lalibala are unique, not so much for their beauty and architectural distinction, remarkable as this is, but because they were located in close proximity to each other. Eleven churches, all cut out of red volcanic tuff, are situated within little more than a stone's throw apart. Over a dozen other churches, several very remarkable, are also to be found within a day or so's journey of the town.

The first foreign traveller to describe the Lalibala churches was the early sixteenth-century Portuguese traveller Alvares. Recalling the impression they made on him, he concludes:

> I weary of writing more about these buildings, because it seems to me that I shall not be believed if I write more, and because regarding what I have already written they may blame me for untruth, therefore I swear by God, in Whose power I am, that all that is written is the truth, and there is much more than what I have written, and I have left it that they may not tax me with its being falsehood.[2]

The eleven Lalibala churches are clustered in two main groups, linked together by a number of tunnels and/or semi-subterranean passages. The first group comprises six places of worship, namely those of Madhané Alam (by far the largest), Maryam, Denagel, and, in close proximity to each other, Sellasé, Golgotha and Mika'él. The second group consists of four churches, those of

---

[1] Plant, 1985.
[2] Beckingham and Huntingford, 1961, I, p. 226.

Plate 3   Lalibala: the church of Madhané Alam, the largest of the town's notable rock churches. Photo: Alula Pankhurst.

Amanu'él (the largest in this group), Marqoréwos, Abba Libanos, and Gabr'él-Rufa'él. There is in addition a single isolated structure, that of Giyorgis, or St George.

The largest, noblest, and perhaps historically most interesting, of the Lalibala churches is that of Madhané Alam, or Saviour of the World. It is may well have been modelled on the old Church of St Mary of Seyon at Aksum, which was then extant, and has been described, as we have seen, by Alvares.

Madhané Alam, which is no less than 33.5 metres long, 23.5 metres wide, and 11 metres high, is unusual in having an external colonnade of pillars on all four sides. These columns extend from its main plinth to its gabled roof which they support. Like the old St Mary of Seyon, the church has a nave and four isles, and four rows of seven pillars, each carved from the single block of stone which forms the church. These pillars rise straight from the stone floor, without any bases, and are surmounted by stone brackets to support the continuous barrel vault of the nave and the lateral and traverse semi-circular arches of the aisles. The principal door is in the centre of the west front. There are also doors on the north and south sides. These doors have semi-circular arches supported by brackets. There are also two rows of windows. The upper, which are decorated with diaper patterns, have round arches supported by brackets. The lower windows on the other hand are rectangular, and filled with panels of pierced stone ornamented with a central cross. The beauty of the interior lies in the gracious lines of its many columns and arches. These are often fitfully illuminated by rays of light, which glance upon them through the arched doors and interstices of the pierced stonework.[3]

Also of special interest at Lalibala is the church of Amanu'él, the second largest structure, and an edifice of almost perfect workmanship, which harks back to the church of Yemrahana Krestos. The walls thus project and recess alternately, and, though cut from a single block of stone, are carved to make them appear as if made of horizontal bands of timber and stone. Some of the windows are cut in the same shape as the decorative device on the top of the principal Aksum obelisks, while others have arches supported by brackets resembling those of Madhané Alam. The interior has five bays. Rectangular columns separate nave and isles. There is a dome over the sanctuary, a barrel vault over the nave, and a beautifully carved frieze. A spiral staircase, likewise cut out of the living rock, leads to the upper gallery with several small chambers.

The church of Maryam differs from the other Lalibala places of worship in having three exterior porches built out from the main structure. Above the west porch is a fine bas-relief, one of very few ever carved in the country, of St George engaged in combat with the dragon. The church has a nave and two aisles formed by two rows of five piers. There are three chapels at one end, each with its own altar, and an upper story or loft over each aisle. The church is unusual in being situated in a courtyard with two other monolithic structures. The church's interior is richly painted, with remarkable frescoes. The capitals, the soffits of some semi-circular

---

[3] For detailed descriptions and photographs of these churches see Monti della Corte, 1940; Pankhurst, 1955, pp. 157–62.

arches, and some of the piers are beautifully carved in low relief, with such ornament as foliage, birds and animals, and a two-headed eagle.

Very different again is the Church of Giyorgis, or St George, which stands somewhat apart from the two main groups of churches. One of the most elegant of the Lalibala structures it is excavated in the form of a Greek cross. It too imitates Aksumite architecture, as evident from its representation of horizontal wooden beams and stonework, its doors and windows, which are reminiscent of the finest obelisks, and its numerous 'monkey heads'.

Two other churches deserve special mention; Golgotha because it is the structure in which Lalibala is believed to have been interred, and Abba Libanos, because it is thought to have been excavated after the death of Lalibala, by his widow, Masqal Kebra.

Not all the present churches were perhaps originally intended for religious purposes. Marqoréwos differs from most Ethiopian churches in that it is not oriented to the east. This would suggest that it was probably not conceived as an ecclesiatical building. Gabr'él-Rufa'él has a monumental facade, which has given rise to the belief that it may have been designed as a palace, rather than as a church. This view is reinforced by the fact that iron shackles have been found within its precincts, leading to the assumption that it may have served as a prison. (It was not unusual in Ethiopia for palaces to have a room, or rooms, of detention attached to them.)

Lalibala established this remarkable group of churches, it is believed, in order to make them, and hence his capital, a major place of pilgrimage. Support for this view is found in the *Gadla Lalibala*, or Acts of Lalibala, which claims that visiting the churches was equivalent to seeing the face of Christ. In establishing his capital as a place of pilgrimage Lalibala may have been influenced by the fact that Jerusalem, hitherto the country's principal pilgrimage site, had been captured by the Muslims, and had therefore become difficult of access. He may also have felt that Jerusalem was too far from Lasta and its environs, which were of course much further inland than Aksum. Be that as it may, there seems to have been a deliberate attempt at Lalibala to simulate the Holy City. A number of places in and around the Lasta capital were thus given biblical names. A local hill was called Calvary and a stream Jordanos, after the Jordan river, while several graves were referred to as those of Adam, Jesus Christ, and other biblical personages.

Lalibala's efforts to make his capital a pilgrimage centre were remarkably successful. Over the centuries innumerable pilgrims from far and near made their way to the city, and on religious festivals congregated around its remarkable churches, as they indeed do to this day.

The Decline of the Zagwé Dynasty

Lalibala, generally regarded as the greatest of the Zagwé rulers, was succeeded by his nephew Na'akweto La'ab, who built a beautiful church in a cave half a day's journey from Lalibala, and which to this day bears his name. His reign was, however, reportedly fraught with difficulties, as a result of which he abdicated, or was deposed, in favour of Lalibala's son Yetbaraq.

Difficulties within the ruling family appear to have coincided with increasing regional opposition to Zagwé rule. This appears to have centred mainly in Tegray, Amhara and Shawa, and to some extent in the south-westerly province of Damot, that is to say from lands all around Lasta. Opposition also came from prominent churchmen, several apparently related to one of the Zagwé's principal opponents, the Shawan prince Yekuno Amlak. Church opponents included Abba Iyasus Mo'a, abbot of the monastery of Dabra Hayq, and Abba Takla Haymanot, abbot of Dabra Libanos, i.e. in two of Ethiopia's principal monasteries.[4]

Such combined opposition proved decisive. It led, around 1270, to the overthrow of the Zagwé dynasty, and resulted in another major shift in the centre of political power, this time to Shawa, where Yekuno Amlak established himself on the throne. He thereby established a new dynasty, which was to dominate Ethiopia for over half a millennium.

Yekuno Amlak, the 'Solomonic Restoration' and the *Kebra Nagast*

The antecedents of Yekuno Amlak are uncertain. Some traditions claim that he was descended on his father's side from

---

[4] Taddesse Tamrat, 1972, pp. 66–8.

Delna'od, the last king of Aksum, and on his mother's from a prominent Amhara family. Others suggest that he had been involved in earlier struggles within the Zagwé dynasty, and had used the position he had acquired to wrest power for himself. Accounts as to exactly how the Zagwé were ousted, and the amount of force involved, differ significantly. It is, however, generally agreed that Yekuno Amlak had powerful regional support from the north and south of the country, as well as from the Church, many of whose prominent leaders were reportedly related to him on his mother's side.

More significant than Yekuno Amlak's actual parentage was his claim to descent, through Delna'od, to King Solomon and the Queen of Sheba. This claim was soon to find expression in the country's national epic, the *Kebra Nagast*, or Glory of Kings. This work, written in Ge'ez during the reign of Yekuno Amlak's great warrior grandson Amda Seyon (1312–42), was based on the biblical story of Solomon and the Queen of Sheba as told in 1 Kings 10: 1–13, which begins:

> And when the queen of Sheba heard of the fame of Solomon concerning the name of the Lord, she came to prove him with hard questions. . . . she came to Jerusalem with a very great train, with camels that bore spices, and very much gold, and precious stones; and when she was come to Solomon, she communed with him of all that was in her heart.

The text goes on to claim that 'king Solomon gave unto the queen of Sheba all her desire, whatever she asked, beside that which Solomon gave her of his royal bounty'. After this she reportedly 'turned and went to her own country, she and her servants'.

The Ethiopian version, which was far longer and more elaborate than the biblical, claimed (1) that Sheba, also known as Makeda, was an Ethiopian queen; (2) that she gave birth to a son by Solomon, a boy by name Menilek; (3) that Menilek, after visiting his father in Jerusalem, took the Ark of the Covenant to Ethiopia which is specifically referred to by that name; and (4) that it was from Menilek that the country's later emperors were all descended.

The origins of the *Kebra Nagast* are perhaps deliberately shrouded in obscurity. The text, according to its colophon, which was in Arabic, was composed by an Ethiopian cleric, Yeshaq, the Nebura'ed, or lay governor, of Aksum, who lived in the early fourteenth century. The colophon also claims that the work had been translated into that language from a Coptic manuscript belonging to the throne of St Mark, i.e. the Patriarchate of Alexandria, and had been found at Nazret. No Coptic or Arabic version has, however, ever come to light, and it may be assumed that the text was in fact originally written in Ge'ez.

In the colophon Yeshaq asks why the work had not been translated earlier. He replies that this was because it had become available only during the time of the Zagwés, who had not had it translated because of a passage in it which declared: 'Those who reign not being Israelites [i.e. descendants of Solomon and Sheba] are transgressors of the Law'. Yeshaq adds, by way of conclusion, that in writing the work he had 'toiled much' for the 'glory of Ethiopia' and its king, and, having consulted Ya'ebika Egzi'e, the 'God-loving governor' of the Aksum, had been encouraged to complete his writing.[5]

The *Kebra Nagast*, it should be emphasized, was not the first work to claim that the Ark had been taken to Ethiopia. This belief had been expressed a century earlier by the Armenian author, Abu Salih. He declares that the Ethiopians possessed the Ark of the Covenant, in which 'were the two tables of stone, inscribed by the finger of God with the commandments which he ordained for the children of Israel', and, adds that the Ark was 'attended and carried' in Ethiopia by a large number of Israelites descended from the prophet David'.[6]

The *Kebra Nagast*, unlike Abu Salih, seeks to explain how the Ark supposedly reached Ethiopia. Basing itself on the Bible, but, greatly elaborating on it, it claims that the Queen of Sheba, whom it calls Makeda, visited Solomon to learn of his wisdom, after which she accepted his religion. She was then prevailed upon, by a stratagem, to share his bed, so that he could 'work his will with her'. Further embellishing the story the text goes on to claim that the Jewish monarch then had a dream, or perhaps more correctly, a nightmare, in which he saw the sun, which had hitherto shone over Israel, move away above Ethiopia, over which it shone brightly for ever more.

---

[5] Budge, 1928, pp. 228–9. See also Taddesse Tamrat, 1972, p. 64.
[6] Evetts, 1895, pp. 287–8.

The queen, according to the *Kebra Nagast*, then returned to her own country, Ethiopia, where she gave birth to a son by Solomon. The child, Menilek, on attaining manhood, travelled to Jerusalem to see his father. The latter recognized him as his first-born son, and entreated him to remain in Israel, but the young man insisted on keeping a promise to return to his mother. Solomon agreed, but gave his son the first-born of his leading courtiers and clerics to accompany him. Reluctant to depart on so long a journey without divine protection they decided to abduct the Ark of the Covenant so as to take it with them. Menilek, on being subsequently informed, declared that since God had allowed this to happen it must have been His wish that the Ark be taken to Ethiopia.

Another Ethiopian version of the legend claims that the Ethiopians of old had worshipped a serpent to whom they had been obliged to give a young girl as tribute each year. Eventually a stranger called Angabo appeared, and offered to dispose of the hated animal, if the people agreed to make him their king. A pact to that effect was duly concluded, after which Angabo fed a poisoned goat to the snake, and then cut off its head. He was duly crowned, and in the passage of time was succeeded by his daughter, Makeda, Queen of Sheba. The remainder of the story then continued more or less along the lines of the *Kebra Nagast*, and concluded by asserting that Menilek, Makeda's son by Solomon, brought back the Ark to Ethiopia. This version telling of the worship of the snake, and of the latter's destruction by Angabo, seems to have gained greater popular currency than that in the *Kebra Nagast*.[7] The snake story was later illustrated in many twentieth-century popular paintings of the Queen of Sheba's visit to Solomon, presented in 'cartoon strip' form, and produced to this day.[8]

The traditions embodied in the *Kebra Nagast* were politically most powerful. Sheba's association with Solomon, and the birth of their son Menilek, seemed to show that the rulers of Ethiopia had a unique lineage, and deserved special respect – and obedience – as befitted the descendants of the biblical kings of Israel. Solomon's dream, followed by the Ethiopian acquisition of the Ark – suppos-

[7] Littmann, 1904.
[8] McCall, 1968, pp. 34–43; Pankhurst, 'Some Notes for the History of Ethiopian Secular Art', 1966, pp. 57–73.

edly by God's wish, likewise appeared to indicate that the Ethiopians had replaced the Jews as God's chosen people.

Such beliefs duly found their way into the country's royal chronicles, which began to be written in the early fourteenth century, during the reign of Emperor Amda Seyon. These writings are important in reflecting Ethiopian political thought of the time. They present God as the Almighty Old Testament God of War, who, having fought on behalf of the children of Israel, had transferred his support no less exclusively to Ethiopia, its rulers and people. The king of Ethiopia was thus, it was claimed, the instrument of God. *Psalm 110, 2*, was quoted as saying to the monarch, 'The Lord shall send the rod of thy strength out of Zion', while Psalm 2: 9, speaking of his subjects, and enemies, was cited as declaring, 'Thou shall rule them with a rod of iron; thou shalt dash them to pieces as a potter's vessel'.

Since the Ethiopians, according to the *Kebra Nagast*, were beloved of the Lord, and their rulers descended from the kings of Israel, the chroniclers found little difficulty in identifying the monarch's foes with the unrighteous, described and defeated, in the scriptures. Enemies of the Ethiopian monarchy were thus likened to Sennacharib king of Assyria, David's enemy Goliath, the wicked Pharaoh, the treacherous Judas Iscariat, and even terrible Satan himself.[9]

The Royal Chronicles, the *Fetha Nagast* and the Growth of Ge'ez Literature

The early 'Solomonic' period was an important one for the growth of Ge'ez literature. Besides the *Kebra Nagast*, with its legendary account of the Queen of Sheba's visit to Solomon, Amda Seyon's reign witnessed the composition of the country's first real work of history: a detailed, and seemingly fairly factual, though highly sychophantic account of the monarch's victorious campaigns against his Muslim adversaries to the east. This was the first of a series of royal chronicles, which were written for 'Solomonic' emperors down to modern times. Scarcely paralleled in Africa

[9] Pankhurst, 'Fear God, Honor the King: The Use of Biblical Allusion in Ethiopian Historical Literature', *NorthEastern African Studies* 8, 1 (1986), pp. 11–30; vol. 9, no. 1, pp. 25–88.

south of the Sahara, they provide a not too unbroken chronological narrative for the entire period. Also dating from this time were a number of historically interesting war songs in honour of Amda Seyon and later sovereigns.[10] The monarchs of this time all explicitly refer to themselves as rulers of Ethiopia.

A no less important work produced during Amda Seyon's reign was the country's legal code, the *Fetha Nagast*, or 'Law of the Kings'. Translated into Ge'ez from an Arabic text of a Copt called Ibn al-Assal, and based largely on biblical writ, it contained passages codifying the legal and social ideas of the time, among them the divine right of kings, and the right to own slaves. This code was consulted by Ethiopian monarchs when giving judgement, and remained in use until the early twentieth century.

Several major Ge'ez religious works were also written in this period. They included the Mysteries to Heaven and Earth, and four translations from the Arabic: the History of the Prophet Habbakuk, the Acts of the Apostles, the Acts of the Martyrs, and an early draft of the Synaxarium, or Lives of Saints – to which the acts of a number of later Ethiopian holy men, were subsequently added. Also of no small literary value was the *Zéna Eskender*, a legendary account of exploits of Alexander the Great, differing versions of which were then common throughout the East.[11]

Not a few other important Ge'ez literary works were written during the fifteenth century, notably during the reign of Emperor Zar'a Ya'qob (1433–68). A life-long devotee of the Virgin Mary he was himself reputedly an author of renown. He is believed to have drafted several religious texts, among them the *Mahsafa Milad*, or Book of the Nativity, the *Mahsafa Sellasé*, or Book of the Trinity, and the *Mahsafa Berhan*, or Book of Light. Other works of the period composed in honour of the Virgin included the *Ta'amra Maryam*, or Miracles of Mary, many copies of which were profusely illustrated, and the *Arganona Maryam Dengel*, or Harp of the Virgin Mary. The period also saw the composition of Acts, or Lives, of numerous Ethiopian Saints, or holy men. Notable among them were the fifth- or sixth-century Nine Saints (Aragawi, Garima, Pantaléwon, Asfé, and others), the Zagwé rulers (Yemrahana Krestos, Lalibala, and Na'akweto La'ab), and later holy men of Shawa (Filipos, and Takla

[10]   Guidi, 1889, pp. 53–66.
[11]   Cerulli, 1956, pp. 35–68.

Plate 4   A medieval Ethiopian manuscript: opening page of the Gospels. Note, left, representation of the Evangelist, writing, with two ink-wells beside him, for black and red ink. Photo: Alula Pankhurst.

Haymanot), Amhara (Ba-Salota Mika'él), and Wallo (Iyasus Mo'a).[12]

Also dating from this period are Ge'ez lives of several foreign saints. They include St George, a popular figure throughout the Christian Orient; and Gabra Manfus Qeddus, a European or Egyptian monk, who settled on the Shawan mountain of Zeqwala.[13]

These and other saints are depicted to this day, in many a church painting, according to strictly stylized iconography. Takla Haymanot is thus frequently shown, with wings, standing on one leg, or sometimes falling, unhurt, down a precipice. Gabra Manfus Qeddus, dressed in a costume of feathers, stands patiently, with lions and leopards on either side, kindly allowing a bird to drink from his eye. Abba Aragawi is carried to the summit of Dabra Damo by his friend, the snake. Samwél, i.e. Samuel, of Waldebba, rides a very docile lion. St George, who often appears in icons featuring the Virgin and Child on an adjacent panel, rides a horse,

[12] Cerulli, 1956, pp. 71–156.
[13] Budge, 1928, II, pp. 567–72. See also Ullendorff, 1973.

and spears a dragon beneath him, thereby rescuing a damsel taking refuge in a tree. In Ethiopia, unlike other lands of the Christian Orient, she has a name, and is referred to as Brutawit, literally the girl from Beirut.

4

Life in the Middle Ages: Contacts with Muslim Neighbours and Far-off Christians

Medieval Ethiopia may be said to date from the assumption of power of the Shawan, or 'Solomonic', dynasty, in 1270. The ensuing period, thanks to the royal chronicles and the writings of several foreign travellers, is far better documented than that of earlier times. Such sources reveal that Ethiopian medieval civilization owed much to that of Aksum and Lalibala. The powerful monarchical and religious institutions of the time were in particular highly reminiscent of those of the past.

Two significant differences between medieval and earlier times should, however, be noted. Firstly, the use of coined money, which had been minted in the Aksumite period, had long since come to an end. Trade was instead based on either barter, or 'primitive money', i.e. commodities such as bars of salt or pieces of cloth or iron, used instead of currency. The second difference was that stationary capitals, such as Aksum or Lalibala, were things of the past. They had been replaced by one of the most characteristic features of the medieval period: roving, or 'instant', capitals, which were often no more than temporary military camps.

The Powers of the Monarch and the Royal Succession

The monarchs of medieval Ethiopia stood, like their predecessors, at the apex of a great hierarchy of state. The status of the ruler was defined in the *Fetha Nagast*, or Law of the Kings.[1] Enunciating the

---

[1] For text and English translation see Guidi, 1897–9 and Paulos Tsadua, 1968.

Divine Right of Kings on the basis of Holy Writ, the code quoted Christ's command, in the *Gospel of St Matthew* 22: 21, 'Render . . . unto Caesar the things that are Caesar's; and unto God the thing's that are God's'. Even more pertinent were the words of St Paul in his *Epistle to the Romans*, also cited in the text, which declared:

> Let every soul be subject unto the higher powers. For there is no power but of God: the powers that be are ordained of God.
> Whosoever therefore resisteth the power, resisteth the ordinance of God; and they that shall resist shall receive to themselves damnation.
> For rulers are not a terror to good works, but to evil . . .
> (Romans 13: 1–3)

Ethiopian monarchs were theoretically endowed with immense powers. This was recognized by Hiob Ludolf, the seventeenth century German founder of Ethiopian studies in Europe, who emphatically declares: 'The Power of the Abessinian Kings is absolute, as well in Ecclesiastical as Civil Affairs'.[2]

The ruler's supremacy in fact, however, varied greatly from reign to reign. Imperial power was probably at its greatest during the time of the great centralizing emperor Zar'a Ya'qob (1434–68). His chronicle states that he inspired 'a great terror among the people of Ethiopia', who, 'trembled' in front of him, and, when he appeared, 'fled before him and took up a craintive and respectful position'.[3]

The authority of the monarch rested in large measure on his ability to appoint and dismiss provincial and other officials virtually at will, as well as to transfer land to or from them at his pleasure. This was noted by the Portuguese traveller Francisco Alvares. Describing the powers of Emperor Lebna Dengel (1508–40) over officials, he states that the king, whom he terms the Prester, appointed and deposed officials whenever he pleased, 'with or without cause'. These changes of personnel were so widely practised, he comments, that it created 'no ill humour', or if there was any it was kept secret, for during his six years in the country he saw:

[2] Ludolphus, 1684, p. 198.
[3] Perruchon, 1893, p. 16.

great lords turned out of their lordships, and others put into them, and I saw them together, and they appeared to be good friends (God knows their hearts). And in this country, whatever happens to them, of good fortune or of loss, they say of all of it, that God does it.[4]

Alvares also vividly portrays the manner in which the monarch overawed his governors. Describing the recall of one such official, the way in which he had to humble himself before entering the royal presence, and the general uncertainty surrounding his position and future prospects, the Portuguese author reports:

A lord approaches the court with great pomp and takes up quarters at least a league from the court, and there he often stays a month or two without stirring; and they treat them [the chiefs] as if they were forgotten as long as the Prester chooses. They [the chiefs] do not, however, refrain while thus forgotten from coming to Court and speaking to the other lords, but not with pomp or robed, but with two or three men, and stripped from the waist upwards, and with a sheepskin over their shoulders, and so they return to their tents until they have permission to come. When they get this permission, they enter it with great pomp, and playing kettledrums and instruments, encamp in their place, which is already ordained for each. When he [the chief] encamps he does not appear clothed as he does when he makes his entry, but walks about as before his entry, naked from the waist upwards . . . So they say: 'so and so is not yet in favour with our lord, for he still goes about stripped.'

However, as soon as the monarch had deigned to speak with the chief, the latter:

comes out dressed, and they say: 'So and so is in our lord's favour'. Then it is divulged and said why he was summoned, and sometimes and often they return to their lordships, and at others not. If they return to them they are sent away more quickly; and if they are taken away from them, they let them go five, six, and seven years without going away from the Court. By no manner of means can they go from the Court without permission, so obedient are they, and so much do they fear their King; and as they used to be accompanied by many people so now are they neglected, and they go about on a mule with two or three men, because the many

---

[4]   Beckingham and Huntingford, 1961, I, p. 116.

people who used to accompany them belonged to the lordships that have been taken away from them, and transfer themselves to the new lord; and this we used to see every day.

Emphasizing the weakness of a provincial ruler *vis-à-vis* the monarch, Alvares recalls that when the former 'sets out from the land of which he is lord', he:

> does not leave either wife or children or any property there because he goes away in the expectation of never returning, since . . . the Prester gives when he pleases, and takes away when he pleases; and if he happens to take it away, from that moment they take from him [i.e. the governor] whatever they find belonging to him in the lordship; that is to say the lord who comes to succeed him in that place [does so]. For this reason they [departing governors] carry everything away with them without leaving anything, or at least without putting it in another lordship.[5]

Despite its immense power the monarchy suffered from major weaknesses in connection with the succession. Until the reign of Emperor Naʻod (1494–1508) every emperor, according to Alvares, 'had five or six wives', and sons by them, or 'most of them'. Such children were all actual or potential claimants to the throne. The royal inheritance was in consequence often very uncertain. Alvares recalls that it was often said that 'the eldest born inherited', but others claimed that it was on the contrary 'he who appeared to the Prester the most apt and prudent'. Others again declared that the inheritor was he 'who had the most support'. The Portuguese author, for his part, believed that this latter assertion was the most correct, for the then *Abun*, or Patriarch, had told him that he and the Dowager Queen Great-Grandmother, Empress Eléni, had placed Lebna Dengel on the throne 'because they had all the great men and all the treasure in their hands'. 'Thus it appears to me', Alvares concludes, 'that besides primogeniture, supporters, friendships and treasure enter the question'.[6]

Another difficulty, arising from the absence of any clear line of succession, was that minors were often selected in place of seasoned or experienced princes. This was because the nobles, who preferred freedom under a youth than to chafe under a strong

[5]   Ibid., II, pp. 445–6.
[6]   Ibid., I, p. 241.

emperor, in many instances were able to choose a child king whom they could manipulate, at least until he came of age.

One final problem connected with the succession was that the death of an emperor frequently led to the collapse of royal authority. Government after that was at least temporarily not fully resumed until a successor had effectively taken over the reins of power. This difficulty was particularly serious when a monarch was unexpectedly killed in battle, whereupon his army, as we will see more than once in these pages, would often disintegrate, and his soldiers disappear from sight.

To protect the society, and government, from conflicts over the succession, the custom developed of detaining unwanted royal contenders to the throne. This practice dated back to Aksumite times, when the mountain of Dabra Damo had served as a royal prison. It was replaced, in the medieval period, by Amba Geshen, a high flat-topped mountain in Shawa where sundry 'Solomonic' princes were later imprisoned.

Land Tenure: *Gult* and *Rest*

The powers of the monarchy, when strong, extended far into the area of land tenure and taxation. Emperors owned sizeable pieces of land, described by Alvares as 'large farms and estates'.[7] They could, however, also grant the revenue from any piece of land, by waiving their rights of taxation to it in favour of anyone they wished: members of their own family, nobles, local rulers, the priesthood, or religious establishments. Such land was known as *gult*, and gave *gult*-owners the tribute or taxes otherwise payable to the state. Such dues would usually be provided in kind, mainly in cattle and grain, but also in honey and butter, and, last but not least, in labour services. These could include a wide range of activity, such as ploughing, harvesting and threshing, building and repairing lords' houses, preparation of banquets, and military service in time of war.

Grants to churches and monasteries were in most cases virtually permanent, and would often be confirmed in writing by successive sovereigns. Secular grants, on the other hand, were generally revocable at the monarch's pleasure. They were given on the

[7] Ibid., I, p. 248.

expectation that the recipient would serve the sovereign by supply-
ing provisions, by helping to administer the country, and by raising and commanding troops in times of both peace and war. A
gult-owner's heir did not necessarily inherit *gult* rights, but, if able
to meet the obligations associated with the land, were often allowed to do so, at the ruler's will.[8]

Most peasants probably owned their own land, which was
known as *rest*, and inherited from father to son. Though the
monarch could, and often did, grant *gult* rights to such land, he
could not deprive *rest*-owners of it, except in very special circumstances. These might occur if *rest*-owners were held to be guilty of
rebellion or treason.

Moving, or 'Instant', Capitals

Trade throughout most of the country in this period was too
limited to permit the growth of mercantile towns, except for a few
settlements on the principal trade routes, located mainly towards
the eastern borders, on the way to the coast. Ethiopian emperors
and important chiefs, who were often accompanied by hundreds
of courtiers and innumerable soldiers and camp-followers, in most
cases had no fixed capitals. State affairs, which consisted largely of
the monarch's personal inspection of the provinces, the collection
of taxes, and the frequent waging of wars against internal or
external enemies, obliged rulers, and those who accompanied
them, to travel extensively throughout the far-flung empire. Monarchs and their cohorts thus lived a fairly nomadic, or semi-
nomadic, life. This was facilitated by the fact that, because of the
need for frequent movement, they dwelt largely in tents, or temporary wooden huts, which could easily be transported from one site
to another.

Monarchs spent much of their time travelling around the countryside, but often halted wherever grain, cattle, firewood and
water were available. The ruler and his numerous companions and
camp-followers lived at the expense of the peasantry, through
whose lands they passed, and whose resources they soon exhausted. The Florentine trader Andrea Corsali reported in 1517
that the emperor's retinue and army was often so considerable,

[8]   For an elaboration on these points see Pankhurst, 1966, pp. 29–31.

and its depredations so considerable, that it could not remain in any locality for more than four months, or return to the same place in less than ten years. Changes in the location of capitals also often resulted from the destruction of forests, and the consequent depletion of fire wood. Once this happened camps were obliged almost willy nilly to move.[9] The custom of moving camps frequently was so well established that the chronicle of Emperor Galawdéwos (1540–59) went so far as to observe that it was the practice of kings to travel from place to place, until the hour of their last sleep, the day of their eternal repose.[10]

The emperor's army, and its camps, were in many cases immense. It was 'unbelievable', Alvares declared, how many people accompanied the ruler on his marches. Describing one such camp he noted that its members, spread over more than twelve miles, were 'so numerous' and 'so close together' that they resembled 'a procession of Corpus Domini in a great city, without getting fewer in any part of the road'. The camp consisted of 'innumerable pavilions and tents', which were 'pitched like a city in a great plain', and occupied 'a good six miles'. Each of the 'great lords' travelled with 'a city or a good town of tents'. Important persons likewise took with them vast numbers of attendants, both on foot and on mule-back. The result was that the court never travelled with less than 50,000 riding mules, and could reach as many as 100,000, besides innumerable pack animals.[11]

Royal camps, according to Alvares, were 'always situated on a plain', for they needed a vast amount of space for their many tents. Those of the emperor were pitched on the highest available ground. Four or five in number, they stood in a cluster almost invariably facing west, that is to say away from the rising sun. The area around these royal tents was at that time often surrounded by tall woven curtains, designed like a chess-board, half white, half black. If, however, the camp remained in one place for more than a day or two, the tents would be surrounded by a 'big hedge', or fence, a mile and a half or so round. It had twelve gates, the principal situated to the west, and two other major ones to the north and south. Each was carefully guarded by royal pages. Near the royal tents there was 'one very large red tent', used for great

[9] Pankhurst, 1982, p. 41.
[10] Conzelman, 1895, p. 149.
[11] Beckingham and Huntingford, 1961, I, pp. 320–1.

receptions. The land in front of the royal tents, for a distance of some 800 yards, was, however, left empty, apparently to isolate the monarch from his subjects, as well as to provide an open field for martial displays.

Several other tents were reserved for religious purposes. The two largest such tents, as described by Alvares, were those of St Mary, situated to the north of the camp, and of the Holy Cross, to the south. Beside each was 'a very beautiful and good tent', used to store church vestments, and another for the fire, cooking equipment, and supplies needed to make bread for Holy Communion. The emperor's clothes, and those of the queen and her great ladies, were stored in adjacent tents.

There were likewise fairly large tents reserved for the principal courtiers of state, among them the two Behtwaddads, or 'Beloved' ministers of state, each of whose followers occupied 'as much space as a city'. The tents of the judges likewise took up 'much space', as they had 'plenty of people under them'. The *Abun*, or Patriarch, also had 'a great many tents', on account of the 'endless people', who came from all over the country for him to ordain.

The tents of the great lords were followed by those of persons of lesser rank. After the 'gentlemen' thus came more humble, but still well-dressed persons, then 'the common people', such as bakers and taverners, and, finally, the prostitutes, the merchants, and the blacksmiths, all of whom together occupied a 'very big space'. Tents were similarly set aside for the cooks, and their kitchens.

The camp also contained a 'long tent', which served as a court of justice, and two other tents as prisons. Beyond them was a sizeable market-place, where there was 'much trading'. Further on again were the tents of the two chief justices, and, between them, a third tent church, called the Church of the Justices. In front of them were chained four lions, traditional Ethiopian symbols of royalty, which always accompanied the emperor, and, some distance away, a fourth tent church, referred to as the market church. It was the place of worship of such merchants as were Christians. The latter, however, represented only a small part of the trading community, for most of its members were Muslims. The market was always situated in front of the emperor's tent, but at some distance, out of sight of its door.

The above arrangements were long and well established. They endured, Alvares insists, from camp to camp, for although the court was constantly moving, its 'mode of encampment' never changed.[12] This statement was later endorsed by Ludolf. Describing the manner in which a camp came into existence, he declares that, within 'a few hours . . . the whole Camp appears in the same Order as it was before. For everyone knowes his place and his proportion, there being never any alteration of the order, but the same streets and lanes, the same distance of tents, so that were it not for the variation of the prospect, other mountains, other rivers, and another face of the country, you would think yourself in the same place'.[13]

Soldiers and Peasants

Military service was closely related to the system of land tenure. Vassals held land, as we have seen, on the understanding that they would provide service to their master in time of war or other emergency. Vast numbers of warriors could thus be mobilized, with remarkable speed. The early sixteenth-century Italian traveller Francesco Suriano stated that the emperor never took the field with 'less than two or three hundred thousand', while Alvares reported that Ethiopian monarchs were able to call '100,000 men, if they want as many, to assemble in two days'.[14]

Soldiers had – or forcibly asserted – the right to seize whatever they wanted from the peasantry, and when passing through any area, friendly as well as hostile, looted extensively. The chronicle of Emperor Eskender (1478–94) thus states that his soldiers 'ruined all the people', while that of Sarsa Dengel (1563–97) quoted that monarch on one occasion as sadly observing, 'If I prolong my stay in Tegray the country will be ruined because our soldiers are numerous, indeed innumerable'.[15]

The Church and its *Abun*, or Patriarch

The Ethiopian Church in this period was headed, in accordance with long-established tradition, by an *Abun*, or Patriarch, sent, at

[12] Ibid., II, pp. 437–42.
[13] Ludolphus, 1684, pp. 214–15.
[14] Crawford, 1958, p. 45; Beckingham and Huntingford, II, p. 447.
[15] Perruchon, 1893, p. 357; Conti Rossini, 1907, p. 94.

the emperor's request, from the Coptic Church of Egypt. This latter church, it will be recalled, had a millennium or so earlier ordained Ethiopia's first Christian bishop, Frumentius, later named Abba Salama.

The Ethiopian Church, and its Patriarch, enjoyed immense prestige, wealth, and influence. Many of the more important churches and monasteries were endowed with considerable landed property, for the most part as *gult* though other terms, such as *samon*, were also used for it. The *Abun* was also provided with extensive lands, and, though a foreigner, could at times play a major role in state affairs, even, as we have seen, in some instances influencing the selection of the monarch.

Barter and 'Primitive Money'

The Ethiopian highlands throughout this time, as previously, had a largely self-sufficient, subsistence economy. Trade largely took the form of barter, the exchange for example, as Alvares says, of a cow, sheep or chicken for a certain amount of grain, limes or red pepper. Various types of 'primitive money' were, however, also in extensive use. They consisted invariably of commodities in considerable demand, which for geographical or other reasons could not easily be obtained in any particular area. The most important of these articles was rock salt, a type of 'primitive money' which had been mentioned, it will be recalled, early in the sixth century by Kosmos. The mineral was in great demand by man and cattle alike, but in restricted supply as it came from the torrid Afar, or Dankali, depression east of Tegray. The salt, which circulated instead of money throughout virtually the entire highlands, was cut, Alvares reports, into blocks, known as *amolés*, which were nearly a span long, and three or four fingers thick and wide. Though virtually identical in shape, size and composition, they varied considerably in value from one place to another, in direct proportion to distance from the mines. They were thus 'very cheap' where they were obtained, but 'very dear' at the court, then situated in the southern highlands of Shawa.[16] Variations in value were due partly to the cost of transporting the relatively heavy and fragile mineral over a long and arduous

[16]   Beckingham and Huntingford, 1961, I, pp. 180–1.

journey, partly to loss or damage *en route*, and partly to heavy taxation levied by provincial rulers through whose territory the bars of salt were conveyed.

Two other types of 'primitive money' also circulated. One consisted of pieces of cloth used as wraps. In great demand for clothing their supply was limited because it depended on the availability of cotton from the lowlands, as well as on production by a limited number of weavers, who alone had access to looms, had the skill to use them, and were willing to work in a culturally despised occupation. The other main form of 'primitive money' comprised thin bars of iron, three inches long and two wide, smelted for making plough-shares or other agricultural tools. Such pieces were in restricted supply, as iron ore was found only in certain parts of the country, and was produced, with specialized smelting equipment, by skilled blacksmiths, whose work was also generally held in disrepute.

Most farmers or other land-holders paid their taxes, to their local chief or immediate overlord, in kind, mainly in grain or cattle. Honey and butter, as we have seen, also served as articles of tribute. Major provincial taxes, on the other hand, were usually paid in gold, which was locally panned, and obtained from Enarya and other areas of the south-west. The valuable metal was generally weighed on hand-scales, and often balanced against specific imported coins, which served as units of weight. Money was virtually unknown in the country at large, though foreign merchants visiting some of the larger markets made limited use of silver or gold coins, mainly Austrian or Turkish.

Relations with Muslim Neighbours

During the first centuries of the 'Solomonic' dynasty the Shawa-based Christian state was in close contact both with its Muslim neighbours, and with Christian co-religionaries in Jerusalem and far-off Europe.

Christian Shawa was tied to Muslim Egypt, and to Ifat and Adal, the Muslim amirates between the Ethiopian highlands and the sea, by bonds of mutual dependency. The Christians of Ethiopia were dependent on the Church of Alexandria for their *Abun*, and consequently regarded Egypt, then under Muslim control, as the spiritual source of their faith. The Egyptians on the other hand were dependent on Ethiopia, the principal source of the Nile, its water and its silt, for their prosperity, and feared that the Ethiopians might, if provoked, divert the river's flow.

Shawa was likewise heavily dependent on Ifat and Adal, because of their location on the trade routes to the Gulf of Aden ports. Shawan trade to the sea passed by way of these territories, through which almost all the hinterland's imports and exports had likewise to pass. Muslim merchants and caravans based on the coast handled a large part of the commerce of the interior, and at times acted as commercial agents for the Christian kings. The coastal areas were on the other hand heavily dependent on Shawa and other parts of the hinterland, which were the source of the raw materials, and slaves, they exported, as well as the market for a considerable proportion of the imports they handled.

Despite this inter-dependency the rulers of the Christian interior and of the Muslim coastal lowlands often fought against each other, largely with the aim of gaining control over the trade routes between their respective territories. Fighting was, however, almost invariably carried out in the name of religion. Neither side ever achieved a truly decisive victory, for they were for long periods of time militarily fairly equally balanced. The Christian rulers were able to deploy large armies, which made them for centuries almost invincible, particularly when fighting in the mountainous interior. Christian soldiers, as highlanders, however, found it difficult to penetrate the torrid, often malaria-infested lowlands, and well-nigh impossible to occupy them on any permanent basis.

The Muslim rulers of the coast, because of their proximity to the sea, and greater involvement in international trade, had on the other hand better access than the emperors to military material imported from abroad. These included sharp daggers, stout swords, and some coats-of-mail, as well as, from the beginning of the fifteenth century onwards, increasing numbers of firearms, which were thereafter often destined to play a decisive role in Ethiopian warfare.

The Shawa-based Christian state at the time of its inception, enjoyed close relations with the Islamic rulers of both Yaman and Egypt. The first important Shawan ruler, Emperor Yekuno Amlak, on coming to the throne in 1270, was much concerned that his country had been for two decades without an Abun. He accordingly wrote for one, around 1273–4, in a friendly letter to Sultan Barbars of Egypt, and entrusted it to the Hamadid sultan of neighbouring Yaman. In this letter, he described himself as the protector of all Muslims visiting his kingdom, and observed, interestingly enough, that his army included many Muslim horsemen.[17]

Relations between Ethiopia and Egypt, however, later deteriorated, apparently because the bishop requested from Alexandria was not despatched. Yekuno Amlak's son and successor Yagba-Seyon (1285–94) nevertheless attempted a rapprochement. Writing to Cairo he asserted that his father had been 'the enemy of the Muslims', but that he for his part afforded them protection throughout his realm.[18]

The early fourteenth century witnessed the growing power of Shawa, and the consolidation of its dynasty under Yagba Seyon's warlike successor Emperor Amda Seyon (1312–42). Conflict between the Christian state and the Muslim amirate of Ifat over trade to the coast then came to the fore. Passionately interested in this commerce, he is quoted in his chronicle as complaining that the Afar ruler, Amir Haqq ad-Din, had seized one of his subjects, a certain Teʿeyentay, who had probably been on a mission to the coast.[19] Angered by this act of *laissez-majesté*, Amda Seyon launched a major expedition to Ifat. In the course of it he killed Haqq ad-Din, and captured and sacked his capital. Doubtless encouraged by this success, he then despatched his forces to ravage a wide range of nearby lowland territory.

The Muslims of Ifat, determined on regaining the military initiative, later rallied around Haqq ad-Din's son Darader, who inflicted heavy casualties on the emperor's forces, but was soon defeated, captured and killed. Amda Seyon was then free to conduct a further series of campaigns. In the course of one of them he made his way to the provinces of Damot and Hadeya, in the west. He thereby brought them under imperial control, thereby breaking their earlier links with Ifat.

Conflict with Ifat erupted again in 1332, by which time Haqq ad-Din's brother Amir Sabr ad-Din had become ruler of Ifat. Determined to control, and tax, the trade from the interior he interfered with royal or other caravans travelling to and from the coast. Amda Seyon later referred to this when he indignantly

---

[17] Maqrizi, 1840, p. 122.
[18] Quatremère, 1811, II, p. 268.
[19] Huntingford, 1965, p. 56.

complained, 'You took away the commodities belonging to me obtained in exchange for the large quantity of gold and silver I had entrusted to the merchants. And you imprisoned the traders who did business for me'.[20]

Sabr ad-Din was by then well prepared for war, and, if we can believe the Ethiopian royal chronicle, was actually planning the invasion, and permanent occupation, of the Christian highlands. To this end, he rallied many Muslim soldiers from far and wide. Amda Seyon, wishing to prevent Hadeya from throwing in its lot with Ifat, then marched into the province, whereupon Sabr ad-Din began a full-scale invasion of the Angot, Amhara and Shawa highlands. The emperor, though often out-numbered, fought, his chronicle claims, with matchless skill and determination. He succeeded, supposedly almost single-handed, in defeating Sabr ad-Din, after which he destroyed the latter's capital. The Ifat ruler was obliged to surrender, together with his two principal allies, Haydera, ruler of Dawaro, and Amano, that of Hadeya. Amda Seyon then appointed Sabr ad-Din's brother Jamal ad-Din as ruler of Ifat, with the imposing title of 'king of all the Muslims'.

Apparently not satisfied with this military success Amda Seyon considered advancing further into the lowlands. This angered the Muslim leaders of nearby Adal and Mora, who decided to attack him before he could enter their territories. Jamal ad-Din, doubtless feeling his position ambiguous, begged the emperor to return home, and declared that if he did so the Muslims would serve him peacefully as traders. Amda Seyon, however, proudly refused to withdraw, whereupon his erstwhile governor joined forces with the Adal ruler to continue the war against him. Further fierce fighting followed, in which the emperor was eventually once more victorious. He then proceeded into the semi-desert regions of Mora and Adal, after which he advanced into the Afar, or Danakil, country, an inhospitable land which no previous Christian ruler of Ethiopia is said to have ever traversed.

One of the results of Amda Seyon's victories was that the rulers of the Muslim sultanates on the borders of Shawa for the most part accepted the emperor's overall suzerainty. An Egyptian courtier Ibn Fadl Allah al-Omari, himself a Muslim, shortly afterwards observed:

---

[20]   Cited by Taddesse Tamrat, 1972, p. 85.

Although all the sovereigns of these [Muslim] kingdoms transmit their power on a hereditary basis, none of them have their own authority other than that invested by the sovereign of Amhara [i.e. the Ethiopian Emperor]. When one of these kings passes away, and there are males in his family, they use all their means to gain his favour, because it is he who will choose the one on whom he will confer power. Once the latter has been invested with power he has supreme authority over them, and in front of him they are only his lieutenants.[21]

The struggle in the east continued during the reign of Amda Seyon's son Emperor Sayfa Ar'ad (1342–70), who, faced by a rebellion in Ifat, on one occasion reportedly despatched a considerable force of 30,000 soldiers to the area. One of his successors, Emperor Dawit (1380–1409), subsequently chased a local rebel, Sultan Sa'd ad-Din, as far as the Gulf of Aden port of Zayla', where he killed him in battle in 1415.[22] This was the most easterly point apparently ever reached by the Ethiopian empire, which soon thereafter began to contract.

Medieval Ties with Muslim and Coptic Egypt

Despite occasional religious animosity, and Ethiopian irritation at failures by the Egyptians to despatch *Abuns* as requested, relations between the two countries were often cordial, and from the economic point of view not unimportant. This was notably the case during the reign of Emperor Yeshaq (1412–27) when a group of Mameluks, led by one al-Tabingha, made their way to Ethiopia as refugees. The Egyptian, who was known, according to the Arab historian Maqrizi, for his 'skill in arms and equestrian art', was received by the emperor with 'dignity and honour', and taught the latter's soldiers to make flame-throwers and fight with the swords.

Another Egyptian visitor of this time was an unnamed Copt, 'well versed in the science of government', who 'reorganized the kingdom, and collected so much wealth for the Hati [*Hasé*, or Emperor] that he enjoyed the king's authority'. This able Copt

---

[21] Gaudefroy-Demombynes, 1927, pp. 22–7.
[22] Rinck, 1790, pp. 6–7.

is said to have also differentiated the king from his subjects, by having him wear 'splendid' clothes, and a red head-dress, and carry an exquisite cross decorated with precious stones, which gleamed in the sun. Yeshaq, unlike his predecessors, thus reportedly stood out from the crowd by his 'kingly splendour'.[23]

Links with European Christendom

The rise of the 'Solomonic' dynasty also coincided with increasing contacts between Ethiopia and European Christendom. The country's Christian rulers, threatened by Muslim armies equipped with superior weapons obtained from Arabia, realized the value of alliances with the technologically more advanced powers of Europe. They regarded the latter as a potentially valuable source of firearms, but, because of their dependence on Egypt for their Abun, could not afford a too visibly pan-Christian, or anti-Muslim, policy.

Many European Christians in the period of the Crusades, which began in the early twelfth century, were on the other hand keen on military cooperation with Ethiopia, then virtually the only Christian power outside Europe. They believed that this would be of major importance in their efforts to wrest Jerusalem and the Holy Land from the followers of Islam.

Ethiopian and European Christians over the centuries became increasingly conscious of each other's existence – and of the military advantages to be drawn from collaboration on the field of battle, no less than the spiritual advantages of mutual communion in Christ.

European interest in having a Christian ally against the Saracens, or followers of the Prophet Muhammad, found expression in the Prester John legend. This held that there existed a great Christian ruler, somewhere in the East, who had dedicated himself to liberating the Holy Sepulchre from 'infidel' rule. This belief was embodied in a fictitious letter, written in Latin, around the middle of the twelfth century, in which that imaginary monarch supposedly invited the kings of Europe to join in his mission. The epistle, which exercised no small influence on European thinking, was later translated into the principal European languages, and

[23]   Ibid., pp. 6–7.

Hebrew. Efforts to find its author, who was thought to reside north of India, proved fruitless, which was scarcely surprising, as he did not exist.[24]

Contacts between European and Ethiopian Christians over the ensuing centuries developed slowly, but steadily, and at times dramatically. They resulted from the travels of Europeans to the east, as well as Ethiopians to the west. Both peoples contributed significantly to an increasing realization of each others' existence.

Some of Europe's first information on far-off Ethiopia was collected in the late thirteenth century by the famous Venetian explorer Marco Polo. Writing in 1298 he reported, albeit at second hand, that Abash, i.e. Abyssinia, was ruled by a Christian king, who was in direct contact with Jerusalem, and in possession of 'excellent soldiers' and 'many horsemen'.

The Ethiopian rulers of this time were also interested in relations with their co-religionaries in Europe. Shortly after the appearance of Marco Polo's account Emperor Wedem Ar'ad (1297–1312) despatched a large embassy of thirty men to 'the King of the Spains', with an offer of help against the infidels. The mission visited Rome, and its then religious rival Avignon. On their return journey, while waiting at Genoa for a favourable wind, the ambassadors were questioned in 1306 by Giovanni da Carignano, rector of the church of St Mark's, who embodied his findings in a treatise on Ethiopian government, customs and religion. This work, unfortunately no longer extant, had a major impact on European knowledge of Ethiopia. It established the country's approximate geographical location, and for the first time indicated that the so-called Kingdom of Prester John was in the mountains of north-east Africa, and not, as hitherto supposed, in the Indian region.[25]

The strategic importance of Ethiopia was shortly afterwards emphasized by a Dominican monk, Guillaume Adam. Having visited the island of Socotra beyond the mouth of the Red Sea and made several abortive attempts to enter the Christian empire, he had a good idea of its geographical location. In 1317 he drew up a plan whereby the French, with Ethiopian help, would eradicate the Saracens. Later, in 1332, he wrote to the king of France to

---

[24] Ullendorff and Beckingham, 1982.
[25] Crawford, 1958, pp. 212–15.

explain the political importance of the Ethiopians, whom he described as a strong Christian people 'enclosed by the mountains in the direction of Egypt'. Throughout this period the Ethiopians and their rulers also remained in close contact with Jerusalem, where Emperor Amda Seyon is known to have made a donation to the Ethiopian community.

Relations between Europe and Ethiopia grew closer in the late fourteenth and early fifteenth centuries. Perhaps the earliest European communication to an Ethiopian ruler was despatched by King Henry IV of England, to the 'King of Abyssinia, Prester John', in 1400. Its author was prompted to write because prior to his coronation he had himself been in the Holy Land, where he was informed that the then Ethiopian monarch, Emperor Dawit I (1380–1411), wished to capture the Holy Sepulchre from the Saracens. A year or so later, Dawit despatched an embassy to the 'King of the Franks'. It reached Venice in 1402, and subsequently returned to Ethiopia with many sacred relics, including, it was claimed, a piece of the 'True Cross'.[26]

A Florentine trader, Antonio Bartoli, had meanwhile entered Ethiopia in the 1390s, and was followed by a Sicilian, Pietro Rombulo, in 1407. The latter spent no less than thirty-seven years in Ethiopia before being sent by its then ruler on an embassy to India and China. Rombulo returned to Sicily, in 1450 with an Ethiopian priest, Fré Mika'él, on a diplomatic mission from Emperor Zar'a Ya'qob (1433–68) to Alfonso, king of Aragon, Sicily, Sardinia and Naples. The embassy appears to have reached its destination, for the king later wrote that he was sending the Ethiopian ruler artisans and masons 'to please his dearest friend and brother'.

The first European embassy to Ethiopia had in the meantime been despatched to Emperor Yeshaq (1412–27) from France, by the Duc de Berry. It consisted of a Neapolitan, a Frenchman and a Spaniard. While in Naples, Rombulo met a Dominican monk Pietro Ranzano of Palermo, who wrote a rambling account of Rombulo's travels, still preserved in a Palermo library. Rombulo stayed in Ethiopia for several years, during which time he married an Ethiopian woman. He was later involved in recruiting, or trying to recruit, foreign craftsmen for Emperor Yeshaq.

European interest in Ethiopia was shortly afterwards height-

---

[26]   Tedeschi, 1974.

ened by news that an Ethiopian delegation was to attend the Ecclesiastical Council of Florence, in 1441. The embassy, it later transpired, consisted only of two monks, who had come not from Ethiopia, but from their country's convent in Jerusalem. Their arrival nevertheless caused a considerable stir, and greatly interested the Pope. They seem moreover to have provided much geographical information about their homeland. This data reached the Florentine painter, Pietro del Massaio, who subsequently produced a notable map, the *Egyptus Novelo*, of 1454, which contains the first really accurate cartographic glimpse of the country.

Ethiopia was by then also attracting the attention of Spaniards and Portuguese. In 1428 King Alfonso of Aragon received a letter from Emperor Yeshaq, proposing an alliance against Islam, to be cemented by a double royal marriage. This failed to materialize, but Alfonso later despatched a message to King Zar'a Ya'qob, in 1450, offering to send some craftsmen which the Ethiopian ruler had requested.

This period also witnessed the arrival in Ethiopia of a handful of European adventurers, mainly Venetians, Genoese, and Portuguese. They received honourable treatment at the Ethiopian court, and were given wives and land, but were for the most part prevented from leaving the country, lest they revealed its secrets to the outside world. These Europeans included two Venetian artists, Nicolo Brancaleone, and a certain Bicini, both of whom painted for the Ethiopian state and church. Bicini also served as a secretary to Emperor Lebna Dengel, and reportedly spent many hours playing chess with him. Another foreigner, the Florentine merchant Andrea Corsali, established 'warehouses' in the country, and it is said planned to print in Ge'ez, or Ethiopic, letters.

Two Italian travellers of this time also wrote about the country. Paolo Trevisano, probably a Venetian, arrived around 1480, and produced an account of his travels, in Latin, sadly long since lost. Francesco Suriano, of Perugia, at about the same time, drew up a brief description of his journey, in which he provides details of some of the foreigners then resident in the country. Venetian contacts with Ethiopia also found expression a few years later in another cartographic masterpiece: Fra Mauro's *Mappamondo* of 1460, which contains indications of several mountains, rivers and provinces until that time scarcely known abroad.

A number of Ethiopians in this period also continued to make their way to Italy. At least five were interviewed between 1519 and 1524 by the Venetian scholar Alessandro Zorzi, who recorded details of their journeys, and thus produced valuable, if brief, glimpses of the country's geography.

Most Ethiopians making their way to Rome were attached to the Church of Santo Stefano, later known as Santo Stefano dei Mori, i.e. 'Moors', which became a cradle of Ethiopian studies in Europe. It was there that a German typographer, Joannes Potken of Cologne, heard Ethiopians singing their mass, and was inspired to print the first Ge'ez *Psalter* in 1513. Later, in 1539, the Holy See purchased a nearby hostel for the Ethiopian community, just behind St Peter's. It was in Rome too that another scholar, Marianus Victorius, studied with an Ethiopian cleric, Tasfa Seyon, and published the first rudimentary Ge'ez grammar in 1548.

The presence of Ethiopians in Italy also contributed to growing Venetian, Italian and indeed European, consciousness of their country. This continued, and developed, throughout the sixteenth century, as exemplified by half a dozen maps published in Venice during that time. They included Giovanni-Batista Ramusio's map of Africa, printed in 1550, which turned the African continent on its head, with the south of the map at the top, and the justly renowned maps of Jacopo Gastaldi and Livio Sanuto, published in 1561 and 1578 respectively.

5
Ahmad ibn Ibrahim, Oromo Migration, and Ottoman Seizure of Massawa

The first decades of the sixteenth century constituted another major turning point in Ethiopian history. Three major events took place in this period, in the east, south and north, respectively. First, the power of the Shawa-based Christian monarchy, which had once advanced, as we have seen, as far as Zaylaʿ, was threatened from the east, almost to the point of destruction, by the increasingly well-armed Muslim rulers of Adal, and was restored only with great difficulty. Secondly, escalating pressure from a people to the south, the Oromos, then better known as Gallas, led to a major change in the ethnic composition of much of the region, as well as to a significant contraction of the empire, and of its revenues. Thirdly, Massawa, the empire's principal port in the north, was seized by the Ottoman Turks, who were to remain in occupation of it for the next three centuries.

Imam Mahfuz and the Conflict with Adal

The last years of the fifteenth century witnessed an intensification of the old commercial-cum-religious struggle between the Christian empire and the Muslim amirate of Adal. Both sides had long been concerned, as we have seen, with control of the trade route between the interior and the Gulf of Aden ports, through which a substantial proportion of the country's imports and exports passed. This trade was by the early sixteenth century all the more important on account of the increasing significance of firearms, which could be obtained by the rulers of the amirate far more easily than by those of the formerly almost overwhelmingly powerful interior.

Conflict between the empire and Adal erupted in the 1490s, when an able warrior and charismatic Muslim religious leader called Mahfuz arose in the east. He was ruler of the rich port of Zayla', and the principal commander of Amir Muhammad of Adal. Mahfuz, who was in contact with Sharif Barakat, the Amir of Mecca and conqueror of Hijaz, soon adopted the title of Imam. This designation was important as it symbolized his claim to religious leadership, and in effect committed himself to a *jihad*, or Holy War.[1]

Mahfuz is said to have undertaken no less than twenty-five annual raids into the Christian highlands of Shawa, Amhara or Fatagar. These operations were generally carried out in Lent, when the Christians had been weakened by their long fast, and were dispersed with their families preparing for the coming Easter feast. In the course of these campaigns the victorious Muslim warrior carried off vast numbers of slaves and cattle. This achievement gained him immense popularity among his soldiers and supporters, and enabled him to despatch many slaves to his co-religionaries in Arabia.

Such depredations were finally brought to an end in 1517 when Emperor Lebna Dengel, travelling rapidly with his soldiers almost day and night, reached Mahfuz's camp. The Imam challenged any Christian to fight a duel with him unto death. A monk called Gabra Endreyas at once offered to do so. A fierce contest ensued, which ended in victory for the monk, who killed Mahfuz, and cut off his head, whereupon the Adal soldiers, deprived of their leader, fled the field.[2]

The First Portuguese Diplomatic Mission

Mahfuz's annual raids took place at a time when major international developments were taking place in the Red Sea region. Two mutually hostile powers, Portugal and the Ottoman Empire, had established themselves in the area, and were consolidating their

---

[1] Erlich, 1994, p. 30.
[2] Beckingham and Huntingford, 1961, II, pp. 413–14; Trimingham, 1952, pp. 83–4.

power. The Portuguese seized the east African port of Kilwa on the Indian Ocean coast, south of Ethiopia in 1505, and the island of Socotra, beyond the eastern mouth of the Red Sea, in 1507. Ten years later the Ottoman Empire overran Egypt and Yaman in 1517, and began extending its rule on the Mediterranean and Red Sea coasts. The advent of these two rapidly expanding powers, one Christian, the other Muslim, each bent on exclusive domination of the region, was bound to have a profound impact on the Ethiopian Christian Kingdom, which had hitherto remained largely isolated from such international struggles.

In the course of these developments, two Portuguese envoys, Fernão Gomes and João Sanchez, arrived in Ethiopia, from the east African port of Melindi, in 1508. Emperor Na'od had died only a short time earlier, and the country was governed for his young son Lebna Dengel (1508–40) by a regent, Empress Eléni, the widow of Emperor Zar'a Ya'qob. The daughter of the Muslim ruler of Hadeya in the south-west, she had become a Christian on marrying into the Christian royal family. An able and far-seeing ruler, she was well aware of the potential danger of further conflict with Adal, particularly if the latter was supported, as seemed likely, by the rapidly expanding Ottoman Empire. She therefore adopted the policy of previous Ethiopian rulers, in seeking an alliance with a Christian European power, and attempted to do so with the Portuguese, who were then entrenching themselves on the coast. She accordingly despatched Matthew, an Armenian merchant in her service, on a diplomatic mission to the Portuguese in India, in 1512.[3]

Matthew, a pale-skinned Armenian, encountered many difficulties with the Portuguese, who could not believe that he was an Ethiopian envoy, and for a time regarded him as an impostor. Travelling first to India and later to Portugal he nevertheless eventually established his credentials. The king of Portugal thereupon at last responded to Eléni's request, by despatching an embassy, which landed at the port of Massawa in 1520. Matthew, to the surprise of the Portuguese, was at once warmly received by his many Ethiopian friends.

The Portuguese mission duly proceeded to Shawa, where Eléni's great-grandson Emperor Lebna Dengel had come of age.

---

[3] Girma Bashah and Merid Wolde Aregay, 1964, p. 23; Beckingham and Huntingford, 1961, pp. 1–4.

Mahfuz, as we have seen, had by then been killed, and the young emperor, a proud and self-confident youth, saw no need of the proposed Portuguese alliance. He did, however, appeal for crafts-men, first to King Manoel I of Portugal, and later to the latter's son and successor, King João III. In the second of these letters, for example, he wrote:

> Lord, brother, hear another word now: I want you to send me men, artificers to make images, and printed books, and swords and arms of all sorts for fighting; and also masons and carpenters, and men who make medicines, and physicians, and surgeons to cure ill-nesses; also artificers to beat out gold and set it, and goldsmiths and silversmiths, and men who know how to extract gold and silver and also copper from the veins, and men who can make sheet lead and earthenware; and masters of any trades which are necessary in [these] kingdoms, also gunsmiths. Assist me in this, which I beg of you, as a brother does to a brother, and may God help you and save you from evil things.[4]

Nothing seems to have come of this request, for what would now be termed foreign economic and military assistance. This was scarcely surprising, as Lebna Dengel kept the Portuguese embassy in the country for no less than six years without concluding any agreement. The advent of the mission was nevertheless of immense scholarly importance. Its chaplain, Francisco Alvares, wrote the first detailed description of the country: the *Verdadera Informacam das terras do Preste Joam das Indias*, or Truthful Information about the Countries of Prester John. This remarkable work, which was extensively quoted in the previous chapter, remains to this day by far the most important account of the country prior to the wars which were almost immediately to envelop it.

Imam Ahmad ibn Ibrahim and his Expeditions

The Portuguese departure served as the signal for further, and considerably more extensive, Adal incursions. The leader of these new attacks was another charismatic warrior, Ahmad ibn Ibrahim al Ghazi, whom his Christian enemies nicknamed Gragn, i.e. in Amharic the 'left-handed'. He began his career by overthrowing

---

[4] Beckingham and Huntingford, 1961, II, p. 505.

and killing Sultan Abu Bakr of Harar, thus making himself the master of that rich Muslim walled commercial city, and assuring him the possibility of acquiring a significant number of fire arms imported from the coast. Though essentially a soldier, Ahmad was also a religious leader. He followed Mahfuz's example by adopting the religious title of Imam, and, no less significantly, married the latter's daughter, Bati Del Wanbara. He thus gained the support of her father's followers, who were committed to continuing his *jihad*, or Holy War. This was popular among many of his followers, the more so in that it involved the acquisition of extensive loot from the rich and fertile highlands.

Ahmad's life, which was destined to have a major impact on virtually the entire Christian highlands, as well as on the 'pagan', or animist, territories to the south and west, is extensively documented. It is the subject of a chronicle, the *Futuh al-Habasha*, or History of the Conquest of Abyssinia, written in Arabic by the victorious warrior's Yamani chronicler, Shihab ad-Din Ahmad ibn ʿAbd al-Qadir. This work covers all but the last decade of Ahmad's career, and can be supplemented by several Ethiopian and Portuguese writings of the time.

Imam Ahmad began his conflict with the Christian empire in 1527, as the *Futuh* reports, by ordering the Muslim towns of Adal to refrain from paying the tribute customarily due to it. Emperor Lebna Dengel responded by ordering Déglahan, his governor of Bali, to march into Adal, but the Imam defeated him decisively at the battle of ad-Dir. Ahmad thereupon proceeded eastwards to subjugate the Somalis, many of whom he later recruited into his army.

Ahmad then undertook a series of expeditions which took him much further westwards into the highlands than his father-in-law Mahfuz had ever penetrated. In the course of these operations Ahmad captured innumerable slaves, many of whom he despatched as gifts to the Muslim ruler of Zebid in south Arabia, who in return supplied him with arms.[5] The loot Ahmad acquired on such expeditions thus directly funded, and made possible, further conquests, in which he was supported by many of his co-religionaries. On reaching the Shawan town of Amajah for example its Muslim population warned him that the emperor had 'a mighty force', innumerable horses, and God knew how many

5   Basset, 1897, pp. 43–4.

foot-soldiers, shields, helmets and coats-of-mail. They declared
that neither Mahfuz nor any other previous ruler of Adal had ever
dared to attack the emperor in the latter's own country, but had
merely raided the periphery of the empire, which they would
plunder before returning to their own country. Addressing the
Imam they added, 'Beware, lest you do not bring ruin upon the
Muslims!' Ahmad, who was not a man to be deterred by such
warnings, refused, however, to listen. He declared that a *jihad*
conducted for God was 'no hardship for Muslims'. These words
reportedly satisfied his listeners, who declared, 'Our only desire is
for the *jihad*. Whoever of us is killed will go to Paradise, and
whoever survives will enjoy happiness'.[6]

After several further raids Ahmad fought a major battle with the
emperor, early in March 1529, at Shembera Kuré, literally Swamp
of Chick-peas, 80 kilometres south-east of present-day Addis
Ababa. Lebna Dengel was decisively defeated, and his men suffered immense casualties. Many of the Imam's soldiers were also
killed or wounded, and were obliged to withdraw to their own
country for several months.[7] Before long, however, they were once
more able to take the offensive, and carried out several more
successful raids, mainly south-eastwards into Dawaro and Bali.

The Imam had at about this time finally decided to embark on
the conquest of Christian Ethiopia. To this end he made up his
mind to occupy the southern provinces on a more permanent
basis. This move was not at first accepted by many of his supporters. The *Futuh* reports that when he 'sent to the country of the
Muslims, urging them to join his *jihad*', the soldiers said to him,
'We will not live in the country of the Christians; we would rather
return to the country of the Muslims'. The Amirs took a similar
view, declaring, 'Our fathers and ancestors never wanted to settle
in Abyssinia. They would instead send raiding parties to the
outermost borders of the country for booty, cattle and the like,
and would then return to the country of the Muslims. We have no
precedent for making our homes there', i.e. in the Christian
highlands.[8]

Despite such opposition the Imam was able to carry out extensive operations in the southern areas in 1530–1. At this time he

6   Ibid., p. 96.
7   Ibid., p. 109.
8   Ibid., pp. 146–7.

sent frequently for military assistance to Zayla', and on occasion to Mahra in south Arabia.[9] He received numerous rifles, and at least seven cannons, which were to play a crucial military role, and on one occasion seventy well-armed Arab soldiers. The significance of such help was apparent at the battle of Antukyah, south of Lake Hayq, in the spring of 1531. The Imam began the engagement by ordering his men to fire a cannon at the Christian army. The shell landed in the middle of the enemy ranks, where it hit an olive tree, which was cleft in two. Lebna Dengel's men, according to the *Futuh*, thereupon 'tumbled the one on the other', and fled before an Adal charge.[10] The importance of imported weapons in the struggle later caught the imagination of Ludolf. He observed that 'the Turks, out of their inbred hatred to Christianity, had supply'd their Muhumetan Friend [i.e. Imam Ahmad] with Fire-Arms, and such as knew well how to use them'. Lebna Dengel's men, he adds, were 'unable to endure' the 'Thunder' of the Turkish artillery, and did not know how 'to cure the Wounds which the Bullets made, as not being accustom'd to them'.[11]

By the summer of 1532 the Imam's well armed troops had overrun almost all Ethiopia's eastern and southern provinces, among them Dawaro, Bali, Hadeya, Ganz, Waj, Fatagar and Ifat. The *Futuh* claims that only a third or a quarter of Abyssinia remained unconquered. Ahmad at this point called together his principal followers, and after thanking God for his successes, declared that it was 'no longer possible', for them to return to their own country, or to abandon the lands they had occupied. He therefore ordered them to summon their wives and children, so that the army could establish itself permanently in the highlands. His demands were this time finally accepted, without opposition. Each Adal soldier accordingly sent his spouse what she needed for the journey, as well as for the upkeep of those she left behind. Some men, we are told, sent thirty ounces of gold, others twenty, others ten, each according to his means.[12]

Ahmad and his men then embarked on the last phase of their historic campaign. This took them northward to Amhara and Lasta in 1533, and to Tegray in 1535. They then gained the

---

[9]   Ibid., pp. 146, 172, 179, 184–5, 199.
[10]   Ibid., p. 186.
[11]   Ludolphus, 1684, p. 221.
[12]   Basset, 1897, pp. 394–5.

allegiance of the Muslim rulers of Taka, or Kassala in the north-west, and of Massawa on the Red Sea coast. Emperor Lebna Dengel, by then totally defeated, had become little more than a hunted fugitive, obliged to flee from one mountain fastness to another. He finally died, at Dabra Damo, in 1540.[13]

Conversions and Looting

The fighting of these years was accompanied by widespread apostasy. After the Imam's spectacular early victories large numbers of apparently staunch Christians adopted Islam. Conversions, which appear to have been mainly opportunistic, were so common that a subsequent Ethiopian royal chronicle asserted that of the Christians 'hardly one in ten retained his religion'.[14]

The Imam was passionately interested in conversion. His armies were accompanied by religious zealots, who actively sought to proselytize newly occupied areas. Conversions, as indicated by Shihab ad-Din, were, however, also in many instances based on force, or the threat thereof. While in the Dabra Berhan area of Shawa for example the Imam was informed that the locality had been largely, but not completely, converted. He ordered that anyone who had failed to embrace Islam should be brought before him. An armed detachment was accordingly despatched against the 'infidels', i.e. Christians, two of whose chiefs were brought to him. He asked, 'Why have you not become Muslim when the whole country is converted?' Finding them adamant, he declared, 'We have decided to cut off your head.' 'Very well!', they replied. He was 'surprised', but ordered them to be put to death.[15]

Under such pressure many entire communities converted. Shihab ad-Din, reporting one such mass act of apostary, notes that the people of Jan Zalaq 'had not yet embraced Islam', but had 'hidden themselves in the deserts and mountains'. Ahmad, determined on bringing about their speedy conversion, sent one of his followers, Khalid al-Warradi, with a force of cavalry to attack them. The chief duly arrived, and sent a message to the inhabitants ordering them to 'become Muslims before he came to close quar-

[13]   Trimingham, 1952, p. 78.
[14]   Conzelman, 1895, p. 123.
[15]   Basset, 1897, pp. 271–2.

ters with them'. Faced with this threat they consulted together, saying, 'If we reject Khalid al-Warradi's proposition he will send to his master [i.e. the Imam], who will despatch an army against us . . . The majority of Abyssinians have embraced Islam, and the Muslims have expanded all over the country. If they know that we are resisting, none of us will escape. Our master Wasan Sagad [a prominent Christian noble] has been killed; let us [therefore] now embrace Islam'. This said, they sent a message to Khalid, asking for *aman*, or protection, and declaring that they all wished to become Muslims, and to join the Imam, who would give them peace.[16]

Ahmad, though often ruthless in his demands for conversion, did not always insist on it, especially if the individuals or communities concerned submitted to him willingly, and agreed to pay *jizya*. This was a special tax on 'infidels', and was not payable by Muslims, who were expected instead to provide military service. Refusal to pay *jizya* often resulted in dire punishment for the defaulters. When the Imam reached the Abba Garima area near Aksum, for example, two localities consented to pay him tax, apparently without converting, but a third refused. He accordingly attacked it, routed its inhabitants, and, according to the *Futuh*, 'exterminated them to the last man'.[17]

One of the most interesting, and politically important, apostates of this period was Awra'i 'Uthman, a Balaw from the far north-west of the country, who had earlier been forcibly converted from Islam to Christianity. Emperor Lebna Dengel appointed him governor of Ifat, and gave him half of his army to command. After the Imam's victorious advance Awra'i decided to re-convert to Islam. He wrote a fulsome letter to the triumphant chief in which he said:

I was once a Muslim and the son of a Muslim; the infidels [i.e. Christians] captured me and made me a Christian; but my heart has always been attached to the true faith. I am still an adherent of God, His Prophet and yours. If you accept my repentance, and do not punish me for what I have done, I will return to God. These troops of the King which are with me, I will deceive so that they may come over to your side and embrace Islam.[18]

[16]   Ibid., p. 268.
[17]   Ibid., pp. 425–6.
[18]   Ibid., p. 273.

Awra'i's defection from the imperial army contributed greatly to the Imam's victories in Ifat and neighbouring lands.

Though this period witnessed extensive conversion to Islam some apostasy in the opposite direction also occurred. Prominent Muslims quarrelling with their co-religionaries would on occasion defect to the Christian camp, and, warmly welcomed by their new comrades-in-arms, could often count on appointment to important posts in Lebna Dengel's administration.[19]

After the Imam's subsequent defeat and death, many Muslims returned at once to Christianity, and not a few Muslim converts from that religion reverted to their former faith. A case in point was the father of the Bahr Nagash, or ruler of the lands towards the Bahr, or Red Sea, who had turned Muslim, it is said, because he thought that 'the kingdom could never be restored'. Ahmad regarded him so highly that he made him a tutor to one of his sons. After the Imam's death, however, the chief escaped with his ward, and sent a message to Lebna Dengel's son Galawdéwos, who had by then become emperor, stating that if the latter pardoned him he would hand over the child. The monarch agreed. He also amnestied many other converts, doing so, as the Portuguese writer Miguel de Castanhoso slyly remarked, because, if he had killed all the apostates, he 'would have remained alone'.[20]

Ahmad's campaigns, which took place over a wide stretch of territory, resulted in considerable destruction throughout the Christian highlands. Adal soldiers ravaged the countryside, and, as the *Futuh* claims, looted and burnt down many historic churches, and manuscripts, not a few of them exquisitely decorated, besides innumerable Christian villages. Shihab ad-Din, describing his master's arrival at the church of Makana Sellasé in Amhara for example relates that Ahmad 'entered it with admiration', and continues, conceivably with some exaggeration:

> He entered with his companions, and in contemplating it they almost lost the power of sight. It was ornamented with sheets of gold and silver on which incrustations of pearls had been placed. A wooden door ten cubits long and four wide was covered with sheets of gold and silver, and over the gold had been placed incrustations of various colours . . . The ceiling and interior courts were covered with sheets of gold . . . The Muslims were amazed at this work.

[19] Ibid., pp. 274–5.
[20] Whiteway, 1902, pp. 84–6.

Those who had not entered cried out to the Imam. 'Open the door so we can come in!' He opened it, they crowded in, and he said to them, 'Whatever anyone takes shall be for himself, except for the [gold] sheets'. They set to work with a thousand axes, tearing down the gold and also the incrustations which were inside the church, from mid-afternoon until night; each one took as much gold as he wished, and was rich for ever. More than a third of the gold was then burnt with the church.[21]

The church of Atronsa Maryam and an adjacent storehouse, according to the Muslim chronicler, were pillaged from mid-day until the following morning. The loot, which was carried off both by porters and on mules, included rich brocaded velvets and silks, gold and silver in heaps, gold and silver cups, plates, and censers, a gold *mambara tabot* (i.e. container for the *tabot*, or symbolic representation of the Ark of the Covenant) weighing over a thousand ounces, an illuminated religious manuscript bound in sheets of gold, and innumerable other riches. When they were tired of collecting the loot the soldiers set fire to the church, and everything was consumed by fire. Some of the monks were reportedly so stricken with grief that they threw themselves into the flames.[22]

The Imam later visited one of the rock-hewn Lalibala churches, where he ordered the priests to submit to a trial of strength, but seems to have carried out only limited damage. Shihab ad-Din reports that Ahmad and his companions:

> arrived at the church [where] the monks were collected to die for it. The Imam saw a church the like of which he had never seen. It was cut in the mountain, as were its columns . . .
> The Imam called together the priests, and collected wood which he set on fire. When the pyre was hot Ahmad, wishing to see what they would do and test them, said to them, 'Let one of yours and one of ours enter'. Their chief replied, 'So be it, I will go in!', but a woman who had embraced the religious life, rose, and cried out, 'It is he who expounds the Gospel to us; will he die before my eyes!' She then threw herself into the fire. The Imam cried out, 'Drag her out!' They pulled her out, but part of her face was burnt. He then burnt their shrines, broke their stone idols, and took all the gold plates and silk carpets he found.[23]

21　Basset, 1897, pp. 310–11.
22　Ibid., pp. 312–13.
23　Ibid., pp. 409–10.

The Arrival of Christovão da Gama

Lebna Dengel, to return to our narrative, was in such a difficult position by 1535 that he reverted to Empress Eléni's earlier idea of seeking assistance from Portugal. He accordingly despatched João Bermudes, a member of the earlier Portuguese mission of the 1520s, who had been detained at his court for over a decade, to the king of Portugal, with an urgent appeal for help. Bermudes tarried on the way, and his mission ran into sundry bureaucratic difficulties, but the Portuguese eventually despatched an expeditionary force in support of the Christian Ethiopian state. Led by Dom Christovão da Gama, a son of the famous mariner Vasco, the force consisted of 400 hand-picked, and particularly well armed, musketeers, who landed at Massawa in February 1541. Lebna Dengel had died in the previous year, but his son Galawdéwos had by then succeeded to the throne, and was resolutely endeavouring to continue the struggle.

News of the coming of the Portuguese, and of their powerful military equipment, spread rapidly through northern Ethiopia. Many soldiers who had sided with the Imam now abandoned him, and flocked to Lebna Dengel's widow Empress Sebla Wangél. Dom Christovão and his companions were able to cross the greater part of Tegray, and join up with the empress, and with Bahr Nagash Yeshaq, the ruler of the coastal province, without encountering any opposition. They then proceeded westwards to Dambeya, north of Lake Tana, where they confronted the Imam, who in April 1542 for the first time in his career encountered an enemy well equipped with cannons. Wounded in battle he was obliged to retreat, but managed to send an urgent appeal to Zebid, and promised, in return for renewed Turkish aid, to become a vassal of the Ottoman emperor, Suleiman II. The Turks responded by immediately providing him with ten field-guns and 700 well-armed soldiers. Thus greatly strengthened he succeeded in defeating the Portuguese in August, when Dom Christovão was captured and beheaded.

This victory gave the Imam a false feeling of security, as a result of which he appears to have made no effort to prevent his Turkish allies from returning to Zebid. The strategic balance thereupon shifted once more in favour of the Christians. Emperor Galawdéwos, who had by this time joined forces with his mother

Sebla Wangél and a hundred or so Portuguese survivors of Dom Chistovão's army, confronted the Adal army at the battle of Wayna Daga, in Western Bagémder, on 21 February 1541. The Imam was killed, probably by a shot from a Portuguese musket, and his son Muhammad was taken prisoner, whereupon his followers fled. The fourteen year Muslim ascendancy thereupon crumbled almost overnight.[24]

The long drawn out struggle between Imam Ahmad and the Christian empire, one of the most traumatic in Ethiopia's millennia-old history, had taken a considerable toll of life and material wealth. Both warring parties had suffered immensely. The Christian monarchy, which Amda Seyon and Zar'a Ya'qob had forged, was almost destroyed, and, though restored through the fortitude of Emperor Galawdéwos, backed up by the armed strength of the Portuguese, had lost most of its former mystique. Many of its holiest and most beautifully decorated churches and monasteries were in ruins, and countless fine manuscripts and other works of art had been destroyed. The Muslim state of Adal, which for over a decade had seemed virtually all-powerful, had, despite Imam Ahmad's military skill and his soldier's heroism, also collapsed. Its prosperity, based on loot, had been dissipated by the war. Lebna Dengel's son Galawdéwos, and Imam Ahmad's nephew Nur ibn al-wazir Mujahid, both strove hard to restore the states over which their predecessors had ruled, but succeeded only very partially. A new era had in fact dawned.

Galawdéwos and his Confession of Faith

After the Imam's defeat, the Portuguese, who had contributed so greatly to Galawdéwos's victory, remained in the country. The emperor rewarded them generously with fine estates. Relations between the monarch and his former allies, however, soon clouded. Bermudes, who claimed the status of Patriarch, and several of his compatriots, who felt that the assistance they had given the Ethiopian ruler entitled them to dictate to him, insisted that Galawdéwos should embrace the Catholic faith, and accept the primacy of the Pope. The emperor, a staunch supporter of the

[24] Girma Bashah and Merid Wolde Aregay, 1964, pp. 45–52; Erlich, 1994, p. 31.

Orthodox faith, refused. Instead he astutely moved the Portuguese from the vicinity of the capital to distant areas on the empire's periphery, where they could defend the realm against Muslim or other enemies without being in a position to meddle unduly in its internal affairs. Bermudes and his companions were thus cleverly outmanoeuvred.

The dispute between the Ethiopian ruler and his Portuguese allies, and would-be dominators, had an important outcome in that it led him to draft a historic *Confession of Faith*. In it he (or his religious advisers) enunciated what he considered to be the principal religious beliefs of the Ethiopian Orthodox Church. He sought, in places somewhat disingenuously, to refute Portuguese Catholic suggestions that it was following 'Jewish' practices in Sabbath observance, circumcision, and food prohibitions.

On the question of the Saturday Sabbath the *Confession* declared:

> We do not honour it like the Jews ... For the Jews do not draw water, or light a fire, or cook a dish of food, or bake bread, or go from one house to another. But we celebrate the Sabbath as the day in which we offer up the Offering [i.e. the Sacrament], and we make feasts thereon, even as our Fathers the Apostles commanded us ... We do not celebrate the Sabbath as the first day of the week, but as a new day, whereof David said, 'This is the day which the Lord hath made, let us rejoice and be glad in it'. For on the Sabbath our Lord Jesus Christ rose from the dead, and on it the Holy Spirit descended upon the Apostles in the upper room in Zion, and on it the Incarnation took place in the womb of Saint Mary, the perpetual Virgin, and on it [Christ] will come again to reward the just and to punish sinners.

As for the rite of circumcision, the text declared, 'we do not circumcise after the manner of the Jews, for we know the word of the doctrine of Paul, the fountain of wisdom, who saith, "circumcision availeth nothing, neither doth non-circumcision help, but rather the new creation, which is the faith in our Jesus Christ" ... the circumcision which we have [is performed] as the custom of the country, like the scarification of the face in [Western] Ethiopia and Nubia, and the slitting of the ears among the Indians. What we do is not done to observe the Law of the Pentateuch, but in accordance with the custom of the people'.

Regarding 'the eating of swine', or pork, the *Confession* added:

we do not prohibit it in order to keep the Law of the Pentateuch, as do the Jews. We do not hold in detestation the man who eats the flesh of the swine, and we do not condemn him as unclean; neither do we hold him as eateth it not as one who does. Even as our Father Paul wrote to the Romans, saying, 'Let not him that eateth despise him that eateth not, for God receives them all. For the kingdom of God consisteth not in eating and drinking; to the pure all things are pure. It is an evil thing for men to eat and [create] offence [by so doing]'. And Matthew the Evangelist saith, 'Nothing defileth a man except which goeth out of his mouth. That which enters the belly is disposed of, is poured forth and cast out in a secret place'. And this makest pure all meats. In saying these words he overthrew the whole edifice of the error of the Jews, which they had learned from the Book of the Law.[25]

Fortified by this *Confession of Faith*, and their essentially conservative attitude, Galawdéwos's Orthodox Christian compatriots resisted the pressures of Bermudes and his colleagues; and remained steadfast in their adherence to Sabbath observance, circumcision, and the prohibition against pork and other 'unclean' foods.

Literary Developments

Despite the destruction wrought by Imam Ahmad's invasion of the highlands, the period which followed was one of no small literary achievement. Perhaps the most interesting Geʿez author of the period, curiously enough, was Salik, a Yamani Arab. Arriving in Ethiopia as a young man around 1489, he was converted to Christianity, and adopted the name Embaqom, or Habakkuk. He was so able, learned and devout that he became Abbot of the renowned Shawan monastery of Dabra Libanos, and translated at least five works from his native Arabic. These were John Chrysostom's Commentary on St Paul's Epistle to the Hebrews, the Apocalypse of St John, a theological treatise entitled *Anqasa Amin*, or the Gateway of the Faith, Abu Shakir's Chronology, and, in more literary vein, a Christianized Buddhist Romance of Baalam and Yewasef.[26]

---

[25] Budge, 1928, II, pp. 352–6.
[26] Donzel, 1969, pp. 29–32. See also Cerulli, 1956, pp. 169–75; Pankhurst, 1986, pp. 463–74.

This period also witnessed the composition of several other important Geʿez texts. These included the Miracles of St George, one of the most popular Saints in Ethiopia, as in other parts of the Christian Orient. Shorter royal chronicles likewise began to be produced around this time. Sometimes misnamed 'abbreviated' chronicles, they constituted summaries of the annals of individual kings, but also often included valuable historical and other information not found in the longer works.[27]

The Beginnings of the Oromo Migration

The years after the death of Imam Ahmad were politically, and militarily, important in that they coincided with the beginning of two centuries of armed confrontation between the empire and the Oromos, then better known as Gallas. The latter, whose existence seems to have been first recognized in Fra Mauro's *mappamondo* of 1460, were a Cushitic people with a society based on age-groups, the so-called *gada*-system.[28] They appear to have formerly inhabited lands outside the area of imperial rule, or only on its margins, in what is now southern Ethiopia or northern Kenya. In the early fifteenth century, however, they began a dramatic northward migration, which was to take them over a wide stretch of then imperial territory.

Oromo expansion, which apparently started in Balé, in the far south of the empire, seems to have begun immediately before or at about the time of Imam Ahmad's first incursions. The Oromo advance gained momentum, however, after the Muslim warrior's death in 1543, and the resultant collapse of his government, which created a power vacuum in the area. This enabled the Oromos to occupy much of the southern and eastern Ethiopian highlands.

The Oromo advance was described by a contemporary Ethiopian monk Abba Bahrey, who dates it in relation to a succession of Galla *lubas*, or age-groups. He states that the Oromo migration initially took the form of a series of raids or forays. The first was

[27] Cerulli, 1956, p. 161.
[28] On the Oromo migration, and the *gada*, or age-group system, see Bahrey, 'History of the Galla', in Beckingham and Huntingford, 1954, pp. 111–39; and Mohammed Hassen, 1990.

during the *lubaship* of Mélbah (1522–60), who, he claims, first invaded Bali. Later, during the *luba*ship of Kilolé (1522–30), the Oromos, he says, penetrated into the Dawaro lowlands, and subsequently made their way into Fatagar at the time of the *luba* Bifolé (1546–54). It was then that the Oromos began to establish themselves in the area on a more permanent basis. Their advance then continued during the *luba*ship of Meslé or Michelle (1554–62) when they came in contact with the Amirate of Harar. This resulted in fierce fighting with Amir Nur ibn al-Wazir Mujahid. At about this time, Bahrey reports, the Oromos developed the custom of riding horses. This skill doubtless enhanced their mobility, and hence their ability to expand.[29]

The coming of the Oromos was accompanied by extensive assimilation, both by the new-comers and by the peoples into whose lands they penetrated. The Oromo advance was important in that it separated the Christian Ethiopian empire from its former rival, the Muslim amirate of Adal. The Oromo migration also led to a major contraction of the empire, and its revenues.

The Jesuits and the Ottoman Occupation of Massawa

The sixteenth century witnessed three further major developments, which were to have long-term ramifications on the entire Ethiopian region: the coming of the Jesuits, the Turkish occupation of Massawa, and a renewed spate of fighting between the Ethiopian empire and Adal.

The Spanish religious divine, Ignatius of Loyola, who had founded the Society of Jesus in 1534, was greatly interested in reports by the Portuguese of their involvement in the struggle against Imam Ahmad, and of Emperor Galawdéwos's stubborn refusal to adopt the Catholic faith. Grieved by this check to the advancement of his creed Loyola contemplated going himself to Ethiopia as a missionary, but, for one reason or another, was unable to do so. However, he later arranged for several of his disciples to travel there in his stead. A six-man Jesuit mission, led by a Spanish cleric André de Oviedo, duly landed at the mainland Red Sea port of Arkiko in March 1557, and proceeded inland, where, as we shall see, it was to play a major role in ensuing

---

[29] Beckingham and Huntingford, 1954, pp. 109–17.

decades. Though Loyola and Oviedo were both Spaniards, the Jesuits going to Ethiopia over the years were of several nationalities, and the majority Portuguese.[30]

The Ottoman empire, the region's superpower which had supported Imam Ahmad's advance into the Christian highlands a generation earlier, had meanwhile become more directly involved in the area. Five days after the Jesuit arrival at the coast a force of three thousand well-armed Turkish troops seized the port of Massawa, which they were to control for the next three hundred years. They then advanced rapidly inland to occupy the highland village of Debarwa, until that time the capital of the Bahr Nagash, or ruler of the coastal area; control of the settlement was to be bitterly disputed for over a generation.[31]

In the south-east of the empire meanwhile Emperor Galawdéwos was determined to complete his triumph over Adal by occupying its then capital, Harar. His expedition was, however, badly planned. He reportedly advanced on the city hastily, and without awaiting for his army's support. His impetuosity had disastrous consequences, for he was killed, in 1559, by one of the defenders' bullets. Amir Nur, the then ruler of the city, was thus avenged for his kinsman Imam Ahmad's death sixteen years earlier.

---

[30] Caraman, 1985, pp. 11–16.
[31] Erlich, 1994, pp. 33–7.

6

The Move of Capital
North-West and the Roman
Catholic Interlude

Imam Ahmad's invasion of the highlands from the east, and the steady migration of the Oromos from the south, marked the close of an era in Ethiopian history. For two and a half centuries the emperors had striven to dominate the Muslim lands to the east of Shawa, and to obtain unrestricted access to the Gulf of Aden ports, and to their valuable imports. Prominent among the latter, by the early sixteenth century, were firearms, which were to prove of no small military importance.

The empire's pressure to the east culminated, as we have seen, in Emperor Galawdéwos's disastrous attack on Harar, and his death in battle in 1559. This was a major historical turning point. His brother and successor, Emperor Minas (1559–63), who had been captured by the Imam's warriors, but later ransomed, proved himself a realist. He seems to have recognized the complete futility of trying to rule the lands to the east, beyond Shawa, into which the Oromos were then advancing. He accordingly abandoned any hope of controlling the trade routes to the Gulf of Aden, and thus brought the empire's age-old, and hitherto largely irreconcilable, conflict with Adal to an end.

Minas took this shift of policy to its logical conclusion. Having lost interest in the trade routes from Shawa to the east he abandoned the province altogether. He transferred his centre of government to the Lake Tana area, a particularly fertile region in the north-west of the empire, where he and his successors established a series of short-lived capitals. Unlike those which preceded them they afforded relatively easy access to the western and northern trade routes, to Sudan and the Red Sea port of Massawa respectively. This resulted, a quarter of a millennium after the shift of power from Lasta to Shawa, in yet another major move in the centre of Ethiopian political power.

Minas and his Successors

Despite the ending of the conflict with Adal the ensuing period was far from peaceful. Minas, who reigned for only four years, carried out two major campaigns. The first, in the north-west of the empire, was conducted against the Falashas, or Judaic Ethiopians, in the mountains of Samén.[1] The second, in the far north, was against the Turks, who were supported by a local rebel, Bahr Nagash Yeshaq, ruler of the coastal province.

Minas was succeeded by his son, Emperor Sarsa Dengel, who ascended the throne in 1563 while little more than thirteen years old. He was chosen, like several other Ethiopian monarchs before and later, on account of his infancy, for the nobles tended, as we have seen, to favour boy kings, whom they could more easily control.

Sarsa Dengel, despite his youth, gradually emerged as an able ruler. During a long reign of over thirty years he carried out successful campaigns in many parts of the empire. These included Gambo in the west; Enarya, where he introduced Christianity, and Hadeya, both in the south-west; the country of the Boran Oromos and Guragé in the south; the Falasha-inhabited mountains of Samén in the north-west; and the land of the Bahr Nagash, in the north, where he wrested the local capital, Debarwa, from the Turks.[2]

On his death in 1597 Sarsa Dengel was succeeded by another child emperor, his seven year old son Ya'qob, who was born of a Falasha wife. At first no more than the puppet of one of the nobles, he managed to free himself from the latter's control in 1606, but was soon afterwards deposed, and exiled to Enarya. His uncle, Za-Dengel, was thereupon placed on the throne. Seeking to consolidate his precarious position, he summoned to his aid the leader of the Jesuits, Pero Pais, a Spaniard, who, it is generally agreed, was to prove one of the ablest and most dedicated missionaries ever to

[1] Bruce, 1790, II, p. 390.
[2] Conti Rossini, 1907, pp. 83–7.

visit the country. Za-Dengel assured the latter that he wanted to become a Catholic, but could not do so without Portuguese military support, which he needed to subdue opposition from the nobles. Pais, an astute observer, warned him that the time was not ripe for such action, but the monarch ignored this advice, and proceeded to issue a proclamation forbidding the age-old Ethiopian Orthodox observance of a Saturday Sabbath.

This move, as Pais had anticipated, evoked immediate popular indignation, and provided the nobles with an excuse to overthrow the too hasty monarch. They thereupon recalled the half-Falasha ex-king Ya'qob from his place of exile, and reinstated him as emperor. The newly installed ruler, realizing, like his uncle, the value of contacts with the Jesuits, and through them of a Portuguese alliance, called Pais and several of the latter's colleagues to his presence. He told them that he would declare himself a Catholic if only they would bring him Portuguese soldiers from India. Pais despatched letters to the Portuguese-Indian town of Goa explaining this, but they were lost on the way. Ya'qob, failing to receive the military assistance he had anticipated, was defeated, in March 1607, by Susneyos, another pretender to the throne. He was destined to implement the pro-Catholic policies his two predecessors had earlier envisaged.[3]

First Capitals in the North-West

The period after Minas's abandonment of Shawa witnessed the establishment, as we have seen, of capitals in the prosperous Lake Tana area. The first such settlement was at Emfras, in the mountains north-east of the lake, where Minas set up his abode. This locality, also known as Guzara, subsequently attracted the attention of his son Sarsa Dengel, who built there a strong stone castle. This building, or another later erected in its place, can be seen to this day, within sight of the Bahr Dar–Gondar highway.[4] Apparently the first such structure in this part of the country, its construction was a notable event. Such buildings marked a significant step, as the British scholar David Mathew has suggested, in the

[3] Girma Beshah and Merid Wolde Aregay, 1964, pp. 69–74.
[4] Pankhurst, 1982, pp. 94–100.

transition by which the hitherto Ethiopian 'nomadic empire' became 'accustomed to the idea of a static capital'.[5]

Sarsa Dengel, apparently not satisfied with Guzara, later moved his capital to ʿAyba, in Wagara province immediately north of the lake. There he had a second castle built.[6] Two other capitals were shortly afterwards chosen by Sarsa Dengel's short-lived successors. Qoga, just south of Guzara, became the headquarters of Emperor Yaʿqob in 1603, and Wandegé, south-west of the lake, of Za-Dengel in the following year.[7]

Oromo Confrontation

The confrontation between the empire and the Oromos advancing from the south continued throughout this period. Abba Bahrey claims that the Gallas, after mastering the riding of horses, advanced extensively. This was particularly the case, he claims, during the *luba*ship of Harmufa (1562–70), when they made their way into Amhara, as far as Bagémder and Angot. The Oromo thrust gained further momentum, he states, during the *luba*ship of Robalé (1570–8) when Oromo warriors reportedly 'devastated' Shawa, and proceeded to Gojjam. The Oromo migration was at this time strongly opposed by Emperor Sarsa Dengel, who fought, his chronicle reports, against 'Galla' forces near Lake Zway, in the south of the empire, drove them south-eastwards towards Fatagar and Dawaro, and seized a vast number of their cattle.

Notwithstanding these engagements, which are presented in Sarsa Dengel's chronicle as great victories, the Oromos before long returned to the areas from which they had been repulsed. Sarsa Dengel was soon fighting them in Shawa, and later again in Waj, as well as, north of Lake Tana, in Dambeya. The military prowess of the Oromos was reportedly enhanced during the *luba*ship of Birmajé (1578–86) when they are said to have adopted the use of body-length shields. This enabled them to attack, and defeat, the Mayas, a formidable group in eastern Shawa, whose poisoned arrows had hitherto impeded penetration into their area. The Oromo advance was then resumed, and led to the

[5]   Mathew, 1947, p. 36.
[6]   Pankhurst, 1982, p. 100.
[7]   Ibid., p. 101.

occupation in the *luba*ship of Mul'ata (1586–94) of much of Shawa and Damot.[8]

Pressure from the Oromos continued during the ensuing reign of Emperor Susneyos, and was a major factor causing him, and his immediate predecessors, to seek an alliance with the Jesuits.

Susneyos, Danqaz and Catholicism

Susneyos, who came to the throne in 1607, was then thirty five years of age, and hence much more mature than either of his predecessors, Ya'qob or Za-Dengel. He nevertheless shared their wish to establish a Catholic alliance, but was careful to avoid their mistake of announcing any such policy prematurely. He confined himself at first to writing secretly to King Philip III of Portugal and to Pope Paul V appealing for military help against the Gallas, or Oromos. He did not reveal his intention of abandoning the Orthodox faith until 1612, after his influential brother, and potential rival, Ras Se'ela Krestos, had been converted to the idea. The hitherto cautious monarch then issued a proclamation repudiating the Orthodox Monophysite belief in the unity of the human and divine natures of Christ. He was encouraged in this move by Pais, who felt that the time had at last arrived for the sucessful introduction of Roman Catholicism. In support of this view he told Susneyos that a comet, seen over Lake Tana on 9 November 1618, was a sign that the monarch's enemies would flee before him.

Susneyos was also responsible for further changes of capital. He moved at about this time to Gorgora, on the northern shore of Lake Tana. There Pais proved himself as skilful at masonry as at diplomacy. He built the emperor a fine stone palace at Gorgora in 1614, and a few years later two major churches, one at Gorgora, and the other a little to the north-east, at Azazo. He also erected several other buildings, at Bahr Dar by Lake Tana. One of them, a solid two-storey stone structure, with an outside staircase, was built near the high waters of the Blue Nile, and can be seen to this day, in the compound of the present-day Giyorgis church.

No less important was the development north-east of the lake of the town of Danqaz, which Susneyos made his capital around

[8] Beckingham and Huntingford, 1954, pp. 119–29.

1618. The settlement was situated on a hill, and consisted, the Portuguese Jesuit Manoel de Almeida reports, of 'as many as eight or nine thousand hearths', which would suggest a large settlement probably in excess of 50,000 persons. Most of the houses were round, and made 'of wood, or stone and thatched', the general appearance being 'more like a mountain of ricks than a city'.[9]

The emperor's palace by contrast was a fine stone structure, apparently one of the first in the country to be erected with mortar since ancient times. The use of the latter, according to Almeida, began around 1621. An 'intelligent person from India', doubtless brought by the Jesuits, at that time 'discovered a kind of fine, light and as it were worm-eaten stone', similar to that used for the manufacture of lime in Gujarat, in India. The importance of this innovation, he says, was recognized both by the emperor and by the grandees', who 'valued it greatly'.[10]

Almeida, much impressed by the palace, described it as 'a wonder . . . something that had never been seen nor imagined' in the country, and 'would have value and be reckoned a handsome building anywhere'. The work was designed, according to Susneyos's chronicle, by an Indian called Abdal Kerim, who was assisted by an Egyptian head-workman called Sadaqa Nesrani. Many foreign workmen were also employed in the building operations. The chronicle claims that they came from Egypt and 'Rome', the latter possibly a reference to Syria. Almeida, who was probably better informed as to the workers' precise identity, tells us that they were in fact Indians. If so they may well have been among those who had come with the Portuguese.[11] The emperor's initiative was duly followed by 'some of the grandees', who also erected 'houses of stone and lime'.[12]

Rebellion and Abdication

Susneyos's decree against the Monophysite faith gave rise meanwhile to widespread fear that the monarch was planning, like his two predecessors, to convert to Catholicism. This fear was rein-

[9]   Ibid., p. 188.
[10] Ibid., pp. 83–4.
[11] Pankhurst, 1982, pp. 107–8.
[12] Beckingham and Huntingford, 1954, p. 84.

forced when he, to the surprise and horror of his subjects, appeared in Portuguese dress. Fears of the emperor's apostasy provoked several popular rebellions, which however were easily crushed. Their defeat encouraged Susneyos to issue a second proclamation, in 1620, condemning the Monophysite doctrine, and forbidding the observance of the Saturday Sabbath. He subsequently decreed severe punishment for anyone infringing his orders. These edicts provoked a further rebellion, this time in Damot, but, undeterred, he continued to attack Orthodox doctrines. Finally, in March 1622, he officially took Communion from Pais, and by so doing in effect officially established Roman Catholicism as the country's state religion.

Susneyos's pro-Catholic policy, which had been initiated in order to obtain Portuguese military assistance, had thus led to a religious reformation perhaps comparable only to King Ezana's introduction of Christianity thirteen centuries earlier. The unfortunate emperor's initiative was, however, largely futile, for the Portuguese firearms and musketeers, which he had hoped to obtain, for one reason or another failed to arrive. He had incurred the wrath of his people, and of the clergy, in vain.

Pais, who had advised Susneyos throughout the first part of his reign, died two months after the latter's adoption of the Catholic faith. The missionary's death marked a turning-point in the history of the conversion. His successor, Afonso Mendes, a 'rigid, uncompromising, narrow-minded, and intolerant' man,[13] urged the emperor to accelerate the pace of conversion at all costs. Susneyos, thus goaded, launched a fierce attack on many long-established Ethiopian practices. Traditional fasts and festivals were abandoned, and priests re-ordained. The old Coptic–Ethiopian calendar was abolished, and replaced by the Gregorian, which had superceded the Julian in Europe half a century earlier. Circumcision was forbidden. People were encouraged to eat hitherto forbidden food, notably pork and rabbit, and a number of pig farms were established. Divorce was rendered illegal. Disputes between husband and wife were transferred from civil to ecclesiastical courts. Several important Orthodox church and monastic lands were transferred to the Jesuits. Many persecuted and dispossessed priests and monks fled the capital for the provinces. Not a few of their flock, however, adopted the new faith; no less than

[13]   Budge, 1928, II, p. 390.

100,000 Orthodox Christians are said to have been converted to Catholicism in the districts of Dambeya and Wagara alone.

The new policies initiated by the emperor at the behest of Mendes were bitterly resented, particularly in provinces where imperial writ was difficult to enforce. Rebellions broke out almost all over the country, in Tegray, Amhara, Bagémder, Shawa, and above all Lasta and Angot. In all these areas large numbers of peasants enthusiastically joined with the local nobility and clergy in fighting against the new beliefs and practices. Susneyos and his army fought back, on the whole successfully. By 1629, however, he and some of his closest advisers were beginning to contemplate making concessions to the popular feeling. Mendes, on the other hand, pointed to the victories of the imperial forces, and urged the monarch to remain steadfast in the Catholic cause. Susneyos, however, was unconvinced, and in 1630 officially permitted the resumption of the Orthodox liturgy and traditional fasts.

This limited concession failed, however, to achieve its end. In 1631 the governor of Gojjam and many of the peasantry of Bagémder rebelled. Susneyos, though already wavering, defeated the latter in battle in June of the following year, when over 8,000 peasant warriors were reportedly killed on a single day. The Emperor's son Fasiladas, saddened by this bloodshed, told his father that the dead were neither pagans nor Muslims, but the emperor's 'own subjects and countrymen, and some of them his relatives'. Mendes, in a letter to the Pope, blamed the consequences of the battle squarely on:

> disturbers of the peace who took the Emperor aside and showed him the fields strewn with corpses. 'Look', they said, 'not one of these men whose bones cover the earth is a foreigner; there is not one of us who but has lost a brother or son or someone bound to us by ties of blood. Whether we are vanquished or whether we vanquish, it is the same, we are the losers. It is five years since we did not have arms in our hands; we have neither time nor strength on our side; we can find no men to cut the hay for our horses or guard the mules or bear arms. The cause of our plight is the name of the Roman faith. If you do not permit these peasants and ignorant people their ancient customs the kingdom is lost to you and to your posterity'.[14]

---

[14]   Caraman, 1985, p. 151.

Shocked by the massacre, and by his advisers' words, the weary emperor asked his son Fasiladas, known for short as Fasil, to summon a council of state to consider the restoration of the old faith. The assembly voted overwhelmingly in favour of this proposal. Susneyos accordingly issued a final decree, on 25 June 1632, re-establishing the Orthodox faith. Referring to Roman Catholicism he declared: 'We first gave you this faith believing it to be good. But innumerable people have been slain . . . For which reason we restore to you the faith of your forefathers. Let the former clergy return to their churches, let them put in their altars [i.e. *tabot*s, or holy of holies], let them say their own liturgy. And do you rejoice'.[15]

The defeat of the Jesuits, and of their new-fangled ideas and practices, created immense popular enthusiasm. Ludolf, describing what was in effect Ethiopia's first recorded popular demonstration, later wrote:

> It is a thing almost impossible to be believed, with what an Universal Joy the Emperor's Edict was receiv'd among the People. The whole Camp, as if they had some great Deliverance from the Enemy, rang out with Shouts and Acclamations. The Monks and Clergy, who had felt the greatest weight of the Fathers' Hatred, lifted up their Thankful voices to Heaven. The promiscuous Multitude of Men and Women danc'd and caper'd; The Soldiers wish'd all happiness to their Commanders: They brake to pieces their own and the Rosaries of all they met, and some they burnt . . .
>
> Others ran about Singing for joy that Ethiopia was deliver'd from the Western Lyons, Chanting forth the following Lines.
>
> > At length the Sheep of Ethiopia free'd
> >   From the Bold Lyons of the West,
> > Securely in their Pastures feed.
> > St. Mark and Cyril's Doctrine have o'ercome
> >   The Folly's of the Church of Rome.
> > Rejoyce, rejoyce, Sing Halllelujahs all,
> >   No more the Western Wolves
> > Our Ethiopia shall enthrall.

'And thus', concludes Ludolf, 'fell the whole Fabrick of the Roman Religion, that had bin so long rearing with so much Labour and Expence, and which had cost the Effusion of so much Blood to pull it down'.[16]

[15]   Tellez, 1710, p. 242.
[16]   Ludolphus, 1864, pp. 357–8.

Susneyos, whose policies had thus come to naught, died only three months later, in September, a broken man, and was succeeded by Fasiladas. The latter, though until then willing to follow his father's religious policy, now revealed himself a strong supporter of the Orthodox faith. He at once banished the Jesuits first from his capital, and later from the entire country. Susneyos's Catholic brother Ras Se'ela Krestos was likewise exiled, in his case to the Samén mountains, where he was shortly afterwards found guilty of treason, and executed by hanging.[17]

After the collapse of his father's pro-Catholic policy, Fasiladas rejected all attempts to woo the west. He went so far as to enter into treaties with the pashas of the Red Sea ports of Massawa and Suakin to prevent any European from entering the region through their territories. He also despatched emissaries to both ports, as well as to Mocha on the south Arabian coast, with instructions to report the arrival of any ships carrying Portuguese troops which might be coming to re-establish Jesuit influence.

The Jesuits, whose coming had led to so much unnecessary bloodshed, thus disappeared ignominiously from the Ethiopian stage, leaving relatively little in the country, apart from a few palaces and churches, to show for their efforts. Their advent was, however, by no means entirely discreditable. Several missionaries produced important scholarly writings, essential for any understanding of Ethiopia's history and culture. Pais, the first foreigner to study the Ethiopian royal chronicles, wrote the first serious history of the country. Jeronimo Lobo, Almeida, Emanuel Barradas penned remarkably detailed accounts of its economic, social, and cultural life. The Jesuits also wrote numerous informative letters about Ethiopia, as well as a series of annual reports on their missionary and other activities. All these writings constitute an invaluable source for historical investigation of the period.

[17]   Girma Basha and Merid Wolde Aregay, 1964, pp. 69–104; Basset, 1881, pp. 285–6.

7

The Rise and Fall of Gondar

The Foundation of the City

Fasiladas, like so many of his forebears, decided to found a new capital. Abandoning his father's fine palace at Danqaz, which may have been associated with a period of conflict then happily concluded, he moved some twenty miles to the north-west. There, in 1636, he established himself at the then already existing settlement of Gondar, in the mountains between the Qaha and Angerab rivers. The place, which became his principal headquarters, was of considerable commercial and strategic importance. It provided easy access to the rich lands south of the Blue Nile, as well as to both the northern and western trade routes, which led to Massawa and to Sudan respectively. Gondar was destined to remain Ethiopia's capital, and most populous city, for over two centuries.

The foundation of the city is the subject of numerous legends. One of the most widely known holds that the Archangel Ragu'él had a century earlier prophesied to Emperor Lebna Dengel that his son Minas, having left Shawa, would have a capital at a place beginning with the letter G. This story seeks to explain the establishment of royal capitals at a succession of settlements starting with G, among them Guzara, Gorgora, and, finally, Gondar.

Fasiladas, like his father, endowed his capital with a sizeable palace, known to this day as the Fasil Gemb, or Fasil building. Larger, and more impressive, than any structure erected in the country up to that time, it was described by a Yamani envoy, Hasan ibn al-Haymi, around 1648 as 'a high building' and 'lofty structure' which was 'among the most wonderful of splendid constructions and the most beautiful of glorious marvels, built of stone and lime'. Its 'builder', according to the same authority,[1] was an Indian, conceivably Abdal Kerim, who had earlier worked at Emperor Susneyos's palace at Danqaz.

The construction of the Gondar palace, which was stoutly built with stone and mortar in the form of a crenellated castle, was strategically important. Stout enough to resist anything less than a full-scale artillery attack, it provided the emperor and his court with a convenient shelter during inclement weather. Fasiladas, like his predecessors, spent much of his time on campaign, but almost invariably returned to his Gondar palace, where he spent most rainy seasons. He reputedly also erected numerous other buildings in the city, at least one of them in the vicinity of his palace, as well as a number of bridges.

Fasiladas was succeeded in 1667 by his son Emperor Yohannes, and in 1682 by his grandson Iyasu I. Both built further palaces in the immediate vicinity of the Fasil Gemb. The reigns of the first three Gondarine rulers thus witnessed the growth of a large imperial quarter, as well as doubtless a steady expansion of the city as a whole. The royal compound with its many palaces was later surrounded by a substantial Makkababya, or encircling wall, which isolated, and protected, them from the city, and its inhabitants at large.[2]

The historic importance of Gondar lay largely in its relative permanence, which contrasted with the transient character of the temporary, or 'instant', capitals of earlier times. Enduring as it did from one reign to the next, the city was constantly increasing in both size and population, and over the two and a half centuries of its existence as a capital witnessed considerable building activity.

The Palaces and Court Ceremonial

The Gondar palaces, which were situated more or less in the centre of the settlement, were constructed almost entirely in stone and mortar. Distinctive in design, though differing considerably one from another, they were fine crenellated structures with both

[1] Donzel, 1986, pp. 149–50.
[2] Pankhurst, 1982, pp. 115–38.

barrel and egg-shaped domes, and windows decorated with wine-red volcanic tuff.

Apparently the oldest of these palaces, that of Emperor Fasiladas, is to this day the largest and grandest of all the Gondar buildings. Reached by a great staircase extending to the main doorway on the first floor, this structure, which is built of brown stone, is almost square. It is flanked by four round corner towers, three storeys high, each topped with a simple cupola, rising high above the main building. The latter consists of two lofty storeys crowned by a flat roof with a high crenellated parapet above which rises an arch, also castellated, leading to a balcony. To the rear, facing Lake Tana in the far distance, a rectangular tower, also with a flat roof and crenellated parapet, rises two storeys above the roof of the main structure. The building's doors and windows are topped by semi-circular arches decorated with red volcanic stone.[3] Several further palaces were erected by both Yohannes I and Iyasu I. The latter in particular built a large two-storey crenellated structure immediately adjacent to that of his grandfather Fasilidas's. Iyasu's palace was unusual in that its upper ceiling was not flat, like those of the other buildings, but vaulted, with brick ribs.[4] This or another building erected in this reign is described in Iyasu's chronicle as decorated with ivory, gold, and precious stones, all of which have, unfortunately, long since disappeared.[5]

Numerous other buildings in the area were also constructed in this period. The palace compound by the end of the seventeenth century thus consisted, according to an Armenian merchant, Gosia Murad, of 'more than a hundred and twenty large structures, besides pleasant gardens and plantations'. Most of these edifices had their own particular function, as evident from Iyasu's chronicle. It refers to an Addarash, or Reception Hall, a Dabal Bét, or House of Assembly, a Béta Tazkaro, or House of Mourning, and an Ambassa Bét, or Lion House, as well as an Awaj Mangarya, or open space for announcing *Awajoch*, or proclamations, and an Addababay, or public square, where traitors and other criminals were executed.[6]

[3] For detailed descriptions of the principal Gondarine palaces see Pankhurst, 1955, pp. 368–9.
[4] Powell-Cotton, 1902, pp. 313–14.
[5] Guidi, 1903, p. 89.
[6] Pankhurst, 1982, pp. 133–5.

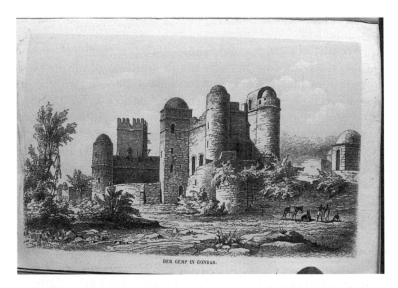

DER GEMP IN GONDAR.

Plate 5   The early seventeenth century castle of Emperor Fasilidas, and other buildings in the imperial compound at Gondar, as seen around the 1860s. From T. Heuglin, Reise nach Abessinien *(Jena, 1874).*

Another notable building, located north-west of the palace compound and attributed, without much real evidence, to the reign of Fasiladas, was a two-storey crenellated stone structure popularly known as Fasil's 'Bathing Pavilion'. This edifice, today a popular tourist attraction, has a flat roof, and two wooden balconies. It is set within, but to one side, of a large rectangular bath, reminiscent of a modern swimming pool.[7] Despite its similarity to a swimming pool, and present designation, it was probably not intended for swimming, but for the annual Temqat, or Epiphany, celebrations, held in the second half of January, which commemorate the Baptism of Christ. That the 'bath' was long used for the Epiphany is evident from the writings of the late seventeenth-century French traveller Charles Poncet. He states that the palace had 'a magnificent bason of water' which 'served for that pious ceremony'.[8] The pool is to this day filled every year for Temqat on which occasion

---

[7]   For early maps of the city see Bruce, 1790, IV, pp. 164–5, and Lejean, 1872, 'Plan de Gondar'. The remains of a similar 'bath' can be seen at Asoso.

[8]   Foster, 1949, p. 130.

the water is brought to it, as in the past, by a pipe running from the nearby Qaha river.[9]

Gondar, as the political capital, was the site of impressive court ceremonial. Poncet, who witnessed this in 1699, during the reign of Emperor Iyasu, provides a detailed account. He states that, having been conducted through 'more than twenty apartments', he:

> enter'd into a hall, where the Emperour was seated upon his throne. It was a sort of couch, cover'd with a red damask flower'd with gold. There were round about great cushions wrought with gold. This throne, of which the feet were of massy silver, was plac'd at the bottom of a hall, in an alcove cover'd with a dome all shining with gold and azure. The Emperour was cloath'd with a vest of silk, embroider'd with gold and with very long sleeves. The scarf with which he was girt was embroider'd after the same manner. He was bare headed and his hair braided very neatly. A great emerald glitter'd on his forehead and added majesty to him. He was alone in the alcove . . . seated upon his couch with his legs across in the manner of the Orientals. The great lords were on each side of him, standing in their ranks, having their hands cross'd one upon the other, and observing an awful silence.

On the following day, Poncet reports that Iyasu was, no less impressively,

> clad with a vest of blue velvet, flower'd with gold, which trail'd upon the ground. His head was cover'd with a muslin, strip'd gold, which fram'd a sort of crown after the manner of the ancients, and which left the middle of his head bare. His shooes were wrought, after the Indian fashion, with flowers beset with pearls. Two princes of the blood, richly cloath'd, waited for him at the palace gate with a magnificent canopy, under which the Emperour march'd, with his trumpets, kettle-drums, flutes, hautboys, and other instruments going before him, which made an agreeable harmony. He was follow'd by the seven chief ministers of the empire, supporting each other under the arms and with their heads cover'd almost like the Emperour; having each a lance in his hand. He that walk'd in the middle carry'd the imperial crown, with his head uncover'd, and seem'd to rest it, with some difficulty, against

---

[9] For modern accounts of Temqat at Adwa see Henze, 1977, p. 180, and Hancock, 1992, pp. 254–67.

his breast. This crown, which is clos'd, with a cross of precious stones at the top, is very magnificent . . .

The ministers, the Frenchmen continues, were:

habited after the Turkish manner and conducted by an officer who held me under the arm. The officers of the crown, supported in the same manner, follow'd, singing the praises of the Emperour and answering as it were in choires. Then came the musketeers, in their closebody's coats of different colours; and were follow'd by archers, carrying their bows and arrows. Last of all, this procession was closed by the Emperour's led horses, richly harness'd and cover'd with costly stuffs of gold hanging down to the ground, over which were the skins of tygers [presumably leopards or panthers], extremely beautiful.

The Patriarch, in his pontifical habits, wrought with crosses of gold, waited for him at the entrance of the chapel, accompany'd with near a hundred religious persons clad in white. They made a lane on both sides, and holding an iron cross in their hands; some within the chapel, and some without. The Patriarch took the Emperour by the right hand at his entering the chapel . . . and led him up thro' the middle of the religious [community], holding each a lighted flambeau in their hands. They carry'd the canopy over the Emperour's head up to his praying place (*priedieu*) which was cover'd with a rich carpet . . . The Emperour remain'd standing almost all the while, unto the time of the communion, which the Patriarch gave him . . . The ceremonies of the Mass are very fine and majestic.

At the close of this colourful ceremony, the soldiers 'discharg'd two pieces of cannon', as they had done at the Emperor's entrance. The monarch then returned to the 'great hall of his palace', where:

he seated himself upon a throne rais'd very high; having on each side the two princes his children, and behind him his ministers . . . All the assembly continu'd standing in a profound silence with their hands across. After the Emperour had taken some metheglin [i.e. mead] and some orange peel, which they presented him with a golden cup, those who had favours to beg came in and advanc'd up to the foot of the throne; where one of the ministers took their petitions and read them with a loud voice. Sometimes the Emperour took pains to read them himself, and made answer to them out hand.[10]

---

[10]   Foster, 1949, pp. 116–19.

Such ceremonial was characteristic of the Gondarine court. A royal chronicle of Iyasu's time observed that when he rode out of his palace in the morning 'the young men saw him and hid themselves, the old men waited upon him, and the brave became mute and did not speak'. The pageantry when he left the city to travel to the provinces was even greater. According to the chronicle, he was on such occasions as 'resplendent as the sun', and resembled 'a bridegroom leaving his nuptial chamber'. Another contemporary text went even further, and likened him to 'a celestial angel'.[11]

Economic and Religious Life

Gondar was not only the political capital, and site of court pageantry, but also a major commercial centre. It was situated at the intersection of three major caravan routes. One ran southwards across the Blue Nile to the rich lands of the south-west, the empire's principal source of gold, ivory, civet and slaves. The two others ran respectively north-eastwards to Massawa and north-westwards to the Sudan, and thence to Egypt. Both routes handled a considerable proportion of the country's imports. These consisted mainly of textiles and manufactured goods, including firearms, and as many valuable exports from the south. Most of this three-way commerce passed by way of the city, where trade was carried out at a large open market, outside the palace compound. Business took place, Poncet says, from morning till evening every day except Sunday in a 'wide, spacious place'.[12]

Trade in Gondar, and indeed in most parts of the empire, was largely in Muslim hands. This was scarcely surprising, as most of the city's trade-routes led to Islamic territories, notably Arabia, Sudan and Massawa, in all of which Muslim merchants received preferential treatment.[13] The result was that while the Christian rulers of Gondar monopolized political power, commerce was mainly controlled by Muslim merchants, who possessed most of the capital's mercantile wealth, and included some of the city's richest inhabitants.

[11]   Guidi, 1903, p. 247; Conti Rossini, 1942, pp. 72, 105.
[12]   Foster, 1949, p. 121.
[13]   On Muslim predominance in trade see Beckingham and Huntingford, 1954, p. 55.

The Muslims of Gondar lived for the most part in their own distinct settlement. Known as Eslam Bét (*bét* being the Amharic for house), or Eslamgé or Salamgé (*gé* signifying country), it lay to the south-west of the city, in a lower stretch of land near the junction of the Qaha and Angerab rivers.

Gondar, like most Ethiopian imperial capitals, was a great religious centre, which, because of its size and population, had several dozen churches, as well as numerous priests, *dabtaras*, or lay clerics, deacons, monks, and nuns. Many churchmen, as was traditional, were attached to the court. Most prominent among them was the Abun, or Metropolitan, who lived in the northern section of the town, and was recruited, as in the past, from among the monks of Coptic Egypt. A scarcely less important ecclesiastical figure was the Echagé, or Head of the Monks, who lived in the west of the town, but at times also resided at Azazo, south-west of Gondar, where the monks of the great Shawan monastery of Dabra Libanos had moved as a result of the Oromo occupation of that area.[14] Both clerics had extensive establishments in the city. The localities around which they lived, known respectively as the Abuna Bét, and the Echagé Bét, were places of asylum, where criminals, civil or political, were normally exempt from arrest.

The Christian monarchs of Gondar, like their predecessors, were great church-builders. Emperor Fasiladas reputedly founded no less than seven places of worship in the city. His son Yohannes I and grandson Iyasu I continued the tradition. One of the churches founded by the latter, on a hill to the east of the city, was that of Dabra Berhan Sellasé, an originally round building which was rebuilt as a rectangular one in the early nineteenth century. This fine structure, with its beautiful wall paintings, and ceiling decorated with winged angels, was later to become one of modern Ethiopia's most renowned tourist attractions.[15]

Gondar, because of its considerable population, and the lucrative patronage afforded by both state and church, emerged as a major handicraft centre. Many of its principal artisans came from minority groups. Some were Falashas, or Béta Esra'él, i.e. people

[14] The history and significance of the monastery is discussed in Crummey, 1972, pp. 22–4.
[15] I. Guidi, 1901, col. 760; Monti della Corte, 1938, pp. 100–1; Pankhurst, 1955, pp. 390–1; Annequin, 1976, pp. 215–26.

of the House of Israel, also known as Kayla, the name of a Falasha regiment in Emperor Fasiladas's service.[16] These were in later times often simplistically referred to by foreigners as Ethiopian, or 'Black', Jews.

The Falashas of Gondar lived west of the Eslam Bét, beyond the Qaha river, and played a notable role in the city's economy. Falasha menfolk worked mainly as blacksmiths and weavers. There were also a number of Falasha masons, some of whom were engaged in both palace and church-building. Most of the Falasha women were potters.[17]

The city also has numerous Muslim craftsmen. They lived in the Eslam Bét, and included numerous weavers and tent-makers. Some of the men also served as tent-carriers for the army.

Another minority group were the Qemants, a 'Judaic-pagan' population, who lived in the countryside north-west of Gondar. Many were engaged in bringing timber and firewood to the city.[18]

The population of Gondar thus comprised people of three main faiths. Perhaps two-thirds were Orthodox Christians, a large proportion of them in imperial service or attached to the church. Possibly a third were Muslims, mostly connected with trade, caravans, or weaving. The Falashas, whose numbers were much smaller, consisted almost entirely of craftsmen: blacksmiths, weavers, masons and potters. Beside these three communities there were in the early days of the city a small number of Catholics, probably made up mainly of half-caste descendants of the Portuguese, as well as, no doubt, a few Ethiopians earlier converted by the Jesuits, or descendants of such converts. Many Catholics were subsequently expelled, but some may have stayed on in the country, practicing their faith in secret.

The three principal religious communities at Gondar tended to live apart from each other. This was particularly noticeable in the case of the Muslims. Al-Haymi observed that they lived in a village, with a mosque and Koranic school, 'exclusively inhabited by Muslims'.[19] Despite this separation there seems to have also been much mixing. This led, the chronicle of Yohannes I states, to

---

[16]   Guidi, 1901, col. 545.
[17]   On Falasha handicraft workers see Quirin, 1992, and Pankhurst, 1995, pp. 1-12.
[18]   For a modern account of the Qemants see Gamst, 1969.
[19]   Donzel, 1986, p. 145.

occasional 'quarrels and disputes', and resulted in the convening in 1668 of a religious council. Presided over by the emperor, as was customary in such gatherings, it decreed that:

> The Afrenj [i.e. Franks, or Catholics] must return to their country and leave ours; but those who have joined our faith and have received our baptism and our Eucharist can remain here with us, or may leave, if they prefer to do so. As for Muslims, they are prohibited from living with the Christians; they must remain separate and live apart, forming a village of their own; no Christian may enter their service, neither a free man nor a slave may serve them, and neither husband nor wife may live with them. As for the Falashas, called *Kayla*, who are of the Jewish religion, they must not live with the Christians, but must separate themselves from them, and live apart, forming a [separate] village.

This edict was proclaimed, by a herald, on pain of excommunication. The council also considered marriage regulations, and decreed that no man should marry his sister-in-law, or woman her brother-in-law.[20]

In accordance with the first of the above ordinances a large number of Afrenj left Gondar in the Spring of 1669. They were escorted westwards as far as the Sennar frontier. In the following year Yohannes ordered the Muslims to move away from the Christians. Separation of the religious communities, however, does not seem to have been fully effective, for Yohannes found it necessary to repeat the decree in relation to the Muslims and Falashas a decade or so later in 1678. He at the same time issued an anti-usury edict, proclaiming that persons lending money or grain should not charge interest.[21]

The age-old Ethiopian custom of detaining unwanted members of the royal family, to prevent them from conspiring for the throne, was continued throughout the Gondar period. Detainees were banished to Mount Wahni forty miles south-west of the capital, where several future emperors were kept in confinement before their accession to the throne.[22]

---

[20]   Guidi, 1903, p. 8.

[21]   Ibid., p. 37.

[22]   On the detention of princes on Mount Wahni see Pankhurst, 1982, pp. 147, 167, and for modern accounts of the site, Pakenham, 1959, pp. 46–55, 91–103; and Toy, 1961, pp. 220–36.

The Early Eighteenth Century: Decline and Conflict

The first phase of Gondarine history came to an end when Emperor Iyasu I, the third of the great rulers of the city, was assassinated in 1706. His death was followed by a period of weak government. Four short-lived monarchs reigned within a span of only twenty-one years. Succession struggles, which almost invariably accompanied a ruler's death, involved not infrequent political turmoil. In the course of these struggles the citizens of Gondar and the monks at Azazo, no less than the nobility, at times played a prominent role.

Such difficulties, however, do not seem to have prevented the city's continued growth, which had probably by then acquired a momentum of its own. Two new churches were constructed by a usurping monarch, Emperor Yostos (1711–16), and two others by his successor, Emperor Iyasu's son Dawit III (1716–21). The latter also resumed building activity in the palace compound, where he erected a small, but attractive, Dabal Gemb, or House of Song.[23]

Political stability was restored for a time by Dawit's brother, and successor, the redoubtable Emperor Bakaffa (1721–30), who temporally re-established the powers of the monarch.[24] His nine year reign witnessed the construction of two further palaces, one of them a long single-storeyed crenellated building still to be seen to the north of the royal compound. He also erected at least one church, and rebuilt the old palace wall, which had by then fallen into disrepair.

Vivid evidence of the way in which Bakaffa apparently revived the royal grandeur of earlier times is provided in his chronicle. Describing his great banquets, which were held at one time or another in half a dozen palaces, it states that the emperor would be seated on a golden stool, before which would be placed a table laden with an immense variety of foods, so many indeed that they could not be counted. The courtiers and learned men would be placed on the emperor's right, and the royal princesses on the left. When all were seated in their allotted places the palace servants would bring water for the guests to wash their hands. Waiters

---

[23] For further information on the city see Guidi, 1901, cols. 759–61; Monti della Corte, 1938, p. 101; and Pankhurst, 1982, pp. 142–8.

[24] Bruce, 1790, II, p. 607.

would then quickly distribute food and drink in accordance with the diners' pleasure. The guests, having eaten to their content, would rise and leave. A curtain would then be stretched out in front of the sovereign, who, screened from view, would wash his hands. Another concourse of men and women would thereupon enter, sit at table, each according to his or her rank, and be plied with drink, until, fully satiated, they too left, be it at midnight or at the crowing of the cock. The table would next be shifted somewhat further from the emperor, after which the chiefs would summon their subordinates, and the soldiers' children, who, standing, would partake of the meal, drink, and go out. It would then be the turn of the more humble members of the army, the shield-bearers and rifle-carriers, who would be duly fed. Up to that time the food was reportedly so plentiful that there was no appreciable sign of its diminishing. After that the palace servants and guards would, however, at last enter, pick up the remaining eatables, and carry them away in their clothes, leaving the hall finally empty.[25]

Bakaffa, like his predecessors, spent much of his time on expeditions. These took him to many parts of the by now greatly diminished empire. His departure for one such journey is described in the chronicle. It tells how the soldiers would collect tents, as well as mules to carry provisions, cattle for slaughter, and all kinds of provisions. These included linseed oil, butter, curds, an incredible quantity of *taj*, or honey wine and *araqi*, and honey to be made into the former. Before leaving the city the monarch, doubtless with an eye to maintaining or expanding his popularity during his absence, made numerous gifts to the poor. He also 'distributed gold without measure to all the churches of the town'.[26]

Bakaffa's reign, perhaps because of its length and stability, was a period of considerable cultural importance. It was a time when literature and the arts revived, and many beautifully illustrated manuscripts were produced by newly established scriptoria in or around the city.[27]

[25]   Guidi, 1903, pp. 316–17.
[26]   Ibid., p. 315.
[27]   On the sizeable number of MSS produced during this reign see, for example, Wright, 1872, pp. 335–6.

Iyasu II and Mentewwab

Bakaffa was succeeded in 1730 by his son Iyasu II, who was then an infant. Power was therefore exercised, as in the case two centuries earlier of Empress Eléni, by the deceased monarch's widow, Empress Mentewwab, who held the position of regent. Her 'first task', according to the subsequent Scottish traveller James Bruce, was to call four of her brother's to court, and place them in positions of well-nigh supreme authority.[28] Her regency, and the rise of her brothers, provided an element of continuity in state affairs.

Iyasu in the first years of his reign was too young to participate in expeditions, and therefore remained in the capital with his mother. Their prolonged residence gave the city even more than ever the character of a fixed capital. It was, Bruce later observed, a time of 'luxury and splendour' at the court.[29] Such expeditions as were carried out were led not by the monarch, but by one of the nobles, often in fact one of Mentewwab's brothers or other kinsmen. At the conclusion of one such foray the young emperor and his mother are said to have climbed to the top of the Fasil Gemb, or palace, to inspect the return of the troops, and were reportedly 'astonished by their great number'.[30]

As he grew older the young monarch grew bored with remaining in the capital, and began to leave on hunting expeditions. On one occasion, in 1738, he brought back a large troop of monkeys, which are said to have so surprised the citizens that they exclaimed, in biblical vein, 'We have neither heard nor seen, nor have our parents told us of such a marvel'.[31]

Before long the youthful emperor turned to more warlike activities. He embarked, in 1741, on what his chronicle claims was a victorious expedition to Sennar. He is said to have returned to Gondar with many prisoners and booty of all kinds, including no less then 300 camels and 20,000 cattle. They were kept for a time within the Makkabaya, or palace walls.[32] A later campaign against

[28] Bruce, 1790, II, pp. 609–11.
[29] Ibid., IV, p. 237.
[30] Guidi, 1903, p. 117.
[31] Ibid., p. 92.
[32] Ibid., p. 191.

Sennar in 1744 was, however, a disastrous failure. The enemy inflicted heavy casualties on the emperor's army, and captured the *Kwer'ata Re'esu*, or icon of Christ with the Crown of Thorns, which Ethiopian imperial forces often carried with them. It, and other sacred relics, had to be purchased from Sennar, at a cost, according to Bruce, of no less than 8,000 ounces of gold. On the icon's eventual return 'all Gondar', according to the Scotsman, 'was drunk with joy'.[33]

Empress Mentewwab throughout this time remained in Gondar, where she had a beautiful, and original, palace erected. This structure, located at the northern end of the royal compound, was far more elaborate than those of Fasiladas and his immediate descendants. It was a two-storey structure surmounted by a square tower, both crenellated in what was by then the Gondarine style. The front of each floor had two rows of doors with curved arches, decorated in red tuff, while the walls, fitted with several balconies, were profusely ornamented with a number of Ethiopian-style crosses, likewise in red.[34]

Another building erected at this end of the palace compound, probably at about the same time, and to be seen to this day, was a *wesheba*, or thermal bath, used in the cure of syphilis. This treatment in Ethiopia was then, as in Europe, based on a sudorific cure, i.e. sweating.

Iyasu is said to have taken a keen interest in palace building, and, according to Bruce, redecorated the old Fasil Gemb. The Scotsman, who perhaps heard the story from some of their compatriots only a generation or so later, states that they were Greeks from Asia Minor, who had fled their native country on account of some 'rebellion, massacre or similar misfortune'. They included twelve silversmiths, 'very excellent in that fine work called filigrane, who were all received very readily by the king, liberally furnished with necessities and luxuries, and employed in his palace as their own taste directed them'.

With the assistance of these craftsmen, and 'several Abyssinians whom they had taught, sons of Greek artists whose fathers were dead', the young monarch completed the presence chamber 'in a manner truly admirable'. The skirting 'was finished with ivory four feet from the ground', over which were placed three rows of

[33]   Bruce, 1790, II, p. 642.
[34]   Pankhurst, 1955, p. 376.

mirrors from Venice, 'all joined together, and fixed in frames of copper, or cornices gilt with gold'. The roof, 'in gaiety and taste, corresponded perfectly with the magnificent finishing of the room'. It was 'the work of the Falasha, and consisted of painted cane, split and disposed in Mosaic figures', and produced 'a gaier effect' than it was possible to imagine. Iyasu, according to the Scotsman, also 'began another chamber of equal expense, consisting of plates of ivory, with stars of all colours stained in each plate at a proper distances', but by the time of his death 'little had been done in it but the alcove in which he sat'.

Iyasu was 'charmed', Bruce says, with this 'multiplicity of works and workmen. He gave up himself to it entirely; he even wrought with his own hand, and rejoiced at seeing the facility with which, by the use of a compass and a few straight lines, he could produce the figure of a star equally exact with any of his Greeks'. Much pleased with these workers he granted them many favours. 'Bounty followed bounty. The best villages, and those near the town, were given to the Greeks that they might recreate themselves, but . . . always liable to his call, and with as little loss of time as possible'.[35]

In addition to her Gondar palace Mentewwab built a number of structures in the hills to the north-west of the city, an area which came to be known as Qwesqwam. It was so called after the place in Egypt where the Virgin Mary is supposed to have resided. It was there that Mentewab and her son Iyasu and grandson Iyo'as were later buried. Their mummified bodies are still extant.

The royal compound at Qwesqwam, like that of Gondar, was the site of many buildings. The largest, which was apparently used for receptions, and also served, according to Bruce, as 'headquarters of the garrison', was a lofty, elongated two-storeyed palace. It was ornamented, like that of Mentewwab in Gondar, in red tuff, with decorations, as today's tourists note, in the form of crosses, as well as a lioness and elephant, St Samwél of Waldebba riding a lion, and a bearded face, said to have belonged to the Abun of the time. A second, somewhat smaller nearby building, now largely in ruins, is reputed to have been the empress's private residence. There Bruce saw 'the queen's own apartments' and those of such of her noblewomen as were her attendants, unmarried, and mem-

---

[35]   Bruce, 1790, II, pp. 633–4.

bers of her court.[36] A third building was a two-storey circular oratory. It was later described by the early nineteenth-century German traveller Eduard Rüppell as having been formerly decorated with painted tiles fastened with brass rosettes, and heavy silk door hangings and alcove curtains, and luxurious scarlet satin couches. The palace compound was surrounded by a 'high outer-wall', which, Bruce says, was about a mile in circumference, with the outer precinct 'all occupied by soldiers, labourers, and outdoor servants'.[37]

Immediately to the west of the palace Mentewwab erected a remarkably fine circular church, known as Dabra Sahay, or Mount of the Sun. Its roof, according to the chronicle of this time, was surmounted by red cloth, which, we are told, shone like fire, and no less than 380 mirrors, which flashed like lightning in the rainy season.[38]

Another interesting structure, which probably dates from around this period, is the huge-domed church of Bahri Gemb, situated thirty two kilometres south of Gondar, just off the present road to Bahr Dar. Unquestionably Gondarine in style, it was reputedly built by Dajazmach Bahri, a prominent nobleman, not of the Solomonic line.[39]

Gondarine buildings, it should be emphasized, were by no means restricted to Gondar and its environs. The rulers of the Gondarine period, with the help of the city's skilled craftsmen, built a number of churches, palaces and bridges well beyond the town's environs. Such structures are to be found on the islands and coast of Lake Tana, northwards towards the Samén mountains, and to the south at several sites in the Gojjam. Gondarine masons also rebuilt the by then ruined old Church of Maryam-Seyon at Aksum.

Oromo Fighting and Integration

The Gondar period witnessed a significant change in relations between the Ethiopian empire and the neighbouring Oromos to

---

[36]   Ibid., IV, p. 272.
[37]   Rüppell, 1838–40, II, p. 116; Bruce, 1790, IV, p. 272.
[38]   Guidi, 1910, p. 99.
[39]   Henze, 1993, pp. 83–92.

the south. Pressure from the Oromos, which had been acute, as we have seen, during the reign of Emperor Susneyos, had continued after the establishment of Gondar as the imperial capital. Considerable fighting with 'Gallas' was reported in the chronicles of Emperors Fasilädäs and Yohannes I. The resultant military activity was concentrated largely in areas further north than previously, notably in Gojjam and Bagémder.

Increasing imports of firearms, particularly during the reign of Emperor Iyasu I, brought about a change in the balance of forces. No longer, like his predecessors, on the defensive, he carried out expeditions into nearby Oromo areas. When he did so the inhabitants either accepted his rule or, as his chronicle more than once puts it, 'disappeared like smoke before the wind'. His declared objective of driving the Gallas back as far as the Awash River was, however, never achieved.

The early seventeenth century, however, witnessed the steady absorption of Oromos into the imperial state. During the time of Susneyos, who was acquainted with Oromo ways, three partially assimilated Oromo groups, the Yahabattas, the Ilma gwozit, and Talatas, had allied themselves to the empire. Many pure Oromos, under the emperor's pressure and that of his brother Ras Se'ela Krestos, were converted to Christianity, or, more specifically, Catholicism.

Later, during the reign of Yohannes I, Prince Iyasu, the heir to the throne, found refuge in the Oromo country, where he befriended the Kordidas, a large group of Amhara defectors or slaves, who wished to return to imperial rule and the Christian faith. On subsequently assuming the throne he assisted no less than 100,000 of them to achieve their ambition. During his reign many Oromos also allied themselves with the imperial state. This period likewise witnessed the rise of several Oromo leaders to positions of prominence in Gondarine service. The most notable among them was the Liban chief Tigé, who attained the rank of Behtwaddad, or the King's Beloved Courtier. A number of Oromos, among them the Bassos, Jawis and Talatas, also contributed contingents to the emperor's army.

Oromo involvement in imperial affairs increased during the reigns of Téwoflos, Yostos, and in particular Dawit III, who on one occasion used Jawi troops to suppress dissident monks. His successor Bakaffa spent part of his youth among the Yajju Oromos, and received hospitality from their chief Amizo. Bakaffa also employed Jawi, as well as Liban and Basso, troops, and showed great favour to an Oromo courtier, Waragna, whom he made governor of Damot.

Jawi, Tulama and other Oromo troops played an even more important role during the reign of Bakaffa's son Iyasu II. Under the influence of his mother Empress Mentewwab he promoted Waragna to a series of high offices, and, married Wabit, the daughter of the Yajju chief Amizo, who had befriended the old empress's husband Bakaffa.

Iyasu was succeeded, in 1755, as we shall see, by his half-Oromo son Emperor Iyo'as, who depended heavily on Waragna, as well as on his Oromo mother Wabit. Many Oromos, including the young monarch's two uncles Lubo and Biralé, came to Gondar, and rose to important positions. The result, according to Bruce, was that before long 'nothing was heard at the palace but Galla', and the emperor 'affected to speak nothing else'.[40] The Oromos, who two centuries earlier had been fighting on the empire's periphery, had gained very considerable influence at the capital of the realm. The result of these developments was that many Oromo lands south of the Blue Nile, as well as Wallo to the east, were to a greater or lesser extent integrated, or re-integrated into the empire.

The Collapse of the Empire and the Rise of Ras Mika'él Sehul of Tegray

Iyasu II died in 1755, whereupon the succession once more fell to the deceased's infant son: Emperor Iyo'as. The accession of the child monarch enabled Empress Mentewwab to serve again as regent, doing so for her grandson as previously for her son. Power as a result continued to be exercised by the redoubtable old lady and her brothers, most notably Walda Lecul, who held the position of ras, and led many of the expeditions of the time.

Iyo'as, because of his age, and Mentewwab, because of her sex, spent most of their time in or around Gondar. Such campaigning as took place was carried out largely under the command of Ras Walda Le'ul and other imperial nominees. Lacking the old charisma of monarchy – as well as an adequate supply of firearms –

---

[40]   Bruce, 1790, pp. 658–9, 665, 667.

they found it difficult to crush provincial separatist tendencies, which were then making themselves increasingly manifest.

The country at this time was seriously affected by bitter regional power struggles. Gondar, early in the reign of Iyo'as, fell, as we have seen, under the sway of a number of Yajju Oromo, or Galla, lords. This happened when Empress Mentewwab, anxious to destroy the influence of her son Iyasu's first wife, who was an Amhara, had her banished, and replaced by the Wallo chief Amito's daughter Wabit. The latter exerted great influence on her half-Oromo son Iyo'as, and succeeded, like Mentewwab before her, in bringing many of her relatives to court.

The weakness of Iyo'as's government, and the increasing Oromo influence at court, was regarded with suspicion by several lords, who began to conspire among themselves. This facilitated the rise of Mika'él Sehul, the ruler of Tegray, who controlled the northern trade route to the coast. He was therefore becoming increasingly rich and powerful, the more so as he had access to most of the country's import of firearms. This gave him military superiority over his rivals. His province's political preponderance, largely based on trade, was later noticed by Bruce. He observed:

> what, in special manner, makes the riches of Tigré, is, that it lies nearest the market, which is Arabia, and all the merchandise destined to cross the Red Sea must pass through this province, so that the governor has the choice of all commodities wherewith to make his market. The strongest male, the most beautiful female slaves, the purest gold, the largest teeth of ivory, all must pass through his hand. Fire-arms, moreover, which for many years have decided who is the most powerful in Abyssinia, all these come from Arabia, and not one can be purchased without his knowing to whom it goes, and after his having had the first refusal of it.[41]

The result, the Scotsman estimated only a generation later, was that Tegray could muster no less than six thousand matchlocks, six times as many as the rest of the country.[42]

The growing power of the Tegray ruler became apparent in 1755 when he set forth for Gondar with his province's taxes, which included rifles, costly carpets, gold, and silver coins. He

---

[41]   Bruce, *Travels*, III, 251–2.
[42]   Ibid., IV, 116.

learnt en route of Iyasu's death and of the accession of the infant Iyo'as, and hence of an apparent power vacuum in Gondar. Empress Mentewwab, realising her weakness *vis-à-vis* the powerful Tegray lord, immediately married off her daughter to the latter's son, after which Mika'él peacefully returned to his province.[43]

In the years which followed, however, he steadily increased his wealth and power. In recognition of this he was promoted to the rank of Ras, and invited to the capital, in 1657. He advanced on it, Bruce claims, virtually as a conqueror, and:

> with his army in order of battle, approached Gondar with a very warlike appearance. He descended from the high lands of Woggera into the valleys which surround the capital, and took possession of the rivers Kahha and Angrab, which ran through these valleys, and which alone supply Gondar with water. He took post at every entrance into the town, and every place commanding those entrances, as if he intended to besiege it. This conduct struck all degrees of people with terror, from the king and queen down to the lowest inhabitant. All Gondar passed an anxious night, fearing a general massacre in the morning; or that the town would be plundered, or laid under some exorbitant ransom, capitation, or tribute.[44]

Mika'él, however, soon revealed that his objective was 'to terrify, but to do no more'. Immediately after his arrival in the city, he paid homage to the young Emperor, who in return invested him with the full insignia of Ras. The chief then moved into a palace previously occupied by one of Empress Mentewwab's brothers, and began holding court. So far from inaugurating the reign of terror the citizens had expected, he proved himself, if we can believe Bruce, a man of peace and justice.

Learning, the Scotsman claims, that marauding parties of his soldiers had entered the town, and had begun plundering houses, Mika'él had a dozen of the delinquents apprehended. They hanged from trees, while he sat on a mule to see the execution performed. He likewise had over fifty other marauders executed in different parts of the city. On the same day he appointed four officers to

---

[43] Guidi, *Annales Regum*, p. 216; R. Pankhurst, 'An eighteenth century Ethiopian dynastic marriage contract between Empress Mentewwab of Gondar and Ras Mika'el of Tegre', *Bulletin of the School of Oriental and African Studies*, 42 (1979) 457–64.
[44] Bruce, *Travels*, II, 682.

enforce the sentences of the town's already existing civil judges. All this, according to Bruce, won the support of the Gondar citizens, who 'dismissed all their fears, became calm and reconciled to Michael the second day after his arrival'. They 'only regretted that they had been in anarchy, and strangers to his government so long'.

On the third after his arrival he held a council, in the presence of Iyo'as. At it he 'expressed much surprise, that both the king and queen, after the experience of so many years, had not discovered that they were equally unfit to govern a kingdom, and that it was impossible to keep distant provinces in order, when they paid such little attention to the police of the metropolis'. He was able to speak thus forcefully as he was by then in full command of the city. His army, according to Bruce, was in control of both its rivers, and permitted 'no supply of water to be brought in', except for 'two jars for each family twice a day'. This kept the townspeople in awe, for they knew that, if any attempt was made to set the city alight, they would be unable to quench it.[45]

Determined to gain the Gondar citizens' support by a dramatic gesture, Mika'él then ordered a loaf of bread, a *berelé*, or glass bottle, of water, and an ounce of gold to be exposed in the market place. His control of law and order was so complete that no one ventured to steal any of these articles, though they were exposed night and day from the Monday to the Friday, without any guards. The result, as Mika'él wished, was that 'all the citizens . . . found the security and peace they had hitherto been strangers to, and everyone deprecated the time when the government should pass out of such powerful hands'.[46]

Mika'él's lordly opponents on the other hand were infuriated by this turn of events, and seem to have decided to destroy the Tegray chief. Not long afterwards while he was holding court in his house, which faced the palace, a shot was fired from it. The bullet missed him, but killed one of his servants, a dwarf who was fanning flies from his face. The incident resulted in pandemonium, in which the palace was set on fire, on which occasion many royal chronicles were reportedly destroyed.[47]

The attempted assassination led to a final breach between

---

[45] Ibid., II, 683–4.
[46] Ibid., II, 685.
[47] Guidi, 1910, p. 246; Bruce, *T*, 1790, II, 703, IV, 251; Weld Blundell, 1922, p. 228.

Mika'él and the Gondarine monarchy. Assuming that co-existence was no longer possible, he had Iyo'as murdered, in the Spring of 1769, and had one of the deceased's great uncles, an old, and very feeble, man proclaimed Emperor Yohannes II. The latter soon afterwards refused to accompany Mika'él on campaign, as a result of which the Tegray ruler, unwilling to leave the monarch out of his control, had him poisoned. The chief, as Bruce remarks, thus in less than six months became 'the deliberate murderer of two kings'.[48] This double murder marked a further decline of the Gondar monarchy, which had begun over half a century earlier with the assassination of Iyasu I in 1706.

In the period which followed, central government disintegrated. The provinces became to varying degrees independent, the emperors were reduced to the status of little more than puppets in the hands of one or other feudal lord, and there was frequent civil war. Ethiopian historians later spoke of this time as the era of the *masafent*, i.e. judges, or princes, for it recalled the biblical time, referred to in the *Book of Judges* 21: 25, when 'there was no king in Israel: every man did that which was right in his own eyes'.

The disintegration they bemoaned was, however, by no means complete. Caravans and travelling merchants, for the most part Muslims, continued to ply the old trade routes. These linked the various provinces, including southern lands beyond the confines of the state, to the ports, and also to Sudan, thereby forming an ongoing economic unity. The institution of a Gondar-based monarchy moreover continued to exercise some prestige, with the result that many chiefs with their retinues still from time to time visited the old capital. Christian and Muslim religious ties were no less strong. The inhabitants of Christian highlands recognized a single capital, Aksum, to which many went on pilgrimage, and a single religious head, the Abun, for the most part resident in Gondar, to whom priests and monks travelled for ordination. Ethiopia also had its renowned centres of scholarship, whither church students made their way, and numerous places of pilgrimage, which were regularly visited by the faithful, Christian and Muslim alike, in bad times as in good.

---

[48] Bruce, 1790, III, p. 200.

8

The Early Nineteenth Century and the Advent of Téwodros II

Disunity and Civil War

The nineteenth century dawned on a divided country in which there was, as for many decades, no real central authority. The emperors, who mostly continued to reside in Gondar, were still theoretically endowed with supreme authority. In practice, however, they had been reduced to the position of puppets. They were controlled by feudal lords, who had become virtually independent, and often fought among themselves.

The situation at the beginning of the century was described by the British traveller, Henry Salt. He observed that the country was 'suffering under all those evils that attend an inefficient government'. Its monarch was 'in the power of one ambitious subject or another', received no revenue but that allowed him by nearly independent provincial governors, and was unable to raise sufficient forces to sustain himself, let alone to control the great feudal barons.[1]

This state of affairs was so serious that an Ethiopian chronicler bemoaned that there was no one to ask, 'How is it that the kingdom has become contemptible to striplings and slaves? How is it that the kingdom is the laughing stock of the uncircumcised . . . ? How is it that the kingdom is the image of a worthless flower that the children pick in the autumn rains?' Reflecting on the decline of the monarchy, he sadly added, 'I

[1] Annesley, 1809, I, p. 264.

lament as I ponder over the kingdom, for I was present at its trial and tribulation. And I weep without ceasing'.[2]

The country formerly constituting the empire was by then divided, Salt notes, into three 'distinctly independent states'. The first, and most important, was the northernmost, Tegray, which had risen to prominence, as we have seen, under Ras Mika'él Sehul. The province controlled the trade route to the Red Sea port of Massawa, and because of its access to the coast, had long possessed the country's largest stock of firearms. Tegray, on account of its vicinity to the Dankali plains, likewise controlled the valuable sale of *amolés*, or bars of salt, which circulated, instead of money throughout the empire, and were a considerable source of wealth. The province enjoyed moreover the unique dignity of being the territory in which Aksum, the spiritual capital, and a major place of pilgrimage, was situated.

The empire's second major political unit, according to Salt, was Amhara, which lay to the west of Tegray, beyond the Takkazé River, and comprised the fertile provinces of Bagémder, Dambeya, and Gojjam. Salt's 'Amhara' should, however, be divided into two virtually independent provinces: Bagémder and Gojjam. Bagémder, with its capital at Dabra Tabor, was under the control of a Yajju Oromo dynasty, which was originally Muslim, but soon Christianized. Founded by a chieftain called Gwanggul (*d*.1877–8) it had produced several influential rulers. The last, Ras Ali Alula, held power at Gondar, on behalf of the 'Solomonic' sovereign, Emperor Sahla Dengel (1832–40), and was the last provincial ruler prior to the advent of Emperor Téwodros (1855–68). Gojjam also had its own dynasty, the most famous member of whom was Dajazmach Berru Goshu. The province owed its independent position to the fact that it was encircled, and hence isolated and strategically protected, on three sides by the Abbay, or Blue Nile. The Amhara area, like Tegray, had considerable commercial potential, largely on account of its contacts with the rich lands to the south, the source of gold, ivory, civet and slaves. The province was also involved in foreign trade through routes to both Massawa and Sudan. 'Amhara', or in effect Bagémder, had the additional prestige of being the province in which Gondar, the nominal capital, was located.

---

[2]   Weld Blundell, 1922, pp. 471–2, 477. For a modern account of this period see Abir, 1968.

Plate 6 Traditional Ethiopian ploughing: a Tegray farmer with his wooden plough, pulled, as customary, by two oxen. From R. Acton, The Abyssinian Expedition *(London, 1868).*

The last distinct part of the empire, Shawa, lay to the south. For the time being militarily the weakest of the political units under discussion, it too had no small economic potential. This was due to the province's commercial contact with the southern and western territories, from which it obtained valuable export articles, as well as to its access to the Gulf of Aden ports of Tajurah and Zayla`, through which firearms could be imported. Shawa had the additional advantage that it had been largely isolated by Oromo incursions, and was thus protected from the debilitating civil wars in which the northern provinces were often engulfed. It had moreover been ruled by a long established dynasty, which was seemingly more stable than those of the northern provinces, whose ruling families seldom held power for more than a generation.

Provincial Rulers and Foreign Contacts

In the first part of the nineteenth century Ethiopia, the then divided empire, began to feel the effects of the Industrial Revolution then underway in western Europe. Improvements in communications, including the development of the railway and the steamboat, facilitated the coming of an increasing number of European adventurers, would-be traders, diplomats, and scholars. Many of them wrote about their experiences, and produced an extensive travel literature, of fundamental importance to this day for any understanding of Ethiopian history and civilization.

The advent of these foreign travellers impinged significantly on the principal early nineteenth-century Ethiopian rulers, of Tegray, Shawa, Bagémder, and even Gojjam. They were all to a greater or lesser extend involved in the opening up of diplomatic or commercial relations with the outside world.

The first contacts in this period between Ethiopia and the West were sparked off by Napoleon's dramatic occupation of Egypt in 1798. This prompted the British to decide on initiating contact with the Christian empire to the south. Lord Valentia, a British nobleman devoted to his country's imperial and commercial interests, sailed into the Red Sea in 1804. He sent his secretary and draftsman, Henry Salt, inland to Tegray, with instructions to investigate the possibility of establishing British commercial ties with the territory. Salt, who arrived early in the following year, succeeded in striking up friendship with its chief, Ras Walda Sellasé (died 1816). The latter, he relates, was an 'independent ruler', personally involved in every aspect of state affairs. 'All crimes, differences and disputes, of however important or trifling a nature', were ultimately referred to the ras, and 'most wars' were 'carried on by himself in person'. What Salt said of Walda Sellasé could have been said of virtually any or every provincial ruler of the era of the *masafent*.

Walda Sellasé was quick to see possible advantages in relations with Britain. He wrote to King George III, in October 1805, begging the latter, in terms reminiscent of Lebna Dengel's appeal to the Portuguese three centuries eatlier, to send him someone 'who understood the raising [i.e. pumping] of water, a medical man, and a carpenter'. He also asked for 'a supply of arms and ammunition'.[3] As for Salt's proposals for inaugurating trade with Britain, the ras promised to encourage such commerce with 'every means in his power'. Revealing himself a realist, and speaking, Salt

---

[3] Appleyard et al., 1985, p. 1.

Plate 7   *Woman spinning. From S. F. F. Veitch,* Views in Central
Abyssinia *(London, 1868).*

says, with 'with great sincerity', he nevertheless expressed the fear
that his country:

> might not be able to supply any quantity of valuable commodities
> sufficient to recompense our merchants for engaging in so preca-
> rious a trade; more especially as the Abyssinians were not much
> acquainted with commercial transactions... Could any plan,

however, be arranged for obviating these difficulties . . . he would most readily concur in carrying it into effect.

The ras also touched on another problem which dated back to the Turkish occupation of the port of Massawa almost three centuries earlier. He declared that his subjects, firmly entrenched in the highlands, found it difficult to gain access to the port. The latter was then under the control of Egypt, which had acquired it in its capacity as part of the Ottoman Empire. He added, most forcefully, that it would be 'useless' for him to 'interfere' in the coastal areas, as long as the Egyptians had 'naval superiority in the Red Sea'.[4]

Lord Valentia's initiative was fruitless, but had important long-term consequences. Walda Sellasé's successor Dajazmach Sabagadis Waldu, who gained control of Tegray in 1822, displayed interest in developing relations with Britain. In 1827, he despatched Salt's former British employee, William Coffin, to England, with a letter to King George IV, asking for 'one hundred cavalrymen', a carpenter, and a church builder 'who will build the way [they do] in your country'.[5] Little came of this request, but the British East India Company later shipped Sabagadis a consignment of firearms, which did not however arrive until after his death in 1831.[6]

Dajazmach Webé Hayla Maryam (1799–1867), the next ruler of Tegray, was far more involved in foreign contacts than his predecessor. On assuming power in 1835 he despatched a messenger to Egypt, in a vain attempt to acquire a new Abun, or Patriarch. Three years later, in June 1838, he joined Ras Ali Alula, the ruler of Bagémder, and the latter's nominal overlord, Emperor Sahla Dengel at Gondar, in an impassioned appeal to Queen Victoria of Britain and King Louis Philippe of the French. The Ethiopian rulers appealed to the two European monarchs for help against the Egyptians, who were then invading the country from the west and were only two days' journey from Gondar. Webé also later reacted not unfavourably to the advances of the French traveller Théophile Lefebvre. He reportedly told the latter, in December 1839, that he would like to obtain arms and munitions

[4]   Salt, 1814, pp. 383–4.
[5]   Rubenson, 1987, pp. 28–9.
[6]   Appleyard et al., 1985, p. 38.

Plate 8 Woman, with baby on her back, grinding grain on a traditional stone grinding-mill. From R. Acton. The Abyssinian Expedition (London, 1868).

from France, and was willing to offer the Red Sea bay of Anfilla in return.[7] Nothing resulted from this, but the French subsequently offered the chief a small quantity of firearms.

Webé followed up these discussions, in May 1841, by despatching Coffin to Britain, with a letter to Queen Victoria, asking for her help in facilitating the passage of an Abun. An Egyptian prelate called Abba Salama duly arrived later in the year, and gave his support to Webé, whose influence was thereby greatly enhanced.[8]

Faced shortly after this by enemy advances at the coast Webé wrote again to Queen Victoria, in February 1849. He appealed for her help, as one Christian to another, and declared:

> In former times, Massawa, as far as the sea, was in the hands of our ancestors. Then, when we quarrelled amongst ourselves, the Turks struck and took it by force. Following [this], two years ago, they sent an army and seized Minkillu and Dahono Bar' [two localities on the mainland].

[7] Rubenson, 1987, pp. 34–7, 42; Rubenson, 1976, pp. 86–90.
[8] Appleyard et al., 1985, pp. 65–6; Rubenson, 1987, pp. 52–3.

The letter went on to recall that the Nayb, or local ruler, of Arkiko (the port referred to above as Dahono Bar), had two years earlier ceased paying his customary tribute. Webé had therefore despatched an army against the 'Turks', i.e. Ottomans, whom he had 'put to flight', and 'enclosed in Massawa'. Addressing Queen Victoria as 'a Christian monarch', who 'loves all Christians', he declared that he sought her friendship because she was strong, 'that you may help us, . . . lest a Muslim army should strike and plunder us and deprive us of our country'.[9]

The British Foreign Secretary, the redoubtable Lord Palmerston, was, however, more interested in Egypt, which was then being modernized by its great ruler Muhammad Ali, than in far-off, and economically backward, Ethiopia. He therefore refused to listen to Webé's appeal. Instead he replied that Queen Victoria would 'gladly do anything' for the ras, but bluntly added that the Sultan of Turkey was 'also a friend to the queen'. He added that it was 'inconsistent with the principles which regulate Her Majesty's conduct towards other Powers to pronounce an opinion on any point on which her friends are at issue without being applied to by both the dissident parties'.

Webé's reaction to Palmerston's response is described by the British consul, Walter Plowden. He recalls that the Tegray ruler had sagely commented, 'This letter . . . is polite, but the substance in three words is, We won't assist you. You say you are more powerful than the Mohammedan: you do not prove it'. Turning to the strategic situation at the coast, and to his hopes of British intervention on Ethiopia's behalf, Webé added, in words not unreminiscent of Walda Sellasé's to Henry Salt, that he could easily take Massawa from the Turks, but 'could not hold it against ships and cannon'. 'His reception of myself', Plowden concluded, 'was polite, but as it is impossible to make him understand the political reasons that bind us to Turkey, it is natural that he should find it strange that we should send assurances of friendship, and yet omit to occupy some place [on the Red Sea coast] that would place us in connection with our allies in religious faith'.[10]

Rebuffed by the British, Webé turned to the French. In a letter to Prince Louis Napoleon, of 2 October of the same year, he

[9]   Appleyard et al., 1985, p. 71; Rubenson, 1987, pp. 158–9.
[10]   House of Commons, 1868, pp. 31, 42.

Plate 9 A nineteenth-century warrior. Note shield, spear, sword in sheath, bare feet, decorations, and colourful items of dress. From R. Acton, The Abyssinian Expedition *(London, 1868)*.

declared himself the rightful ruler of 'all the land on the coast', and urged the prince to make the Sultan of Istanbul withdraw from it. This appeal, like those before it, fell on deaf ears, after which Webé again approached the British. He wrote to Queen Victoria, in 1852, begging her to support the Ethiopian Christians, then suffering persecution in Turkish-occupied Jerusalem. In the following year, he requested Consul Plowden, to help him purchase guns and pistols 'of good quality', in England.[11]

Interest in western contacts, particularly after the British occupation of Aden in 1839, had meanwhile also been voiced further south, by King Sahla Sellasé, of Shawa. In the following year he

[11] Rubenson, 1987, pp. 174, 194–5, 230.

despatched a letter to the British East India Company in Bombay, asking for assistance. He observed that 'arts and science have not yet come to my country, as they have to yours'. He accordingly begged for the company's help, 'particularly in sending guns, cannon, and other things which I have not in my country'.[12]

In response to this initiative the British, and later the French, sent diplomatic missions to Shawa, and concluded treaties with its king, on 18 November 1841 and 7 June 1843 respectively. Sahla Sellasé's interest in foreign contacts, like that of other Ethiopian rulers, was above all military. Captain Cornwallis Harris, the leader of the British mission, later observed that the monarch was primarily concerned with the acquisition of firearms, and quoted him as declaring that the gift of 'a few more muskets' would render him a match for all his enemies, after which there would be 'no further risings' among his vassals. Sahla Sellasé's interest in war material also extended to metallurgy, as a result of which he questioned the French envoy, Rochet d'Héricourt, closely on the making of cannon, rifles and swords.[13]

Relations between Sahla Sellasé and the British and French later soured, but his son and successor Hayla Malakot (1840–56), later sought to re-open contact with Britain. He wrote to Queen Victoria, in the Spring of 1848, asking her for 1,500 Maria Theresa dollars and, if possible, some gold. The messenger entrusted with his letter also carried a verbal request for craftsmen, who could 'make a crown, and make cannons, and paint pictures, and build palaces'.[14]

Foreign contacts were also established by the north-westerly province of Amhara, in the late 1830s and 1840s, during the rule of Ras Ali Alula, who styled himself 'head of the nobles'. He and his nominal superior, Emperor Sahla Dengel, joined Dajazmach Webé of Tegray in 1838 in their above-mentioned appeal to the British and French for help against the invading Egyptians.[15]

---

[12]   Isenberg and Krapf, 1843, p. 251.
[13]   India Office, London, Bombay Secret Proceedings, CLXXXIX, 2060, and CXCVI, 3489, letters of Captain W. C. Harris. Rochet d'Héricourt, 1841, p. 76.
[14]   Appleyard et al., 1985, p. 79; Rubenson, 1987, p. 160.
[15]   Ibid., pp. 34–7.

Plate 10   Priests, and others, outside country church: Reading a large manuscript. Note carved wooden doorway, priests' sticks, or crutches, palm leaves for Palm Sunday celebrations, processional cross, incense-holder, and church bell. From R. Acton, The Abyssinian Expedition *(London, 1868).*

Later, under pressure from British Consul Plowden, Ali agreed to sign a Treaty of Friendship and Commerce with Britain, on 2 November, 1849. In it, ignoring Sahla Dengel, he proudly claimed the title of *Negusa Habasha*, or King of Abyssinia. The treaty, which was drafted by the British to serve British as opposed to Ethiopian interests, provided for the exchange of 'ambassadors' between the two countries. Article 3 which was to acquire special relevance a decade or so later, during the reign of Emperor Téwodros, emphatically declared:

Her Britannic Majesty and her successors will . . . receive and protect any Ambassador, Envoy, or Consul, whom His Majesty of Abyssinia or his successors may see fit to appoint, and will equally preserve inviolate all the rights and privileges of such Ambassador, Envoy, or Consul.[16]

[16]   House of Commons, 1868, pp. 39–41; Rubenson, 1987, pp. 178–87.

Plowden believed, and doubtless told Ras Ali, that the British Government could 'enforce' this, and other articles of the treaty, on the Turks, i.e. Ottomans.[17]

Ali's interest in accepting the treaty was shortly afterwards revealed when he wrote that same month to Queen Victoria. He asked her for a supply of modern firearms, silver coins, i.e. Maria Theresa thalers, with which to pay his soldiers, and the protection of Ethiopian merchants at Massawa.[18]

Though British and French contacts were thus mainly with Tegray, Shawa, and Bagémder, the ruler of Gojjam, Ras Goshu Zawdé, reportedly seems to have also recognized some usefulness in entering into a relationship with Europe. As a ruler of the northwest he accordingly despatched a letter to King Leopold I of the Belgians, in September 1841, asking him to 'chase the Turks from Massawa'.[19]

The Beginnings of Unification and the Legacy of Civil War

Ethiopia, by the middle of the nineteenth century, had long been suffering, as we have seen, from disunity and civil war. This was the more serious in that the Industrial Revolution was then well underway in Europe and was beginning even in Egypt. Britain and France, taking advantage of the new technology, had sent their warships into Red Sea and Gulf of Aden waters. Even more ominously, Ethiopia's northern neighbour Egypt, modernized by her reforming ruler Muhammad Ali, was extending its control southwards into Sudan.

Ethiopia, torn by civil war and deprived of access to the sea, was by contrast in no position to embark on any policy of modernisation. The country was in fact technologically falling relatively backward. Its national integrity was moreover increasingly threatened, for the Egyptians were encroaching on the northern, western and eastern frontiers.

The second half of the century nevertheless witnessed the country's first significant attempts at unification and modernization –

[17] House of Commons, 1868, p. 39.
[18] Rubenson, 1987, pp. 188–9.
[19] Ibid., p. 54.

but also major, and unprecedented, intrusions by foreign powers.

This period, which marked another great turning point in Ethiopian history, may conveniently be divided into the reigns of its three principal rulers, Téwodros, Yohannes and Menilek. Though very different personalities, facing dissimilar problems, and enemies, they were each involved with the same three basic issues: the re-unification of the Ethiopian state, the preservation of its independence, and the increasingly necessary adoption of modern institutions and technology.

Téwodros and his Reform Policies

The rise of Kasa Haylu, the future Emperor Téwodros (or Theodore) II, marked the opening of a new, and crucially important, era of Ethiopian history. Most of his attempted reforms were never achieved, but were nonetheless significant for they seem almost to have charted the course to be taken in the reigns that followed.

Kasa, who was born around 1818, was the son of a chief of Qwara on the western frontier. A distant member of the royal family he was brought up in a monastery, but later became a free-lance soldier, a kind of Ethiopian Robin Hood, who gave what he looted to those in need. His courage won him the loyalty of his followers, and enabled him to gain control of Qwara, and assume the title of Dajazmach. Empress Manan Liban, the mother of Ras Ali Alula, the ruler of Bagémder, despatched an expedition against him, but he easily defeated it. Ali thereupon recognized him as governor of Qwara, and Manan arranged for him to marry her grand-daughter, Tawabach Ali, in 1847.

In the following year Kasa advanced into Sudan as far as Dabarki, where the Egyptians had erected a fort. He tried to capture it, but his soldiers suffered heavy casualties, and were routed. The engagement was noteworthy, for it convinced him, according to the British traveller Henry Dufton, that 'the primitive mode of warfare of his country would have to be superseded by a more modern one if he were ever to accomplish the splendid designs of his ambition'.[20] In the ensuing civil war in Ethiopia,

[20] Dufton, 1867, pp. 138–9.

Kasa nevertheless rapidly defeated his rivals, among them Ras Ali, whose forces he routed at the battle of Ayshal, in eastern Gojjam, on 29 June 1853. By 1854 Kasa had made himself master of the entire north-west of the empire, including Amhara and the old capital, Gondar. The only significant rulers outside his sway were Dajazmach Webé of Tegray and King Sahla Sellasé's son King Hayla Malakot of Shawa.

Webé, who claimed the imperial crown, was then planning to march to Gondar, where the newly arrived Coptic Metropolitan, Abuna Salama, was supposed to crown him as emperor. Kasa, however, defeated, and captured, the would-be monarch, at the battle of Darasgé, south of the Takazé river, on 8 February 1855. The prelate thereupon agreed to anoint Kasa instead. The victorious chief was accordingly crowned three days later, on 11 February, as Emperor Téwodros. The name was significant, as an old and widely believed Messianic legend prophesied that a monarch called Téwodros would one day appear, rule justly, wipe out Islam, and capture Jerusalem. In the following year Téwodros marched into Shawa, the first Ethiopian monarch to do so since Iyasu I undertook a brief expedition to the province a century and a half earlier. There Téwodros captured Menilek, the heir to the Shawan throne, whose father Hayla Malakot had died shortly earlier.[21]

Despite his early victories, Téwodros was throughout his reign in a difficult military position. His power base, in the north-west of the empire, was far from the sea. He was therefore unable to obtain firearms through the Red Sea or Gulf of Aden ports. Such weapons tended only to reach his rivals, the rulers of Tegray and Shawa. The only other trade route through which he might have procured weapons, that to the west, was likewise closed to him, as the Egyptians in Sudan were bent on advancing into Ethiopia.

Notwithstanding this military weakness Téwodros showed himself a remarkable ruler. This is evident in reports by British Consul Plowden, which, because of their bearing on important events soon to unfold, deserve quoting in detail. On 7 April, only a month after Téwodros's coronation, he observed that the king, who was 'capable' of 'great things, good or evil', considered himself 'a destined monarch'. In a later report, of 25 June, Plowden noted that Téwodros was 'persuaded' that he was 'destined' to restore the glories of Ethiopian empire, and to achieve

---

[21] Rubenson, 1966, pp. 39–40, 52–3.

Plate 11 Seal of Emperor Téwodros II (facsimile size). Note Lion of Judah, and use of both Geʿez and Arabic writing. From C. T. Beke, The British Captives in Abyssinia (London, 1867).

great conquests. Elaborating on the monarch's almost fanatical character, he continued:

> When aroused his wrath is terrible, and all tremble; but at all moments he possesses a perfect self-command. Indefatigable in business, he takes little repose night or day; his ideas and language are clear and precise; hesitation is not known to him . . . He is fond of splendour and receives in state even on campaign. He is unsparing of punishment [but] generous to excess, and free from all cupidity, regarding nothing with pleasure or desire but munitions of war for his soldiers . . . His faith is signal: without Christ, he says, I am nothing; if He has destined me to purify and reform this distracted kingdom, with His aid who can stay me: nay, sometimes he is on the point of not caring for human assistance at all . . .

Turning to Téwodros's remarkable personality, which was soon to have a major impact on events, Plowden observed that the Ethiopian ruler was:

> particularly jealous . . . of his sovereign rights, and of anything that appears to trench on them; he wishes, in a short time, to send embassies to the Great European Powers to treat with them on equal terms. The most difficult trait of his character is this jealousy and the pride that, fed by ignorance, renders it impossible for him yet to believe that so great a monarch as himself exists in the world . . .

Plate 12   Emperor Téwodros II inspecting road-building, in north-west Ethiopia. From Hormuzd Rassam, Narrative of the British Mission to Theodore *(London, 1869).*

As for Téwodros's modernizing ambitions, which set him apart from his predecessors, Plowden concluded:

> The arduous task of breaking the power of the great feudal Chiefs
> – a task achieved in Europe only during the reign of many consecu-
> tive kings – he has commenced by chaining almost all who were
> dangerous, avowing his intention of liberating them when his
> power shall be consolidated. He has placed the soldiers of the
> different provinces under the command of his own trusty followers,
> to whom he has given high titles, but no power to judge or punish;
> thus, in fact, creating generals in place of feudal chieftains more
> proud of their birth than of their monarch, and organising a new

nobility, a legion of honour dependent on himself, and chosen for their daring and fidelity . . .
    Some of his ideas may be imperfect, others impracticable, but a man who . . . has done so much and contemplates such great designs cannot be regarded as of ordinary stamp.[22]

Téwodros, as Plowden's reports suggest, was essentially a unifier, reformer and innovator. His first and foremost objective was the military conquest of the country. Abandoning the old capital, Gondar, in favour of Dabra Tabor, a strategically better placed locality some 60 miles to the south-east, he made the natural fortress of Maqdala, about 70 miles further east in Wallo, his principal headquarters. He also carried out a series of well-executed expeditions which brought Tegray, Wallo, and, finally Shawa, into his empire. His first wife Tawabach having died he later attempted to strengthen his control over Tegray by marrying the daughter of its former ruler Dajazmach Webé. She was variously known as Terunash and Teruwarq. Despite Téwodros's well-executed military operations, and his dynastic marriage with one of the principal chiefs in the land, his hold over the provinces was only temporary.

Military Reorganization and Missionary Craftsmen

Struggling to gain control over the empire Téwodros was much preoccupied with military matters. Though a man of war, he was not unaware of the suffering caused by the country's unpaid soldiers. Beside being inefficient they were a social bane, for they ravaged the peasantry in search of food. He was determined to replace such soldiery by a modern-type army that would live on rations, or pay, provided by the state. This 'great reform', as Plowden called it, would have enabled the country's inhabitants, almost for the first time in their history, to live in relative security.[23]
    The reforming monarch, however, found it virtually impossible to establish such an army, for he lacked the resources with which to remunerate his men. He was moreover often unable to make them obey orders which conflicted with their interests. While in

[22] House of Commons, 1868, pp. 143–4, 150–1.
[23] Ibid., p. 150.

Dalanta in 1856, for example, he permitted his soldiers to take whatever they needed from the peasantry, but commanded them to touch neither clothing nor cattle. The men were, however, disobedient. They slaughtered all the livestock they could find, whereupon their exasperated master cursed them, saying, 'As you have killed what belongs to the poor, so will God do unto you!'[24] Looting of the peasantry was thus not infrequent, the more so as Téwodros, an often remarkably ruthless leader, displayed himself particularly vindictive against rebel populations.

Meanwhile, with a view to improving his military equipment, Téwodros accepted an offer by Samuel Gobat, the Anglican Bishop of Jerusalem, in 1855 to send him a group of young craftsmen from the Chrischona missionary institute near Basle, in Switzerland. These missionary artisans, as they were called, brought him gifts of religious books, for the most part in Amharic, but as he later acknowledged, he would have been 'more pleased with a box of English gunpowder' than with books he 'already possessed'. He nevertheless welcomed the missionaries kindly, interested himself in their craftsmanship, and established them near Dabra Tabor, at the village of Gafat. There he also settled several other European artisans, and adventurers, thus making it a veritable craftsmen's centre.

Not long after their arrival Téwodros decided to call the foreign craftsmen to his aid. Though always keen to purchase firearms whenever he could, he found it virtually impossible to procure artillery. Such heavy weapons could scarcely be smuggled into the country through rugged country under hostile control. He therefore bluntly requested his European guests to help him by manufacturing cannon and mortars. The missionaries, who constituted the largest number of the Gafat craftsmen, were entirely unskilled in this field, and had come indeed with more peaceful objectives in mind. They had, however, little option but to obey. One of them, Theophilus Waldmeier, a Swiss, recalls that they were in 'great difficulty, and helpless vis-à-vis the moody king who sent us letter after letter asking whether our work had succeeded. Time after time we were obliged to give a negative answer, but the King's patience was greater than ours; he comforted us, and sent us word: "Begin again from the beginning". This we did, but in vain.'

[24] Moreno, 1942, pp. 160–1.

Plate 13 Téwodros's great mortal 'Sebastapol', dragged towards Maqdala by hundreds of the monarch's followers. From Hormuzd Rassam, Narrative of the British Mission to Theodore *(London, 1869).*

The craftsmen nevertheless persevered. 'After unspeakable effort', says Waldmeier, 'we made a final attempt . . . and, behold, for the first time we were successful. All the Abyssinians of the area, who had for a long time laughed at our work, now came to share our joy and to congratulate us . . . The King was pleased beyond measure with our little piece of metal, kissed it and cried, "Now I am convinced that it is possible to make everything in Habesh. Now the art has been discovered God has at last revealed Himself. Praise and thanks be to Him for it" '. By the early 1860s, the British traveller Henry Dufton reported that 'all the Europeans' at Gafat were engaged in this work. One small mortar they had cast, 'considering the manner in which it was made, was a marvel', for 'the metal was melted in thirty crucibles, on fires in the ground, blown by hand-bellows of the most primitive description'.

By 1866, the craftsmen, according to Waldmeier, were working like slaves, night and day. The emperor soon afterwards asked them to cast a cannon capable of firing a thousand pound shell. 'We were afraid to refuse and were afraid to obey', the missionary recalls, 'but God did not abandon us. . . . He let our work succeed'.[25]

Téwodros's interest in artillery, and the need to transport it from one part of his rebellious country to another, led him to become his country's first road-builder. He began the construction of a rudimentary road network to link Dabra Tabor, with Gondar, Maqdala, and Gojjam. To oblige his men to undertake the back-breaking toil involved he adopted the traditional Ethiopian practice whereby rulers set the example by themselves leading, or beginning, the work. A foreign observer recalls that 'from early dawn to late at night' Téwodros was 'hard at work' on the road; 'with his own hands he removed stones, levelled the ground, or helped to fill up ravines. No one could leave so long as he was there himself; no one would think of eating, or of rest, while the Emperor showed the example and shared the hardships'.[26]

Téwodros, though primarily interested in matters military, also envisaged reforms in other fields. Spurred, it appears, by the need to allocate land to his troops, he attached considerable importance to land reform. He envisaged the extensive expropriation of church land. This brought him into bitter conflict with the clergy, whom previous rulers had almost always sought to woo, and made him extremely unpopular among many of the faithful, as well as with the feudal nobility who hated his attempts to curtail their traditional powers.[27]

The reforming emperor also sought, intermittantly, to abolish the slave trade (though not the instituion of slavery). He likewise tried to persuade his followers to dress more elegantly, and to adopt a more permanent type of marriage. He moreover promoted the use of Amharic, instead of the classical written language, Geʿez, and encouraged the translation of the bible into the vernacular.[28]

[25] On Téwodros's manufacture of artillery see Dufton, 1867, pp. 82–6, 138–9; Beke, 1867, p. 259; Waldmeier, 1896, pp. 7–9, 11–24, 47, 55–8, 87–8.
[26] For a useful account of Téwodros's road-building activities see Blanc, 1868, pp. 342–4.
[27] Pankhurst, 1966, pp. 93–7.
[28] A volume of the Gospels of St Mathew and St Mark, written in Amharic by an Ethiopian scribe called Luqas, is preserved in the British Library, where it is catalogued as Orient 733. See Wright, 1872, p. 34.

Téwodros's Dispute with the British Government

Téwodros's pioneering attempts at unification and modernization
were soon overshadowed, and ultimately brought to naught, by a
serious dispute with the British Government. The emperor had
originally been on excellent terms with two Englishmen, John Bell,
whom he had appointed Court Chamberlain, and British consul
Plowden, whom he treated as an adviser. Both were killed in 1860,
the former fighting by the emperor's side; the latter on a journey to
the coast. Téwodros was left with a perhaps unjustified feeling of
admiration and sympathy for Britain.

Plowden and his successor, Duncan Cameron, had both
pressed Téwodros to renew the Treaty with Britain earlier concluded with Ras Ali, but the emperor, despite his pro-British
feelings, had demurred. Apparently conscious of the danger of
European colonialism, then its infancy, he seems to have feared
that the advent of a British consul, flying the Union Jack, might
infringe Ethiopian sovereignty. He preferred instead to despatch
embassies of his own, as an independent ruler, to Britain, France,
and, it is believed, Russia, like Ethiopia, an Orthodox Christian
country.

Téwodros accordingly wrote two almost identical letters to
Queen Victoria and Emperor Napoleon III of France, on 29 Octo-
ber 1862. Couched in friendly terms, they declared that previous
Ethiopian rulers had 'forgotten their creator', who had accordingly given their kingdom to the 'Gallas', i.e. Ras Ali's Oromo
Yajju dynasty, and to the 'Turks', i.e. the Ottomans, or more
exactly the Egyptians, then in occupation of the Red Sea coast.
God, he claimed, had, however, 'created' him [i.e. Téwodros],
lifted him 'out of the dust', and 'restored' the empire to his rule.
Having defeated Ras Ali's dynasty, he had ordered the 'Turks' to
leave the land of his ancestors, but they had refused; he was
therefore going to fight them.

In his letter to Victoria, which he handed to Cameron,
Téwodros recalled that Plowden and Bell had told him that she
was 'a great Christian queen', who 'loved Christians', and that
they could 'establish friendship' with her. It was, he said, on that
account that he had given them his 'love'. Doubtless remembering
Article 3 of the treaty with Ras Ali, in which the British Government had agreed to 'receive and protect' any diplomatic repre-

sentative appointed by the Ethiopian ruler, he declared that the 'Turks' at the coast were denying him passage by sea, and that he was therefore unable to despatch the ambassador he wished to send to England. He therefore asked where his envoy should take the gifts he wished to send, and appealed to Victoria to 'stand by' him, 'the Christian', at a time when 'the Muslim', i.e. the 'Turks', threatened to attack him.[29]

This letter was couched, it will be perceived, in terms of Christian religious fervour, akin to that of the medieval European Crusaders, who, only a few centuries earlier, would have received it with the utmost enthusiasm. European, and particulary British, modes of thought since then had, however, undergone a great transformation.

Téwodros gave the letter to Cameron, to whom he made several more specific oral requests. These were that the British should (1) receive an embassy from Ethiopia; (2) enable his envoys to pass through hostile 'Turkish', or Egyptian, territory; (3) prevent the incursion of the Ottoman/Egyptian fleet in neighbouring Red Sea waters; (4) help him purchase firearms; and (5) obtain an engineer to build roads.

Téwodros asked Cameron to take the letter, and oral requests, to England in person. The consul, however, chose instead to sent it by messenger, with a cover letter in which he remarked that British craftsmen should have no fear of living in Ethiopia, for the missionaries already working for the monarch were 'very liberally' treated.

The two letters reached London on 12 February 1863, but, like Webé's epistle of 1849, met with Foreign Office disapproval. The British Government, which regarded Russia as a threat to the British Empire in India, considered the Ottoman Empire an ally, and had no wish to alienate it by affording protection to Ethiopia. No reply was therefore returned to the emperor's message, which was instead forwarded to the India Office, and then filed away. Cameron's letter was not answered until 22 April, when the foreign secretary, Earl Russell, despatched an unsympathetic response. He declared that it was 'not desirable for Her Majesty's agents to meddle in the affairs of Abyssinia', and that Cameron should return to Massawa, and remain there 'until further orders'.

[29]   Rubenson, 1994, pp. 198–203.

As time passed and his letter remained unanswered, Téwodros, whose pride in his royal status had earlier been noted by Plowden, became convinced that he was being deliberately slighted. Cameron meanwhile made matters worse, for instead of travelling to the coast as requested, he proceeded to Kassala and Matamma, on the western border. He undertook the journey, as Plowden had done before him, to assist the Christian people of Bogos, whom the Egyptians were taking as slaves. His visit, which took him into Egyptian occupied territory, however, greatly angered Téwodros. The latter, learning of an exchange of courtesies between Cameron and the Egyptians, was left with the impression that the British consul was recognizing the latter's expansion and thus siding with Ethiopia's enemies and invaders.

Not long afterwards the emperor learnt that Henry Stern, a bigoted London-based Protestant missionary, had written a book, *Wanderings among the Falashas*, which contained unfavourable remarks about him. These included the statement that his mother was so impoverished that she had been reduced to selling *kosso*, the traditional Ethiopian cure for tapeworm. Regarding such observations as *laissez-majesté* Téwodros had Stern questioned, and a servant of his flogged to death. The missionary at this point placed his finger to his mouth in a gesture which was interpreted as one of defiance. He was duly whipped, and with another missionary, Rosenthal, sentenced to close confinement.

Soon after this, in November 1863, Cameron's secretary, Kerans, arrived from England with a letter from Earl Russell's secretary James Murray, reminding the consul of his instructions to return to the coast. The message added that Cameron was consul only at Massawa, and had 'no representative character in Abyssinia'. This statement was erroneous, for Cameron, like Plowden, had originally been appointed 'Her Majesty's consul in Abyssinia'. The remark that he was now representative only at Massawa, part of the Ottoman Empire, seemed to signify a change in British policy. It lent itself to the interpretation that the British, so far from responding to Téwodros's advances, were withdrawing from contact with Ethiopia, and might indeed be about to recognize Turkish/Egyptian sovereignty over it. That Murray's letter reflected official policy was apparent from the fact that Lord Russell subsequently wrote to Cameron that the British

Government 'do not approve of your proceedings in Abyssinia nor your suggestions founded upon them'.[30]

Instead of the long awaited reply from Victoria, Téwodros thus learnt the humiliating news that the British Government was withdrawing its consul. His anger crystallized around the paltry gift of a carpet which Kerans had purchased for him, on the British Government's behalf. It bore the effigy of a *zouave*, or turbaned soldier, attacking a lion, and behind the former a mounted European. Téwodros gave the picture symbolic significance. He declared that the animal signified the Lion of Judah, i.e. himself, the *zouave*, the Turks or Egyptians attacking him, and the horsemen, the French, backing up the Egyptians. 'But where', he demanded, 'are the English to back up the lion?'

The emperor's conclusion that the British were abandoning him to the Egyptians was no wild assumption. British policy was then strongly pro-Egyptian. Britain, with its great cotton factories, was anxious, as the contemporary British author Charles Beke observed, to remain on friendly terms with Egypt, which produced 150 million pounds of cotton a year. This consideration was then of especial importance, for the American Civil War, and the resultant suspension of supplies from the United States, had made Britain more than ever dependent on Egyptian cotton.

Further evidence of a British change of heart reached Téwodros almost immediately afterwards. The head of the Ethiopian convent in Jerusalem arrived with news that the Coptic priests in the Holy City, with the help of the Turkish authorities, had endeavoured to seize his convent. Though the former British representative, Consul Finn, had protected the Ethiopians against such depredations, his successor, Consul Noel Moore, declared himself powerless to act without instructions from his superiors, who were in fact unwilling to intervene.[31]

Téwodros, who had waited over a year for a reply to his letter of October 1862, had now reached the end of his patience. He responded, on 4 January 1864, by chaining Cameron and his party.

[30] On these negotiations between Téwodros and the British Government see House of Commons, 1868, especially pp. 198, 218–221, 236, 229, 236, 243, and, for a modern account, Arnold, 1991.
[31] Beke, 1867, pp. 124–5, 129–30.

The Question of Foreign Artisans

News of Cameron's detention led the British Government to search out Téwodros's unanswered letter. A reply was hastily drawn up, and entrusted to Hormuzd Rassam, the Assistant British Resident at Aden, who, after much delay, reached Téwodros's camp in February 1866. On receipt of the queen's letter the emperor released Cameron, Stern, and Rosenthal, but soon afterwards re-arrested them, together with Rassam, apparently in the hope of persuading the British Government to listen to his request for the despatch of artisans. Téwodros shortly afterwards sent one of the Gafat missionaries, Martin Flad, a German, to England to arrange for the recruitment of such personnel.

The detention of Rassam, Cameron and their colleagues at first had precisely the effect Téwodros desired. At the end of July, 1866 the British representative in Egypt, Colonel Stanton, bluntly observed that the captives' release would depend 'very much' on the 'amount of satisfaction' Téwodros received on the question of the artisans. Lieutenant Colonel Merewether, the British Political Resident in Aden, likewise declared that the British Government should seek to gain the confidence of the Ethiopian ruler by meeting his requests 'frankly and most liberally'.[32] This view was accepted by the British Government. Flad was therefore able to report to Téwodros on 1 September, 'The business Your Majestly sent me for to England is, through the grace of Christ our Lord, accomplished. The artists Your Majesty was anxious to get are found, and ready to come with me to your country'. As for the European captives he added:

> Queen Victoria is a little grieved, saying, Why has the emperor Theodore not sent over to me the prisoners, whose relations are daily weeping before me. In reply to this I said, After having conveyed the artists to Your majesty I shall come back, and bring the released prisoners over with me to England. This hope I gave to Her Majesty.

Flad's mission for the next few weeks seemed completely successful. On 18 September the missionary reported that the manufacture of the machinery needed by the artisans was 'progressing

[32]   House of Commons, 1868, p. 482.

well', and should be ready by 10 October. Four days later, however, news was received from Flad's wife in Ethiopia that Téwodros had again imprisoned the Europeans. The emperor's relations with them had indeed taken a turn for the worse. Rassam, in trying to arrange for their departure, had aroused the monarch's anger, while a false report that a British company had a contract to construct a railway in Sudan for the invasion of Ethiopia increased his suspicion of Britain.

Téwodros thereupon ordered the captives to be taken to his mountain fortress of Maqdala. Flad's immediate reaction was to advise Merewether to abandon his plan of sending the workmen to the emperor. 'It is no advantage', he argued, 'to send him the required artisans, because the release of the prisoners would, I fear, not be obtained. Most likely he would go on requiring other things from the British Government to which they could never surrender . . . I deem it advisable that Her Majesty's Government should at once use stronger terms'.

The emperor's attempt to pressurize the British Government by imprisoning its functionaries, though up to then successful, had miscarried. British policy was now reversed. Rassam's imprisonment, wrote Merewether on 25 September, was 'so great an outrage and insult' that adherence to the plan of despatching the artisans to Téwodros was no longer possible. It was therefore decided that they should be sent to Massawa, but not allowed inland until the prisoners were released and sent down to the port.

The workmen duly left Southampton on 4 November, and arrived at Massawa on 10 December, but by then mistrust on both sides was so great that no agreement could be reached. Téwodros declared that he would not release the captives until the workmen arrived at his camp, while the British refused to send up the latter until the former reached the coast.[33]

Maqdala: the British Assault and the Suicide of Téwodros

Téwodros was by this time no longer the powerful monarch he had appeared at the beginning of the dispute. His attempts at

[33]   House of Commons, 1868, pp. 492, 503, 508. On the history of the British craftsmen see Pankhurst, 'The Emperor Theodore and the question of the foreign artisans in Ethiopia', 1966, pp. 215–35.

unification had failed. Menilek, heir to the kingdom of Shawa, had escaped from detention at Maqdala in 1865, and declared his independence. Gobazé, son of the deposed ruler of Lasta, had seized power in that province. Kasa Mercha, a nobleman of Endarta, had made himself ruler of much of Tegray. Gojjam was in revolt. Téwodros, though still nominally emperor of the entire country, was in fact in control only of a small part of Bagémder, and even there faced many rebels. His army, once almost a hundred thousand strong, had shrunk to perhaps a tenth of that number.

The British Government, aware of Téwodros's declining strength, and increasingly angered by the protracted imprisonment of Cameron, Rassam and their colleagues, at last decided, in July 1867, to despatch a military expedition to force the emperor's hand. The task was entrusted to a capable British officer, Sir Robert Napier. An Anglo-Indian expeditionary force, despatched from India, landed at Annesley Bay, near Massawa, on 21 October, and then began the long march inland to the emperor's fortress at Maqdala. Téwodros meanwhile was making desperate efforts to transport the artillery, made with such difficulty by his missionary craftsmen, to that mountain, where he had decided to give battle to the invaders.

The British expeditionary force, which was exceedingly well equipped, was several times larger than what was left of Téworos's army. Napier had over 16,000 fighting men, two-thirds of them Indian, supported by 12,600 transport assistants and 3,200 camp-followers.[34] The British had sixteen cannon, two mortars and sixteen guns for firing rockets. Napier's army advanced inland without encountering opposition. On the contrary it received considerable co-operation from Kasa of Tegray, while the latter's rivals, Gobazé and Menilek, both showed themselves sympathetic to the expedition. The British army, unlike a traditional Ethiopian force, was moreover copiously supplied with Maria Theresa thalers, specially minted for the purpose, and the local population through which the British passed was happy to sell them provisions of all kinds.

The first battle between Téwodros and the British took place at Arogé, just below Maqdala, on 10 April 1868. The invading force enjoyed overwhelming superiority of fire-power, for Téwodros's locally made cannon and mortars proved defective, or were inex-

[34] For details of the British expedition, its personnel and armament see Holland and Hozier, 1870.

pertly fired. The British inflicted heavy casualties on Téwodros's unfortunate men. On the following day Napier wrote to the emperor, declaring:

> Your Majesty has fought like a brave man, and has been overcome by the superior power of the British Army. It is my desire that no more blood may be shed. If, therefore, your Majesty will submit to the Queen of England, and bring all the Europeans now in your Majesty's hands, and deliver them safely this day in the British Camp, I guarantee honourable treatment for yourself and all the members of your Majesty's family.

Téwodros, an intensely proud man as Plowden had noted two decades earlier, refused to accept such humiliation. He replied to Napier with a remarkable letter which in a sense constitutes his last testament to the Ethiopian people. In this letter he refers to himself significantly enough, for the first time for over a decade, as 'Kasa', thus apparently abandoning his kingly title of Téwodros. Addressing his fellow Ethiopians he asks, 'My compatriots, will you not stop running away unless I, by the power of God, attack [lit. come down] with you'. Later, in the same epistle, he turned his attention to his victorious adversaries, the British. He recalled the difficulties he had encountered, as a reforming ruler, and observed, 'When I used to tell my compatriots, "submit to taxation and discipline", they refused and quarrelled with me.' Alluding to the superiority of the British army, organized on modern lines, over his traditional-type forces, but curiously ignoring his enemy's overwhelming superiority of fire-power, he added, 'You have defeated me through men obedient to discipline'. Writing in a way his own epitaph he added:

> My countrymen were giving me ten reasons (for opposing me) saying, 'He has adopted the religion of the Europeans, or he has become a Muslim . . .
> If God had allowed me, I had planned to rule all; if God prevented me, (my intention was) to die . . . From when I was born until now, no man knew (how to) take hold of my hand.[35]

After dictating these heroic words Téwodros attempted to commit suicide. He placed a pistol to his head, but his soldiers

[35]   Rubenson, 1994, p. 354–5.

Plate 14   Suicide of Emperor Téwodros II, at Maqdala in April 1868: an
anonymous Ethiopian painting, of around 1960, in semi-traditional
style, preserved in the Institute of Ethiopian Studies Museum in Addis
Ababa. Note the British commander, Robert Napier, anachronistically
saluting the Ethiopian monarch, who had in fact died prior to the British
entry into the fort. Photo: Institute of Ethiopian Studies Museum.

snatched the weapon from his hand. Negotiations with the British
were then resumed. On 12 April the emperor, who was by then
anxious to resolve the dispute peacefully, sent the latter a sizeable
gift of livestock, according to one account 1,000 cattle and 500
sheep. On being informed that they had been received at the
enemy camp, he released the prisoners. Napier in fact at first

Plate 15   Maqdala in flames, 1868, fired by the British Royal Engineers. From R. Acton, The Abyssinian Expedition *(London, 1868).*

contemplated accepting the gift, but, on learning of the 'magnitude and nature of the offering', which would have been interpreted as agreeing to make peace, refused to accept it. On realizing this the emperor attempted to flee, but, realizing himself surrounded, immediately changed his mind, and returned to Maqdala. The British then launched their final assault, on 13 April. Téwodros, seeing that resistance was useless, dismissed his followers, saying, 'It is finished! Sooner than fall into his hands I will kill myself'. He then put his revolver to his mouth, and committed suicide. He thereby won himself a permanent, and highly honoured, placed in Ethiopian history and mythology.[36]

The British, having thus accomplished their mission, at once prepared to leave. From the outset they had no intention of remaining in the country, and had promised to withdraw as soon as the question of the European prisoners had been solved. It was only on that understanding that Kasa, the ruler of Tegray, had allowed them to pass through his province, and that the Turks had permitted them to land at the coast. The British promise to leave

[36] On Téwodros's impact on Ethiopian art and literature see Taddese Beyene, R. Pankhurst, and Shiferaw Bekele, 1990.

Ethiopia was not difficult to honour, for from the outset they had no interest in the country. Lord Stanley, the British Foreign Secretary, had put the matter bluntly, if cynically, when he wrote: 'Her Majesty's Government have no concern with what might befall [sic] Abyssinia from the removal of King Theodore . . . it will in no way concern them what may be the future that awaits Abyssinia; what Ruler may hold power in the country; what civil wars or commotion may arise in it'.[37]

Before leaving Ethiopia, British troops destroyed most of Téwodros's artillery, and put Maqdala to the flames. They took with them the emperor's young son, Alamayehu, at the request of his mother, and close on a thousand manuscripts. Some of the latter were subsequently left behind in Tegray, but almost five hundred, including not a few of the finest, were taken to Britain. The largest number ended up in the British Museum (now the British Library), the Royal Library in Windsor Castle, and several other British collections. The last act of the expedition was to reward Kasa for his cooperation by presenting him with six mortars, six howitzers, as well as 850 muskets, and a goodly supply of ammunition. This somewhat unexpected military windfall contributed greatly to his subsequent rise to power.

[37] Rubenson, 1976, p. 275.

9

Yohannes, Menilek and the European Powers

The Rise of Yohannes

Téwodros's death in 1868, which, like his life, was a turning point in his country's history, left Ethiopia once again divided, and without a ruler. Three rival personalities then held power in different areas. The first to gain prominence was Wagshum Gobazé, the ruler of Amhara, Wag and Lasta, who was immediately crowned Emperor Takla Giyorgis at Gondar. He was, however, soon effectively challenged by Dajazmach Kasa Mercha of Tegray. The latter was militarily more powerful, in part on account of the gift of arms he had received from the Napier expedition, and assistance given him by a former member of the British force, John Kirkham, who had volunteered to train his army on European lines. Gobazé set out with 60,000 men to capture Adwa, the then capital of Tegray, but Kasa, making good use of his British guns, defeated him at the battle of Assam, on 11 July 1871. He then proclaimed himself Emperor Yohannes IV, on 21 January of the following year. The third contestant for power was Menilek, heir to the throne of Shawa, who had been one of Téwodros's prisoners at Maqdala, but escaped in 1865, and proclaimed himself king of his province. Though then the weakest of the three chiefs, he for a time laid ineffective claim to the imperial throne, which he was eventually to inherit. These two latter rulers, Yohannes and Menilek, were rivals, but their reigns not only overlapped, but were also almost inextricably intertwined.

Plate 16   Seal of Emperor Yohannes IV. From G. Massaia, I miei trentacinque anni di missione nell'alta Etiopia *(Milan, 1885–95).*

Yohannes, the second of Ethiopia's great nineteenth-century rulers, was, like his predecessor, an uncompromising patriot – and a strong opponent of Christian missionaries. He differed from Téwodros, however, in that he did not attempt to re-establish a fully centralized monarchy. Proud to call himself Re'esa Makwanent, or Chief of the Nobles, he accepted the existence of virtually independent rulers, provided that they recognized his overall suzerainty – and paid him some occasional taxes. His principal tributaries were Menilek, ruler of Shawa, and Adal Tassama (later Negus Takla Haymanot), that of Gojjam. Yohannes, unlike Téwodros, was a staunch supporter of the Church, and as such probably enjoyed greater popularity than his impetuous predecessor. Yohannes was moreover in a far better military position than the latter, in that Tegray, his power base, was in the north-east of the country, relatively near the Red Sea coast through which firearms had long been imported. The province's geographical location, had, however, also grave disadvantages. These were particularly evident during his reign, which coincided with the beginning of the age of Imperialism. Tegray was dangerously exposed to sea-born invasion, and blockade. This was the more serious in that rulers of Massawa and the torrid coastal strip, irrespective of their nationality, cast envious eyes on the cool and fertile interior. They were predisposed to invade the Tegray hinterland.

Conflict with the Egyptians

Yohannes, at the beginning of his reign, was under strong pressure from the Egyptians, whose Khedive, Ismail Pasha, had officially received the port of Massawa from his nominal overlord, the Sultan of the Ottoman Empire on 20 May 1868. They shortly afterwards occupied the nearby mainland port of Zulla, and instituted a rigid blockade to prevent the import of arms by the Ethiopian ruler.

Faced with Egyptian hostility Yohannes decided to appeal to European Christendom. In August 1872 he sent his English aide, Kirkham on a visit to Europe, with appeals to the governments of Austria, Russia, Germany, Britain and France. This initiative, which recalled those of Webé and Téwodros earlier in the century, created little attention in Europe. Its rulers, particularly after the opening of the Suez Canal, were far more interested in Egypt than in far-off Ethiopia. This disinterest was exemplified by the German Chancellor Otto von Bismarck. Strangely echoing the British reaction to Téwodros's letter to Queen Victoria a generation earlier, he bluntly wrote to the Kaiser.

> There is no political interest in Germany in interfering in the Ethiopian-Egyptian border dispute. An unfriendly attitude to the Khedive might lead to the damaging of German commercial relations with Egypt, which are quite important. Therefore, it is not desirable to answer Yohannes's letter . . .[1]

A few years later, in 1874, Werner Munzinger, a Swiss adventurer in Egyptian service, seized Bogos on the Ethiopian-Sudanese border, and occupied Karan, one of the principal settlements in the area. At about the same time the local ruler of Aylat, some 30 kilometres inland from Massawa, sold his district to Egypt. Munzinger soon afterwards advanced into the Afar, or Danakil, lowlands, but was attacked, and killed, by the local people. In the following year, 1875, the Egyptians annexed the Gulf of Aden ports of Zayla' and Berbera, and, advancing inland, seized the old mercantile town of Harar.

The Egyptians, perhaps influenced by the ease with which the

[1]   Zewde Gabre-Sellassie, 1975, pp. 49–50.

*Plate 17   A Gondarine processional cross. From 'Magazin Pittoresque'
(Paris, 1871).*

British had overthrown Téwodros, meanwhile decided to attack
Yohannes, and occupy Adwa. A well-equipped Egyptian force, led
by a Danish commander, Colonel Soren Arendrup, accordingly
advanced inland from Massawa. He had with him a number of

American officers, who had formerly served in the Confederate forces in the American Civil War, but with its termination were available as mercenaries. Yohannes responded by declaring war, and the Patriarch excommunicated in adavance any soldiers who failed to respond to the call to arms. The powerful Egyptian army then crossed the Marab river into the heartland of Tegray, but were almost annihilated by the emperor's forces at the battle of Gundat on 16 November 1875.

Ismail, on learning of this unexpected reverse, assembled a much larger army of 15,000 to 20,000 men, armed with the most modern weapons. Yohannes mauled the invaders at the three-day battle of Gura, between 7 and 9 March 1876. His soldiers, who displayed great heroism, captured close on twenty cannon, as well as several thousand Remington rifles. His army as a result emerged as perhaps the first really well-equipped Ethiopian force in the country's history.

Though his victory had been so complete, Yohannes, who claimed sovereignty as far as the Red Sea coast, felt unable to drive the invaders from their strongly fortified position on the island of Massawa. He made no attempt to advance to the coast, which lay tantalizingly only a hundred kilometres from the battlefield. Preferring the course of peace he despatched an emissary, Blatta Gabra Egziabhér, to the Egyptians, whom the latter seized, imprisoned, and eventually repatriated, without their agreeing to a settlement. In an attempt to arrive at an agreement with Yohannes they later sent to him Colonel, subsequently General, Charles Gordon, a Briton serving as their Governor-General of Sudan. This choice of envoy was scarcely felicitous. Yohannes was displeased that Gordon, a Christian, should be serving the interest of a Muslim power guilty of aggression at Christian Ethiopia's expense. Though Yohannes had been twice the victor, the terms Gordon brought were moreover not conducive to a settlement. They excluded any restoration to Ethiopia of Bogos or other frontier areas which the Egyptians had then recently seized. Nor was Gordon, on behalf of the Egyptians, willing to recognize Ethiopia's earlier right to import firearms freely through the port of Massawa. The emperor regarded Gordon's proposals as unacceptable. Talks were therefore broken off, without any conclusion.

The Egyptians, though unwilling to compromise, were not unaware of the extent of their military defeats in 1875–6, as well as the apparent invincibility of the emperor's army. They accordingly

*Plate 18   Emperor Yohannes IV, with royal crown and staff. From L.
De Castro,* Nella terra dei negus *(Milan, 1915).*

abandoned their expansionist ambitions in this part of Africa, as it
turned out for ever.[2]

The débâcle at Gundat and later at Gura did much to discredit
Ismail in the eyes of his unfortunate troops. One of the Egyptian
soldiers participating in the Pasha's disastrous campaign was

[2]   On the war with the Egyptians see Dye, 1882.

Ahmad 'Urabi, who was soon to rebel against the Khedive, and emerge as the founder of Egyptian revolutionary nationalism.[3]

The Ethiopian victories of Gundat and Gura were important in that they helped to consolidate the internal political position of Yohannes, and assisted him forge a considerable measure of national unity. In January 1878 he marched south to Manz, in Shawa. Menilek, who had for ten years been unsuccessfully claiming the title of King of Kings, realized the impossibility of resisting the emperor's superior forces. Meeting Yohannes at Leche, on 20 March, he carried a stone on his shoulder as a sign of penitence, and withdrew his claim to the imperial throne. He also abandoned any effort to control Wallo, the province between Tegray and Shawa, and agreed to pay tribute to Yohannes. The latter reciprocated by recognizing Menilek as King of Shawa. Four years later, in 1883, he arranged that his twelve-year-old son, Ras Araya Sellasé, should wed Menilek's seven-year-old daughter, Zawditu. This dynastic marriage between the Tegray and Shawan royal houses, though politically significant, was doomed to failure. The young Tegray prince died before it could be consummated. Zawditu, on the other hand, was later, as we shall see, to rise to greatness in early twentieth-century Ethiopian political life.

After the Leche agreement Yohannes, as head of the Ethiopian Church, convened an important Synod, at nearby Boru Méda. The gathering supported the official Monophysite creed of Alexandria, that the divine and human natures of Christ were united, and rejected the YaSega Lej, or Son of Grace, heresy. This held that Christ was God's son by adoption, and that Christ had three births: once from the Father from all time, once in the Incarnation in the womb of the Virgin Mary, and once through the subsequent action of the Holy Spirit. This belief was also referred to as the Sost Ledat, or Triple Birth, heresy.

At Boru Méda, Yohannes also decided to take action against the Muslims of Wallo, whose leaders had assumed the militant religious title of Imam. They were reported to be actively propagating Islam among animist populations on the empire's periphery. The emperor feared that such determined protagonists of Islam might be won over to the Egyptian cause. To forestall this he tried to integrate the inhabitants of Wallo more effectively into the empire, by attempting forcibly to convert them to Christianity. The two leading chiefs, Muhammad Ali and Abba Wataw, willingly agreed

[3]   Erlich, 1994, pp. 58–60.

to become Christians. They were respectively christened Mika'él and Hayla Maryam, and inducted into the Ethiopian state structure. Many ordinary people, on the other hand, secretly retained their old religion, and came to be known as 'Christians by day, Muslims by night'.

In the rest of the empire by contrast Yohannes proved a more conciliatory and accommodating monarch than Téwodros. He was in consequence a more successful, if less spectacular, unifier than his predecessor.

Yohannes was also successful, in 1881, in persuading the Patriarch of Alexandia to appoint three bishops for Ethiopia, in addition to the Abun. The latter, Abuna Pétros, who served in Tegray, was thus joined by three colleagues: Abba Marqos, for Bagémder and Samén, Abba Luqas, for Gojjam and Kafa, and Abba Matéwos, who was later to play a prominent role in Ethiopian politics, for Shawa.[4]

The Suez Canal, the British Occupation of Egypt, and Mahdism in Sudan

The reign of Yohannes also witnessed other important international developments, mainly to Ethiopia's disadvantage. The opening of the Suez Canal, in November 1869, made the Red Sea, for the first time since the era of the Pharaohs, an annex of the Mediterranean. This greatly increased interest in the Red Sea and Gulf of Aden area on the part of the Europeans, and in particular of the Italians. The latter, who were to achieve their national unity in the following year, were beginning to look outwards beyond their own peninsula. Symptomatic of Italy's new interest in the Red Sea area was the purchase on 15 November 1869 of the port of Asab. It was bought by an Italian Lazarist priest, Giuseppe Sapeto, on behalf of an Italian firm, the Rubattino Shipping Company, from a local sultan for 6,000 Maria Theresa dollars. This was a remarkable, but not entirely unique, case of a European missionary serving the interests of nineteenth-century European colonialism. The port was subsequently declared an Italian colony, in 1882 – an indication of rapidly escalating Italian Government interest in the region.

[4] Zewde Gabre-Sellassie, 1975, pp. 198–9.

In Egypt meanwhile Ahmad 'Urabi led a military revolt, in 1881, which threatened the *status quo* in that country. This led, in the following year, to its occupation by the British who thereby acquired a direct interest in the Egyptian-occupied Sudan. These dramatic events coincided with the rise in the latter territory of its Mahdi, Muhammad Ahmad. His rebellion was so successful that the British decided in 1883 that Sudan would have to be evacuated of Egyptian and British troops.

This evacuation was of direct relevance to Ethiopia. The Mahdists, or Ansar as they called themselves, had by then isolated a number of towns, with Egyptian garrisons and European inhabitants, in neighbouring western Sudan. The British Government, though anxious to help, was reluctant to undertake a major expedition, which would almost certainly have been much more arduous, and costly, than that to Maqdala in 1867–8. The British took the view that the isolated soldiers and civilians could most easily, and inexpensively, be evacuated with Ethiopian assistance. This seemed appropriate in view of Britain's earlier cordial relations with Yohannes, who was considered moreover to be indebted to the British for their gift of arms at the time of the Napier expedition a decade and a half earlier.

A British naval officer, Rear-Admiral Sir William Hewett, was accordingly despatched to negotiate with Yohannes. The Ethiopian monarch, who was smarting under the recent Egyptian seizure of Ethiopian borderlands, and who remembered his good relations with the British at the time of the Napier expedition, received him courteously, and agreed to assist. He demanded, however, two concessions which Gordon had rejected seven years before. These were (1) that the Bogos area on the western frontier should be restored to Ethiopian rule; and (2) that Ethiopia should be given control of Massawa. The emperor's first demand was accepted, but, as far as the port was concerned, the British promised only free transit, 'under British protection', for Ethiopian goods, including arms and ammunition.

A tripartite treaty, the Hewett Treaty as it is often called, was accodingly drafted. It met the two points above demanded by Yohannes, and declared that it bound, not only the then reigning monarchs, but also their heirs and successors. The agreement was signed, by Britain, British-occupied Egypt, and Ethiopia, at Adwa on 3 June 1884. The emperor's dynamic military leader, Ras Alula Engeda, acting in accordance with the treaty, thereupon relieved five garrison towns in Sudan. They were, according to Augustus B. Wylde, a sometime British consul for the Red Sea area, 'the only ones from throughout the length and breadth of the Egyptian Soudan that did not fall into the hands of the Mahdi'.[5]

Alula's action was followed by the Egyptian withdrawal not only from Sudan, but also from Massawa, and from Ethiopia's northern and western borderlands, which Egypt had occupied only within the previous decades. The disappearance of the Egyptians created a power vaccum, which, as we shall see, was soon to be filled.

The Coming of the Italians

The value of the 1884 agreement to Ethiopia was short-lived, for on 3 February 1885, only eight months after its conclusion, the Italians seized Massawa. This action was taken with the support of the British Government, which favoured Italian expansion on the Red Sea coast as a way of curbing that of France, its principal rival in the European Scramble for Africa. The Italian naval officer responsible for the occupation, Rear-Admiral Pietro Caimi, issued a proclamation to the port's inhabitants announcing that his action had been taken in agreement with the British and Egyptian Governments, and promised, 'No obstacle shall be put by me on your trade'.[6] Such friendly protestations were, however, before long abandoned, for as soon as they were in a position to do so the Italians, like the Egyptians in the previous decade, seized the coast adjacent to Massawa, and instituted a blockade to stop the supply of arms to Yohannes. Italian troops then advanced inland as far as Sa'ati and Wi'a, both around 30 kilometres from the sea.

Ras Alula protested against this unwarranted Italian penetration, but the invaders replied by strengthening their fortifications in the areas they had occupied. He thereupon rode down from the highlands, and attacked the Italian garrison at Sa'ati, on 25 January 1887, but was repulsed, with heavy casualties. The interlopers then sent in more troops, which Alula intercepted and virtually annihilated at Dogali on the following day. Italian troops then

---

[5] Wylde, 1901, p. 35.
[6] Hertslet, 1894, I, p. 3.

evacuated Saʿati and Wiʿa, and declared an intensified blockade on all ships bringing supplies for Ethiopia. The engagement at Dogali had a remarkably mixed impact in Italy. Many Euro-centric Italians bitterly condemned it as a 'massacre', while their anti-colonialist compatriots lauded Emperor Yohannes and Ras Alula as patriots in the tradition of such Italian heroes as Mazzini and Garibaldi.

Wylde, commenting on the British-sponsored advent of the Italians, and the short duration of the tripartite treaty of 1884, later commented:

> Look at our behaviour to King Johannes from any point of view and it will not show one ray of honesty, and to my mind it is one of the worst bits of business out of the many we have been guilty of in Africa . . . England made use of King Johannes as long as he was of any service, and then threw him over to the tender mercies of Italy, who went to Massowah under our auspices with the intention of taking territory that belonged to our ally, and allowed them to destroy all the promises England had solemnly made King Johannes after he had faithfully carried out his part of the agreement. The fact is not known to the British public, and I wish it were not true for our credit's sake, but unfortunately it is, and it reads like one of the vilest bits of treachery that has been perpetrated in Africa or India in the eighteenth century.[7]

War between the Italians and Yohannes at this point seemed imminent, but the intruders, wishing to obtain their objectives without resort to further fighting, persuaded the British Government to mediate. A British diplomat, Sir Gerald Portal, was accordingly despatched to the emperor to ask him to agree to an Italian occupation of the coastal area, including Saʿati and Wiʿa, as well as the Bogos area, which the Egyptians, it will be recalled, had ceded to him only three years earlier. When these terms were read out to him, on 7 December 1887, he proudly replied:

> I can do nothing with all this. By the treaty made by Admiral Hewett, all the country evacuated by the Egyptians on my frontier was ceded to me at the instigation of England, and now you have come to ask me to give it up again.[8]

---

[7]   Wylde, 1901, p. 39.
[8]   Portal, 1892, p. 158.

Much incensed that the British should have asked him to depart from the 1884 treaty, which they had earlier actually pressed him to sign, he wrote to Queen Victoria, on 8 December 1887. In his letter, which was couched in characteristically Ethiopic vein, he protested that the Italians:

> wanted to begin the quarrel, they stopped the traders and came to places in my country called Saʿati and Wiʿa, and fortified them . . . By making me appear the offender when I am not, are you not implying that I should give them the land which Jesus Christ gave to me? Reconciliation is possible when they are in their country and I in mine, but now, sleeping with our swords in hand and keeping our horses bridled, are we not with our armies as good as in combat already?[9]

In the following year Yohannes made his way down to Saʿati, with a large army of 80,000 men, intending to expel the Italians. The latter, however, refused to leave their fort. Yohannes, unable to break into their defences, soon ran short of supplies, and accordingly withdrew to highland Tegray.

Difficulties with the Dervishes

The Egyptian withdrawal of 1884 affected Ethiopia's western borders no less than Massawa. The Mahdists, or Dervishes as they were also called, having triumphantly gained control over Sudan, determined to attack Christian Ethiopia. They did so in part to avenge themselves for Ras Alula's earlier intervention on behalf of the Egyptian garrisons, which had been carried out, it will be recalled, in accordance with the Hewett treaty. The agreement thus contributed to a serious deterioration of relations between Christian Ethiopia and Muslim Sudan. This caused Sven Rubenson, the modern Swedish historian of Ethiopia, to observe that by the treaty Yohannes 'traded one weak enemy', i.e. distant Egypt, 'for two strong ones, the Mahdist state and Italy'.[10]

In the autumn of 1885, little more than a year after the conclusion of the treaty, Dervish forces under the command of the

[9]   PRO, Foreign Office 95/748, No. 209. See also Rubenson, 1976, p. 382.
[10]   Rubenson, 1976, p. 362.

renowned Mahdist leader Uthman Diqna advanced from the Kassala area towards Kufit, almost half way to Asmara. Alula, though primarily concerned with Italian machinations at the coast, rode west to confront the invaders. A fierce battle of Muslim against Christian was fought at Kufit, on 23 September. Alula's horse was killed under him, but he continued to fight, on foot. His men suffered heavy casualties, but eventually won the day.[11]

Further confrontations between the Ansar and Ethiopians took place along the long Ethio-Sudanese frontier in the next two years. Then, at the beginning of 1888 a powerful Dervish force, under another Ansar leader, Hamdan Abu Anga, forced its way into the Ethiopian highlands. It defeated the Gojjam army, on 18 January, and then rampaged into the old capital, Gondar. The subsequent Ethiopian writer Heruy Walda Sellasé recalls that the Dervishes 'burnt all the churches' of the city, and adds:

> Those who were brave were slaughtered on the spot, while the cowardly fled. The remainder, women and children, were made prisoner and taken into slavery.

The booty reportedly included many beautiful Ethiopian girls, and 30,000 Maria Theresa thalers.[12]

Yohannes for his part was unable to resist both the Dervishes in the west and the Italians to the east. Faced with the threat from the latter, he strengthened his defences near to the coast by transferring there his garrison stationed at Qallabat on the Sudan frontier. Finding the border thus unguarded, the Mahdists once more broke into the country. Yohannes hastened to Qallabat to repel them, but, at the close of a victorious battle at Matamma on 9 March 1889, was mortally wounded by a sniper's bullet. He died on the following day, one of the last crowned heads in the world to die on the field of battle. News of his death created great confusion throughout northern Ethiopia. This was intensified almost immediately afterwards by a serious outbreak of cattle disease. It was followed by a famine of unprecedented proportions, and almost immediately afterwards by major epidemics of smallpox, cholera and influenza. Vast number of people all over the county perished.

[11] Zewde Gabre-Sellassie, 1975, pp. 177–9.
[12] Fusella, 1943, pp. 207–8.

Plate 19 Difficulties of traditional transport. Note the characteristic mountains of Adwa, site of the subsequent battle, in the background. From E. A. De Cosson, The Cradle of the Blue Nile *(London, 1877).*

Yohannes and Modernization

Yohannes, unlike his predecessor Téwodros, was more of a conservative than a modernizer. His successive struggles against foreign invaders, Egyptian, Dervish and Italian, left him moreover with little time for technological or other innovation. He nevertheless succeeded, where Téwodros had failed, in sending envoys on important diplomatic missions abroad. Yohannes was likewise the first Ethiopian ruler to appoint a foreign consul, a certain Samuel King, who served as his representative in London, albeit ineffectively.

The reign of Yohannes also witnessed several other important innovations. In the medical field mercury preparations for the treatment of syphilis came into extensive use at this time, at least in the principal Ethiopian towns. Yohannes was futhermore the first ruler of Ethiopia to have a foreign physician at his court, a Greek doctor, Nicholas Parisis. He was similarly the first Ethiopian monarch to be inoculated with modern-style smallpox vaccine, which was then beginning to replace the country's traditional inoculation. The victories over the Egyptians at Gundat and Gura likewise resulted, during the reign of Yohannes, in the extensive distribution of breech-loading rifles, as well as of several pieces of modern artillery.

The Rise of Menilek

Menilek, the third of Ethiopia's notable nineteenth-century monarchs, inherited the throne of Shawa in 1865, after escaping from ten years' captivity at Maqdala. He came from a long established line of provincial rulers, who dated back nine generations, and had exercised virtually independent power for over a century and a half. Menilek was moreover in a geographically more favourable position than his two predecessors, Téwodros and Yohannes. Shawa's isolation in the south-east of the empire had long shielded it from internal and external conflicts, like those which had ravaged the northern provinces, and in particular Tegray. This isolation from the north was extremely advantageous to Menilek, for it enabled him to strengthen his position, without having to pay too much attention to Yohannes, who as emperor constituted his nominal overlord. Shawa, though located safely, far from the coast, lay on a major trade route to the Gulf of Aden ports. This provided its ruler with reasonably good access to firearms, which were destined to improve considerably in the course of Menilek's reign.

Menilek, like Téwodros, by whom he was reportedly much

Plate 20   Seal of Menilek as King of Shawa, prior to his emegence as King of Kings, i.e. Emperor, of Ethiopia. From G. Massaia, I miei trentacinque anni di missione nell'alta Etiopia (Milan, 1885–95).

influenced during his imprisonment at Maqdala, was keenly interested in both unification and modernization. He was also motivated, like his grandfather King Sahla Sellasé, and indeed most other Ethiopian rulers, by an almost unquenchable desire for firearms, but was much more successful in obtaining them than any earlier ruler of the country.

Menilek's accession to power in Shawa, in 1865, took place six years before the rise of Yohannes, in Tegray, in 1871. The ruler of Shawa, who thus had the advantage of being the 'first-comer' to the Ethiopian political scene, did not, however, at first challenge the emperor openly. The two leaders nevertheless soon came into indirect conflict. This took place, in 1874, in Wallo. The emperor recognized the territory's traditional chief Abba Wataw, subsequently known, as we have seen, as Hayla Maryam. Menilek, on the other hand, gave his support to the latter's rival Muhammad Ali, subsequently to become Ras Mika'él. Towards the end of the following year, Menilek captured Maqdala, his own former place of detention, where he imprisoned Abba Wataw. He then appointed his favourite, Muhammad Ali, as governor of Wallo. After Menilek's subsequent capitulation to Yohannes, the chief, however, threw in his lot with the emperor.

Menilek's Occupation of the Southern Provinces

Menilek, as we saw earlier, had accepted the paramountcy of Yohannes, at Leche in 1878. Prevented as a result from expanding his influence northwards into Wallo, where Yohannes had a keen interest, he turned his attention in other directions. Emulating the expansionist policies of earlier Shawan rulers, among them his great-great grandfather Maredazmach Asfa Wassan (d. 1808), whose name, significantly, meant 'Expand the Frontier', Menilek began the occupation of territories to the south, south-west, and south-east. In 1875–6 he advanced into Guragé. The Christians in the northern part of the area accepted him peacefully, but the Muslims to the south resisted, and were occupied only by force.

Menilek's territorial expansion soon brought him into conflict with Ras Adal of Gojjam, who was likewise bent on penetrating into the rich lands south of the Blue Nile. Adal was supported by Emperor Yohannes, who doubtless regarded the ruler of Gojjam as a useful counter balance to Menilek. Adal was accordingly recognized by his overlord, in January 1881, as King Takla Haymanot, of both Gojjam and Kafa. Conflict between Shawa and Gojjam erupted in January of the following year, when Menilek's general Ras Gobana Daché defeated one of Takla Haymanot's commanders. Menilek and the ruler of Gojjam subsequently fought against each other directly, at the battle of Embabo, immediately south of the Blue Nile on 6 June. The Shawan ruler won a decisive victory. This enabled him, between 1882 and 1886, to occupy Leqa Naqamté, Leqa Qellem, Jemma, the rest of the Gibé states, and, later, Illubabor. Advancing into Arsi in 1882, he completed its occupation in 1886, in which year he also annexed Wallaga.[13]

Profiting by the Egyptian withdrawal from Harar, in 1885, and from the weakness and instability of the Muslim theocratic state subsequently established there by a local ruler, Amir Abdulahi, Menilek defeated the latter at the battle of Chalanqo on 6 January 1887. He later completed the acquisition of Guragé, and took control of Kulo and Konta in 1889. He began the occupation of Kambata in 1890, occupied Ogaden, Balé and Sidamo in 1891,

---

[13] For a graphic account of Menilek's Embabo expedition see Guèbrè Sellassié, 1931–2, I, pp. 174–82.

gained control of Gofa and conquered Walamo, also known as Walayta, in 1894, and took over Kafa three years later. Menilek's southward drive met in many areas with little resistance. His conquest of Walamo, on the other hand, was accompanied by the extensive seizure of slaves, and that of Kafa, by much bloodshed, which resulted in considerable depopulation of the area.[14]

The acquisition of these southern territories, which took place in the decade or so prior to the famous battle of Adwa in 1896, was of major political and economic importance. The occupation of Harar in particular greatly facilitated Menilek's access to the not too distant Gulf of Aden ports, through which he was soon to import vast quantities of firearms. His control of the rich southern and western provinces, the source of ivory, gold, slaves, civet and other articles, likewise helped finance his purchase of imported weapons. By the time of the battle his southward drive had, however, almost come to an end. The following years nevertheless witnessed his occupation of Borana in the far south, and Konso, Masongo and Gimirra in the west.

Relations with the Italians

Menilek's contacts with the Italians dated back to 1875 when they first began to take an interest in Shawa. The Italian Geographical Society that year despatched a mission, led by the Marquis Orazio Antinori, to the then Shawan capital Ankobar. Menilek provided the Italian party with a large estate at nearby Let Marafeya. There they established their headquarters, as the Swiss missionaries and others had done at Gafat a generation earlier. Italian explorers, among them Antonio Cecchi, Giovanni Chiarini and Leopoldo Traversi, later proceeded to the south and west, travelling as far as Guragé and Arsi, Jemma and Kafa.

Relations between Italy and Shawa in the ensuing years grew steadily closer. An Italian diplomatic envoy, Count Pietro Antonelli, arrived in 1879, and signed a Treaty of Friendship and Commerce with Menilek on 21 May 1883. Article 3 specified that nationals of the two countries could travel freely in their respective

---

[14]   On the reign of Menilek, his southern campaigns and his relations with the Italians, see Guèbrè Sellassié, 1931–2, and Marcus, 1975.

countries. Article 9 laid down that the two signatories would collaborate to keep open the trade route between Shawa and the port of Asab, while Article 12 accorded Italy some extra-territorial rights in Shawa. Article 13, though in itself of limited importance, was in retrospect of especial interest. It stated that Menilek could make use of the Italians in his communications with Europe, and thus foreshadowed Article 17 of the Wechalé Treaty of 1889, which, as we shall see, was later to be a cause of much controversy.[15]

Italian interest in Shawa increased greatly after Rear-Admiral Caimi's occupation of Massawa in 1885. Italian policy thereafter became markedly far more aggressive, for it aimed at the military penetration of Tegray, the province nearest the port. Emperor Yohannes, as the ruler of that territory, came at once to be regarded by the Italians as the principal obstacle to their colonial ambitions. Aware how he had earlier collaborated with the British at the time of the latter's expedition against his overlord Téwodros, they sought to reverse the situation by befriending Menilek, ruler of far away Shawa. Known as an ambitious aspirant to the throne, and a reluctant tributary of Yohannes, he was therefore considered by the Italians as a potential ally.

To further his country's expansionist aims Antonelli concluded a further agreement with Menilek, on 20 October 1887. It was styled, significantly enough, a Treaty of Friendship and Alliance. Italy, in Article 2, promised the king of Shawa military and other assistance, and more specifically agreed, in Article 4, to provide him with 5,000 Remington rifles. Article 3 laid down, more generally, that Italy would not annex any Ethiopian territories, while Menilek promised, in Article 5, that the arms obtained under the agreement would be used for his own defence, and not against the Italians.[16]

The sudden and entirely unexpected death of Emperor Yohannes almost a year and a half later, on 9 March 1889, little more than four years after the Italian occupation of Massawa, transformed the entire Ethiopian political scene. His demize created a power vacuum in the north of the country, which his survivors, among them his official heir Ras Mangasha, were apparently ill-equipped to fill. Menilek, who had abandoned his

---

[15]   Rossetti, 1910, pp. 7–11.
[16]   Ibid., pp. 23–4.

claim to the imperial crown eleven years earlier in favour of Yohannes, now once more re-asserted it, and in so doing sought Italian support. One of his first acts, on 26 March, was to urge the Italians at Massawa against succouring 'rebels', and instead to occupy Asmara.[17] The Italians, much pleased with this suggestion, were thereafter only too willing to support his claim to the throne.

The Wechalé Treaty and the Additional Convention

The new relationship between Menilek and the Italians found expression in an important new agreement, which the Ethiopian ruler signed with Antonelli on 2 May 1889 – less than two months after the death of Yohannes. Described, unlike its predecessors, as a Treaty of Perpetual Peace and Friendship, it was concluded at the village of Wechalé, in Wallo, and was destined to be perhaps the most controversial agreement between the two countries ever signed.

The treaty of Wechalé (or, in Italian transliteration, Uccialli), as it was almost invariably called, contained articles of major advantage to both parties. It gave Menilek his first foreign recognition of his claim to the imperial throne. Italy did this in the Preamble and several other articles, which specifically referred to him as 'King of Kings'. Article 6, which seemed of major strategic importance to Menilek, afforded him the right to import arms and ammunition freely through Italian colonial territory. This article was reminiscent of the proviso in the ill-fated tripartite treaty of 1884, which had allowed Yohannes free import of war material through Massawa, albeit under British protection.

The Italians on their side also obtained important advantages from the treaty, for Menilek in it agreed to a substantial expansion of their Red Sea colony. He accepted, in Article 3, that Italian rule should extend over most of the highland district of Hamasén, in what was soon to be known as the northern Eritrean plateau. The Italian colonial area was to reach as far as the villages of Halay, Saganayti and Asmara, all of which were defined as on the Italian side of the frontier. The nearby highland districts of Sarayé and Akkala Guzay, further south, were, however, to remain part of

17 Ibid., p. 59.

Ethiopia. Article 4 specified that Dabra Bizan monastery, 15 kilometres east of Asmara, and its possessions, were to be the property of the Ethiopian state.

The treaty's most famous article was, however, Article 17, which was soon to be the basis of irreconcilable dispute between the two parties. The quarrel arose from the fact that the agreement had two texts, one in Amharic and the other in Italian. Their sense was supposed to be identical, as stipulated in Article 19, but they differed materially in Article 17. The Amharic text stated, like the Italo-Shawan treaty of 1883, that Menilek should have the power to avail himself of the services of the Government of the king of Italy for all communications he might have with other Powers or Governments. The Italian text, on the other hand, differed from the earlier agreement by making this obligatory.[18]

Despite the problems soon to arise from this article relations between the two sides at first remained entirely cordial. Menilek shortly afterwards despatched his cousin and close confident, Dajazmach (later Ras) Makonnen, to Italy to negotiate the implementation of the agreement. On 1 October he and the Italian Minister of Foreign Affairs, Francesco Crispi, met in Naples to conclude an Additional Convention. By Article 1 of this further treaty Italy once more recognized Menilek as emperor, or as the text reads Imperatore of Ethiopia. The latter, in Article 2, recognized the sovereignty of Italy over its Red Sea colony, on the basis, according to Article 3, of actual Italian occupation at the time. This latter proviso was later the cause of much bad feeling. During Makonnen's absence from his country the Italians advanced considerably beyond their earlier confines. On 2 August, for example they occupied Asmara. This occupation had been specifically permitted by Article 3 of the Wechalé treaty, but was at variance with Article 3 of the agreement of 20 October 1887 in which the Italians had agreed not to annex further territories. Sven Rubenson subsequently commented that the Convention's 'actual possession' clause probably represented 'the highest level of duplicity reached by the Italians in their dealings with the Ethiopians'.[19]

The remaining articles provided for close economic and monetary cooperation between the two countries. Article 4 stated that

---

[18]   Ibid., pp. 41–4.
[19]   Rubenson, 1976, p. 388.

Menilek could issue coins, to be minted in Italy, which would also circulate in Italian colonial territories, and that if the Italians produced money of their own for use in Africa this would likewise be accepted in the emperor's domains. Articles 5 to 7 laid down that the Italian Government would give the necessary guarantee for an Italian bank to provide Menilek with a loan of four million lire, half to be paid in silver and the other half to be deposited in Italy to pay for purchases which Menilek might wish to make there. It was stipulated that the revenues of the Harar customs would serve as a guarantee for the interest on the loan as well as for its eventual repayment. The treaty, according to Article 10, bound not only Menilek, but also his heirs and successors.[20]

Having concluded this agreement with Makonnen the Italian Government, which had by then established its control over the northernmost rim of the Ethiopian plateau, felt strong enough to take the dramatic step of claiming a Protectorate over the whole of Ethiopia. On 11 October 1889, only ten days after signing the Additional Convention, and presumably as a result of it, the Italian Minister of Foreign Affairs, Francesco Crispi, wrote a brief circular letter to Italian diplomatic representatives in the principal European capitals, Constantinople and Washington. In this communication he asked the envoys to inform the Governments to which they were accredited that 'in conformity with Article 34 of the General Act of Berlin', of 1885, Italy served notice that 'under Article 17 of the perpetual treaty between Italy and Ethiopia [i.e. the Wechalé treaty] . . . it is provided that His Majesty the King of Ethiopia consents to avail himself of the Government of His Majesty the King of Italy for the conduct of all matters he may have with other Powers or Governments'.[21] Crispi referred to Menilek, it will be noted, no longer as King of Kings, as in the Wechalé treaty, or as Emperor, as in the Additional Convention, but merely as King.

The Italian Minister's communication, which was couched in the diplomatic terminology of the time, requires comment. Article 34 of the General Act of Berlin, to which the letter refers, stated that a European power acquiring a Protectorate in Africa should 'send a notification thereof . . . to the other Signatory Powers . . . in order to enable them, if need be, to make good any claims of

---

[20]   Rossetti, 1910, pp. 46–8.
[21]   Ibid., pp. 60–1.

their own'. Crispi's letter contained no explicit mention of any claim to a Protectorate, but reference to the said article left readers of the time in no doubt that Italy was in fact making one.

Whether Article 17 of the Wechalé Treaty could establish a Protectorate over Ethiopia raises three major issues: (1) whether Menilek in agreeing to the article had knowingly accepted Italian protection; (2) whether the Italian text, stating that Menilek was obliged to make use of the good offices of the Italian Government, had greater validity than the Amharic one, which did not do so; and (3) whether the Italian text, even if embodying the article's correct meaning, actually afforded Italy a Protectorate.

(1) There is no evidence that Menilek, who did not understand Italian, was aware when signing the treaty that the Italian text of Article 17 differed from the Amharic or for that matter from Article 13 of the 1883 treaty, which had made Italian good offices only voluntary. Nor is there any evidence that Antonelli, who was responsible for the Italian version, ever informed Menilek that it was materially different from the text of the earlier agreement, let alone that it implied the establishment of a Protectorate. The Ethiopian ruler, it may be concluded, never knowingly agreed to a Protectorate. This would seem confirmed by the fact that when the Italian claim was brought to his attention he immediately repudiated it.

(2) Since the sense of the two texts of Article 17, and indeed of the treaty as a whole, were supposedly identical, as stated in Article 19, and were therefore considered of equal validity, there was no reason why the Italian version should have been regarded as more authoritative than the Amharic. When the two texts were found to differ the only just and reasonable course would therefore have been to cancel both, as Menilek later suggested, rather than to insist only on one, as the Italians attempted to do.

(3) Even were it accepted that the Italian text was alone valid, and that Menilek had in fact consented to make use of Italy's good offices, it is debatable whether this actually constituted a Protectorate. It should be noted that the treaty in no place used the word, or indicated any specific restriction on Menilek's sovereignty, as would be expected in a Protectorate treaty. Any reference to a Protectorate is likewise noticeable by its absence. Article 6, on the contrary, stated, as we have seen, that the Ethiopian ruler was entitled to import arms freely through Italian territory – a right

which would scarcely be allowed to a ruler under Protection. Moreover, had a Protectorate been established the Additional Convention, signed five months later, might be assumed to have mentioned it, at least in passing, but it did not. The Treaty and the Convention in fact both refer to Menilek as either King of Kings or Emperor, and treat him consistently as the King of Italy's equal, not in any way as a subject ruler under Italian Protection.[22]

Article 17, it may be concluded, did not constitute any real or legitimate basis for a Protectorate. The Italian claim was, however, entirely in the spirit of the then European Scramble for Africa, and therefore passed uncontested in Europe. European maps began to indicate Ethiopia as an Italian territory. More importantly, the British Government entered into three Protocols with Italy, signed in Rome on 24 March, and 15 April 1891, and 5 May 1894, defining the frontiers between British territory and the alleged Protectorate, to which they thus gave full recognition.[23]

Menilek, for his part, refused to accept the Italian interpretation of Article 17, or to abandon direct contacts with the European powers, as this would require. On 14 December 1889, only seven months after signing the treaty, he despatched letters to European rulers informing them of his forthcoming coronation as emperor.[24] Surprised by these communications from a ruler whom they understood had consented to approach them only through the Italian Government, the British and German Governments informed him that they could not accept messages from him directly. When Menilek received their replies, in July 1890, he was deeply shocked.

Italian Encroachment and the Establishment of Eritrea

The Italians meanwhile were consolidating their occupation of the northern highlands. By the end of 1889 they had taken over a sizeable stretch of territory. Their advance, Wylde subsequently noted, 'was unopposed, and once they had made good their foot-

[22] For a detailed study of Article 17 see Rubenson, 1964.
[23] Rossetti, 1910, pp. 119–24.
[24] Ibid., pp. 76–7.

Plate 21   Emperor Menilek II, in coronation robes. Photo: A. Holtz, Im
Auto zu Kaiser Menelik *(Berlin, 1908).*

hold on the upper plateau and fortified themselves, no Abyssinian
force could drive them out'.[25]

The Italians, on 1 January 1890, officially named their colony
Eritrea, after the Latin term *Erythraeum Mare*, i.e. Red Sea.[26] They

---

[25]   Wylde, 1901, p. 49.

[26]   On the early history of Eritrea see Tekeste Negash, 1986, and Tekeste
Negash, 1987.

soon afterwards began expanding its confines far beyond those agreed to in the previous year, either by Menilek in the Wechalé treaty or by Ras Makonnen in the Additional Convention. On 26 January the Italian governor of Eritrea, General Baldassare Orero, crossed the Marab river to occupy the great Tegray trading town of Adwa.

Menilek, whose men were suffering severely from the Great Famine and related epidemics, was perhaps understandably slow to react. However, on 17 September 1890 he despatched two entirely separate protests to King Umberto I of Italy. One dealt with the Wechalé treaty; the other with continued Italian encroachment. In his letter about the treaty he declared that the answers to his invitations to his coronation, which he had received from other countries, were 'humiliating' for his kingdom. He added that, on re-examining the two texts of Article 17, he had discovered that they did not agree. He therefore declared:

When I made that treaty of friendship with Italy, in order that our secrets be guarded and that our understanding be not spoiled, I said that because of our friendship, our affairs might be carried on with the aid of the Sovereign of Italy, but I have not made any treaty which obliged me to do so, and, today, I am not the man to accept it.

That one independent power does not seek the aid of another to carry on its affairs Your Majesty understands very well.[27]

In his other letter, on colonial expansion, the emperor declared, perhaps somewhat naively, that he had accepted Italy's initial expansion, with a view to obtaining peace, to avoid war, and to assist the cause of progress. It had been his wish, he told Umberto, that 'my subjects, like yours, could through trade, science and work, live in peace and happiness'. He nevertheless complained of continual Italian territorial penetration, culminating in General Orero's seizure of Adwa. He recalled that at the time of the treaty of Wechalé the Italians had advanced no further than Sa'ati, and at the time of the Additional Convention no further than Asmara, but that they were now claiming jurisdiction as far as the Marab river. Comparing the Italians to merchants, a class which tended to be looked down upon in Ethiopia, he declared that in his

27 Rossetti, 1910, pp. 78–9.

country they were accustomed to ask a high price, so as to lower it later, not subsequently to raise it, as Italy had done.[28]

The Italian Government refused to listen to these protests. The question of Article 17 was therefore the subject of protracted negotiations in Addis Ababa, between Menilek and Antonelli. At one dramatic point the Italian envoy declared to the emperor in an audience at which Menilek's consort, Queen Taytu Betul, was present, 'Italy cannot notify the other Powers that she was mistaken in Article 17, because she must maintain her dignity'. Taytu, who was renowned for her patriotic, almost xenophobic, stance, thereupon intervened. She observed, 'We also have made known to the Powers that the said Article, as it is written in our language, has another meaning. As you, we also ought to respect our dignity. You wish Ethiopia to be represented before the other Powers as your Protectorate, but that shall never be'.[29]

While such negotiations were proceeding in Addis Ababa, the Italians in Eritrea were actively attempting to overawe, and intrigue with, the chiefs of nearby Tegray. The invaders achieved a short-lived measure of success, on 6 December 1991, when Emperor Yohannes's heir, Ras Mangasha, and a number of local chiefs, signed the so-called Marab Convention, whereby they swore an oath of solidarity with Italy.

The Adwa War and the Addis Ababa Peace Treaty

Menilek, enriched, as we have seen, by his control over the valuable lands to the south, meanwhile spent the next two years in strenuously importing firearms. Most were purchased from Italy's colonial rival, France. Sizeable gifts were also received from Russia, a fellow Eastern Orthodox country opposed to Catholic Italy. Thus strengthened militarily, and realizing that the Italians could not be persuaded to abandon their Protectorate claim, Menilek finally decided, at the beginning of 1893, on breaking off cordial relations with Italy. He accordingly wrote to Umberto, on 12 February, to denounce the Wechalé Treaty as a whole. A fortnight later, on 27 February, he notified the other powers that Ethiopia

[28]   Ibid., pp. 80–1.
[29]   Italy, *Documenti Diplomatici* (1890–1), no. XVII, p. 71. See also Work, 1936, p. 118.

should not be regarded as an Italian Protectorate. Alluding to the famous biblical prophesy, which seemed particularly appropriate at that moment, he proudly declared, 'Ethiopia has need of no one; she stretches out her hands to God'.[30]

The Italian effort to win over the chiefs of Tegray collapsed a year or so later, in June 1894, when Ras Mangasha travelled to Addis Ababa to make formal submission to Menilek.

Anti-Italian feelings in Eritrea were meanwhile increasing, at least in part as a result of Italy's then policy of large-scale expropriation of 'native lands'. This was designed to make way for white settlement, as practised further south in British East Africa, later Kenya. Indignation was so intense that on 15 December, Batha Hagos, a supposedly 'loyal' chief of the Eritrean district of Akkala Guzay, rebelled. Speaking of Italian policy, he declared, 'When the white snake has bitten you, you will search in vain for a remedy'. His rebellion was only crushed by the Italians' superiority of weapons.

By the end of 1894 it was thus clear to the Italians that they could achieve their expansionsist aims neither by negotiation with Menilek, nor by subversion of local chiefs. The Italian Government concluded that its objectives could be achieved only by military action, in other words by outright invasion.

Italian forces, led by Generals Oreste Baratieri and Giuseppe Arimondi, and Major Pietro Toselli, had meanwhile advanced further south in Tegray to occupy Addegrat. They were confronted at Kawatit early in January 1895 by Ras Mangasha, who had returned from Addis Ababa, but after fierce fighting was obliged to retreat to Sanafé. A second engagement took place there shortly afterwards, on 14 and 15 January 1895. Mangasha was once more defeated, and forced to fall back on Dabra Hayla, near Antalo. There later in the year, the invaders were again victorious, on 9 October. The Italians, having thus broken local resistance, proceeded to seize Emperor Yohannes's former capital, Maqalé. They were by then masters of virtually all Tegray.

Menilek meanwhile, learning that the Italians had reached Dabra Hayla, at long last decided to mobilize against them. On 17 September 1895, when the rains were drawing to a close, he issued a proclamation, announcing that he was about to march north. He called on all able-bodied men of Shawa to await him, on 16

---

[30] Work, 1936, pp. 134–5.

October, at a site 100 kilometres north-east of Addis Ababa. Soldiers from Gojjam, Dambeya, Qwara and Bagémder were similarly ordered to assemble at Chachaho, and those from Samén, Walqayt and Tagadé at Maqalé. Ras Makonnen's troops from Harar were at about the same time also called forth for battle.

The Ethiopians whom Menilek mobilized were as a whole well armed. They probably possessed a little over 100,000 rifles, somewhat over half of them modern quick-firers, the largest number French *fusils Gras*, known in Amharic as *wejigra*. Menilek's men also had forty or so cannon, some of them, however, antiquated.

The first clash of arms in this stage of the conflict took place on 7 December 1895 at Amba Alagé, a natural fortress and the most southerly place in Tegray which the Italians had reached. The Ethiopian hero of the battle, Fitawrari Gabayehu, led his men up the mountain's steep slopes, and routed the enemy, whose commander, Major Pietro Toselli, was among those killed.

After capturing the mountain the Ethiopian army proceeded to attack the Italian fort at Enda Iyasus, near Maqalé, where they besieged the Italian commander, Major Giuseppe Galliano, and his soldiers from 7 December 1895 for over forty days. On 7 January 1896, however, the Ethiopians captured the fort's water supply, thus rendering further Italian resistance impossible. A truce was thereupon arranged, after which Ras Makonnen, with a gallantry not appreciated by all his compatriots, allowed the Italians to leave the fort and march northwards. Menilek, whose army was acutely short of supplies, chose this occasion to write to King Umberto expressing a desire for peace. A month or so later two chiefs of Agamé, Ras Sebhat Aragawi and Dajazmach Tafari Hagos, who had been collaborating with the Italians, declared that if they had to die they wanted to do so fighting for their Ethiopian motherland. They accordingly began threatening the Italian lines of communication to Asmara and the north.

The Italian commander, General Baratieri, realizing the difficulty of defeating the by then large, and well equipped, Ethiopian army, responded to Menilek's peace initiative. On 7 February he sent an officer, Major Tommaso Salsa, to discuss terms with Ras Makonnen. The ensuing talks were, however, doomed, for the Italian Government insisted on its Protectorate claim, and demanded military control wherever the Italian flag had been hoisted, i.e. over virtually all Tegray. This Menilek considered unacceptable. After the failure of the talks Baratieri, feeling his position insecure, withdrew to a new site, at Sawria. The Ethiopian army, by then increasingly short of food, waited, without attacking.

The Italian evacuation of areas thought to have been securely occupied had meanwhile much incensed the Italian Prime Minister, Crispi. He accordingly despatched a historic telegram to Baratieri, on 25 February, declaring that Italy was 'ready for any sacrifice to save the honour of the army and the prestige of the monarchy'. The Italian commander responded, four days later, by ordering a surprise attack on Menilek's army the following dawn, 1 March.

The terrain through which the Italians had to advance, in the last hours of darkness, was broken by several steep mountains. The invading force, which moved in the intervening flat land, comprized three brigades. They operated as separate units, with faulty maps, and virtually no contact between them. General Vittorio Dabormida led the Italian right flank; General Giuseppe Arimondi, the centre; and General Matteo Albertone, the left. There was in addition an Italian reserve force, under General Giuseppe Ellena, while the overall commander, General Baratieri, made up the rear.

Baratieri's attempted surprise attack miscarried hopelessly. News of it was revealed to Menilek by his spies. According to local tradition, they included a certain Ato Awalom of Entecho, a patriotic Ethiopian in the Italian ranks. He is said to have informed one of the Tegray chiefs, Ras Mangasha or Ras Alula, who duly took the news to Menilek.

The Italians attacked at first light. The engagement began as an artillery duel, and was followed by fierce fighting, mainly with rifles. The Ethiopians, well aware of their enemies' position, were able to do battle with the three Italian contingents separately. The ensuing fighting resulted in heavy casualties. The Italians lost 261 officers and 2,918 men, about 2,000 Askaris, or 'native' soldiers, killed, 954 Italians permanently missing, and 471 Italians and 959 Askaris wounded. The invaders thus lost 43 per cent of their original fighting force. Three out of the five Italian field commanders (Arimondi, Dabormida, and Galliano) were killed, a fourth (Ellena) wounded, and a fifth (Albertone) captured. Baratieri, who had remained in the rear throughout the engagement, was thus the only Italian general to survive the battle unscathed. Fleeing the field of battle the defeated Italian army, like that of the Egyptians at Gura twenty years earlier, abandoned all its artillery, as well as 11,000 rifles and most of its transport. The Ethiopians for their part also suffered greatly, 5,000 to 6,000 were killed and 8,000 seriously wounded. Their victory was, however, complete.[31]

The Adwa defeat had immediate reaction in Italy. Anti-government demonstrations broke out in all the principal Italian towns, and Crispi was obliged to resign. Italian public opinion at this time, as at that of Dogali a decade earlier, was strongly divided in its attitude to the war. The Italian establishment, and some of the officer corps, adopted a highly militaristic stance, and later demanded a war to 'avenge' Adwa. Many Italians on the political left, on the other hand, were bitterly opposed to their country's colonial expansion. The socialist and republican journal *Critica Sociale* thus rejected what it regarded as Crispi's adventurism, and lent its support to the Italian anti-war slogan 'Viva Menilek', i.e. 'Long Live Menilek'.

In Ethiopia meanwhile Menilek, whose army was by then starving, did not feel himself in a position to enforce an Italian withdrawal from Africa. He may well have feared that Italy, whose army was well entrenched at Massawa, an impregnable island, would, if provoked, despatch a much larger force than that earlier employed at Adwa. Ras Alula, who never trusted the Italians, took, however, a stronger position. He declared himself determined to exploit the victory by advancing on the coast, and throwing the invaders into the sea. Menilek, however, refused to countenance any such action.

Thus, though an only limited victory, the outcome of the battle gave Menilek enormous prestige, both within Ethiopia and abroad. The extent of his victory was recognized on 26 October 1896, when the Italians agreed to the Peace Treaty of Addis Ababa. By doing so they at last accepted the annulment of both the Treaty of Wechalé and the Additional Convention, and recognized the absolute independence of Ethiopia. To avoid any ambiguity,

---

[31]   For accounts of the Italian campaign which culminated in Adwa, see Wylde, 1901, pp. 93–121, 196–225, who visited the battlefield shortly after the war, and interviewed Ethiopian and Italian survivors. See also an Ethiopian account of the war in Guèbrè Sellassié, 1931–2, II, pp. 389–448, and subsequent detailed monographs: Berkeley, 1935, and Conti Rossini, 1935.

such as had bedevilled the Wechalé treaty's Article 17, the new agreement was written not in Amharic and Italian, but in Amharic and French.[32]

The battle of Adwa, which was thereafter celebrated annually, left the Ethiopians with immense pride. It led them to believe that they were virtually invincible, and could resist any European enemy, however strong. The outcome of the battle at the same time gave Ethiopia a unique position in Africa. The victory made the country, in the eyes of many Africans, then and, more especially a generation or so later, a beacon of independence in a continent almost entirely enslaved by European colonialism. Menilek's anti-colonial achievement, however, was, as we have seen, strictly circumscribed. Despite his military triumph, the Ethiopian ruler had not felt himself able to insist on an Italian withdrawal from Eritrea. Like Emperor Yohannes after his defeat of the Egyptians a generation earlier, and perhaps even following the latter's precedent, he allowed the invaders to retain the territory from which they had mounted their attack.

Adwa was nevertheless all in all of major diplomatic importance. In the ensuing months the French and British Governments both despatched diplomatic missions to sign treaties of friendship with Menilek. Other missions arrived shortly afterwards from the Sudanese Mahdists, the Sultan of the Ottoman Empire, and the Tsar of Russia.

The French, who had assisted Menilek at the time of his conflict with Italy, later hoped to obtain his collaboration in their imperial designs. These were based on establishing a west–east French African axis from Dakar to Jibuti, in opposition to the attempted south-north British axis from the Cape to Cairo. Menilek responded favourably, and despatched one of his chiefs, Ras Tassama Nadaw in 1898, westwards as far as the White Nile. There he was supposed to join forces with a French force, under Captain Jean-Baptiste Marchand, advancing from the west coast of Africa. The French officer, however, failed to appear when expected, and Tassama was obliged to withdraw because his men, who came from the highlands, were falling victim to malaria prevalent in the Nile marshes. Marchand duly arrived at Fashoda, the hoped for meeting place on the river, but, instead of meeting the Ethiopian chief, was confronted by the British, who had made their way

[32] Rossetti, 1910, pp. 181–3; Work, 1936, p. 280.

south from Egypt. They were there in such strength that the Frenchman felt it wiser to withdraw. The Fashoda incident, as it came to be known, considerably diminished French prestige, in Menilek's eyes, and brought an end to changes of territorial boundaries in the region.

Ethiopia's frontiers were for the most part regulated in this period. Boundary agreements were signed defining the country's borders with the French and British Somali Protectorates, in 1897, Italian Eritrea, in 1900, the Anglo-Egyptian Sudan, in 1904, and British East Africa, later Kenya, in 1908.

10

Beginnings of Modernization: Menilek, Iyasu, Zawditu and Haile Sellassie

Modernization in Addis Ababa and Elsewhere

The last decades of Menilek's reign marked the beginning of Ethiopia's modernization, which had been delayed, among other reasons by almost a century of internal or external warfare. An unprecedented period of peace after the battle of Adwa, the opening up of foreign contacts in the aftermath of the Italian defeat, and the advent of increasing numbers of foreign craftsmen, created an entirely new climate for economic and technological developent. This owed much also to the emperor's almost child-like interest in innovations of all kinds, and to the ability of his trusted Swiss engineer Alfred Ilg. All these factors contributed to the founding at this time of a modern state.

One of the earliest developments in the field of modernization had its origins in 1881, when Menilek, then still only king of Shawa, abandoned the old Shawan capital, Ankobar, and easatblished his camp further south on the mountain of Entoto. Later, in 1886, his consort Queen Taytu, and her courtiers, moved down to the nearby plain, the site of thermal waters. There they set up a new headquarters, at Addis Ababa, literally, New Flower, which was named by Taytu. Five years later it became the official capital of the realm. The settlement, which rapidly acquired the character of a boon town, had by 1910 an estimated population of around 70,000 permanent and 30,000 to 50,000 temporary inhabitants. The town became the site of many of the country's principal innovations, and, because of its sizeable population, enabled a degree of specialization of labour scarcely known elsewhere in the land.

The growth of Addis Ababa, which was particularly rapid after the battle of Adwa, was accompanied by the construction of some of the country's earliest modern bridges. They were important in that the land in and around the capital was broken up by deep ravines, which were filled during the rainy season by unfordable torrents. One of the first Addis Ababa bridges was erected by a group of Russians after one of their number was drowned on the way to or from the then nearby Russian Legation. Other bridges were built over the Awash river on the trade route to the Gulf of Aden coast, and in Gojjam. Its local ruler, King Takla Haymanot, obtained the bridge-building services of an enterprizing Italian, Count Salimbeni.

Partly in view of the impending conflict with the Italians, Menilek subsequently reorganized the system of taxation. He instituted a tithe for the upkeep of the army, in 1892. This marked an important step, which Emperor Téwodros had attempted, but for lack of resources had failed to take towards terminating the old, but iniquitous system, whereby the soldiers lived by looting from the peasantry.

The need to assert Ethiopian sovereignty in the face of Italy's Protectorate claim may well also have helped to prompt Menilek to issue the country's first national currency in 1894. This, according to the Ethio-Italian Additional Convention of 1889, was to have been struck in Italy, but Menilek, after denouncing the Wechalé treaty, had it minted in Paris instead. The at least partially political motive for instituting the new currency was revealed in an official proclamation. It declared that this money was introduced 'in order that our country may increase in honour and our commerce prosper'. The new money bore the then politically relevant biblical motto: 'Ethiopia stretches forth her hands to God', as well as effigies of Menilek and the Lion of Judah. The currency was based on a silver dollar, of the same weight and value as the old Austrian Maria Theresa dollar, or thaler, which had circulated throughout Ethiopia, as well as much of the Middle East, since the mid-eighteenth century. Despite this equivalence Menilek's money failed to supplant the thaler, which for the next half century was to remain the country's principal coin. A mint was later established in the palace, with Austrian help. It was used to strike Menilek's smaller denomination coins, but not the thaler piece itself, which was imported from Paris.[1]

---

[1] On the history of this, and other Ethiopian currency see Gill, 1991.

The year 1894 also witnessed the issue of Ethiopia's first post-age stamps. These too were produced in Paris, and bore representations of Menilek and the Lion of Judah. The stamps were at first little used in the country itself, but were well received by philatelists, and provided the basis for the subsequent development of an efficient postal system. This owed much to the assistance of French advisors, and enabled Ethiopia to join the International Postal Union in 1908. This was the first international organisation to which the country was admitted, but by no means the last.

Another important step taken by Menilek at this time was the granting to Ilg, in 1894, of a concession for the construction of Ethiopia's first railway, to link Addis Ababa with the French Somaliland port of Jibuti. Ilg, whose work confined him to the Ethiopian capital, obtained the support of the French trader Léon Chefneux, who became his partner. Implementation of the project could not, however, take place until after the battle of Adwa, on 1 March 1896, and the consequent elimination of Italy's Protectorate claim. The French Government almost immediately afterwards gave permission, on 5 March, for the laying of the section of the line across French protectorate territory, between Jibuti port and the Ethiopian frontier. The railway project, however, soon ran into numerous technical, financial and political difficulties. Building operations were so delayed that the railway line reached Dire Dawa, half way between Addis Ababa and the coast, only in 1902. The original railway company then went bankrupt. Menilek was obliged to grant a second concession, in 1908, to his personal phycisian, Dr Vitalien, who had the support of the French Banque de l'Indo-Chine. Railway construction work, backed by French finance, was then resumed, and the line duly arrived at Aqaqi, in the vicinity of the capital, in 1915. The coming of the railway, the country's greatest technological achievement of the period, contributed greatly to the expansion, and permanence, of Addis Ababa. Of major commercial importance, the line also led to substantial expansion of the import-export trade.

Railway construction was accompanied by the installation of the country's first telephone and telegraph line, which followed the railway track from the capital to the coast. This line, which was erected by the technicians working on the railway, led from Addis Ababa to Jibuti. The line was supplemented, after the battle of Adwa, by a second one, installed by Italian electricians. It ran from the Ethiopian capital to the frontier of Eritrea, as well as to a number of provincial capitals to the south and west of the country.

Another development of this period was the introduction, by whom is uncertain, of the Australian eucalyptus tree. Some of the first plants were reportedly planted by Menilek's French advisor, Casimir Mondon-Vidailhet, in 1894 or 1895. The tree grew so fast that it was soon extensively cultivated in Addis Ababa. Some landowners planted large eucalyptus forests on their estates, and thereby solved the capital's hitherto serious shortage of both timber and firewood. The eucalyptus tree was, however, a thirsty plant, which dried up rivers and wells, and, by restricting grass cover, increased soil erosion.

The coming of the eucalyptus was of crucial importance in the history of Addis Ababa. The town's shortage of wood had been so acute that Menilek, in 1900, had actually envizaged abandoning the capital in favour of a settlement 55 kilometres to the west, which Taytu named Addis Alam, literally New World. The eucalyptus tree, however, grew so fast that the emperor, in the following year, abandoned the plan to transfer the capital. The move had in any case been strongly opposed by most of the foreign legations, as well as by some of the nobles. Both had invested heavily in Addis Ababa buildings, and were reluctant to see them abandoned. Almost the only support for the Addis Alam project came, curiously, from Italy, which, wishing to please the monarch, went so far as to erect a Legation at the new site.

The country's first modern hospital meanwhile was set up in 1896, immediately after the battle of Adwa, by a Russian Red Cross mission. It had been despatched, by the slow-moving authorities in St Petersburg, to treat Ethiopians wounded in the fighting, but, arriving after the conclusion of hostilities, established itself in the capital instead.

The first years of the twentieth century, the period of peace, that is, after the battle of Adwa, witnessed the construction of Ethiopia's first two modern roads. One, built with the help of Italian engineers, linked Addis Ababa with Addis Alam. The other, constructed, with the assistance of French technicians working on the railway, ran from the old emporium of Harar to the new railway town of Dire Dawa. A shipping service, linking Gambéla on the Baro river, a tributary of the Nile in west, with Khartoum in Sudan, came into existence shortly afterwards, in 1907.

During the next few years, the last of Menilek's reign, a succession of modern establishments came into existence. The first, set up by imperial charter in 1905, was the Bank of Abyssinia. An affiliate of the British-owned National Bank of Egypt, it was run largely under the supervision of British staff. The Bank of Abyssinia was engaged in most ordinary aspects of banking, but also handled most of the emperor's commercial affairs, which were largely undifferentiated from those of the Ethiopian state. The bank was also responsible for the issue of the country's currency, including the issue of paper money, inaugurated in 1914–15.

The country's first government hotel, founded by Empress Taytu, and known as the Etégé, literally Queen, was established in 1907. It was such a novelty that Menilek's chronicler, drawing a distinction with the free hospitality traditionally afforded at state banquets and those of the nobility, found it necessary to explain that guests had to pay for what they consumed.

The first modern school, the Menilek II School, which taught in French, was founded by the emperor in 1908. Having to contend with Church opposition to western ideas, he entrusted it, and three others in the provinces, at Harar, Ankobar and Dasé, to Egyptian Coptic teachers, to whom the local priesthood, and their Egyptian Coptic head, Abuna Matéwos, could raise no objection. Earlier, with Ilg's help, Menilek had despatched three youngsters in 1894 for study in Switzerland. Others were later sent to Russia, which was selected as an Orthodox Christian country, like Ethiopia, with strong monarchical traditions.

The first Ethiopian Government hospital, the Menilek II, was established in 1910, with the assistance of several foreign doctors. Some of them, including several German specialists, had come to treat the emperor, who was then mortally ill. The establishment was located on the site of the earlier Russian Red Cross hospital, which had ceased functioning a few years earlier. A State printing press was set up in 1911. It was used for the publication of the first Amharic newspaper, *Aymro*, as well as various decrees and other official documents. Several small-scale industrial enterprizes were likewise established at this time, among them a hydro-electric plant and a cartridge factory, both at Aqaqi, and saw-mills in the Managasha forest, west of Addis Ababa.

Another innovation was a water pipe, which ran from the Entotto mountains, above the town, to the palace compound. The latter was situated on elevated ground, so that the water had to travel upwards for part of its journey. This at first created considerable amazement, and caused a poet to exclaim that even water worshipped Menilek. A large clock, one metre square, was later installed above one of the palace buildings. It was visible from afar, and chimed every hour, thus, it is reported, enabling the citizens, perhaps for the first time in their lives, to go to work on time.[2]

The early years of the century also coincided with the expansion of Addis Ababa. The city, after the coming of the railway, grew rapidly, and developed an increasingly commercialized way of life. Innovations included stone buildings, which replaced wattle and daub huts; corrugated iron roofing, which replaced thatch; and mechanical grain grinding-mills, which replaced pestles and mortars worked by hand. Among other developments mention may be made of the setting up of bakeries, for the manufacture of European-type loaves, which were beginning to be eaten instead of, or as well as, *enjera*, the traditional Ethiopian-type bread; the sale of *enjara*, which had formerly been made only at home for family use; butchers' shops, for a population which had hitherto slaughtered its own livestock; hotels, restaurants, and drinking houses, for paying customers, who had previously eaten and drunk at home, or in other people's houses as non-paying guests; and commercial, in many cases open-air, tailors' shops, instead of traditional hand sewing. These shops often made use of Singer sewing machines, imported from the United States, and acquired by the tailors on very convenient hire-purchase terms.[3]

Modernization, and urbanization, had thus begun. New employment opportunities were beginning to open, both at the skilled and unskilled level, and modern educated youngsters were starting to graduate. Development was, however, still too slow, and limited, greatly to change the pattern of traditional Ethiopian society.

Menilek's Failing Health and the Tripartite Convention

The last years of Menilek's reign, like those of several earlier Ethiopian rulers, were bedevilled by the problem of succession.

[2]   For a detailed account of these developments see Pankhurst, 1968.
[3]   Ibid., pp. 710–13.

This became particularly serious after 1904, when the emperor's health began visually to deteriorate.[4] The question of the royal inheritance was the more serious in that the ageing monarch by then had no recognized living son. The presumption was that the throne would pass to the monarch's cousin, Ras Makonnen, but he predeceased his ailing master in March 1906, thus leaving the succession wide open.

The impending demize of Menilek, victor of Adwa and founder of the modern Ethiopian state, gave rise to the persuasive idea, on the part of European diplomats in Addis Ababa, that his empire, which they regarded as an anachronism in the era of the Scramble for Africa, would soon disintrgrate. The three neighbouring colonial powers, Britain, France and Italy, whom Menilek had played one against the other, now came together with a view to mutual cooperation. The British Foreign Secretary, Sir Edward Grey, and the French and Italian ambassadors in London accordingly signed a Tripartite Convention, on 13 December 1906. It declared, in Article 1, that it was the 'common interest' of the three powers to 'maintain the integrity of Ethiopia', while 'arriving at an understanding as to their conduct in case of a change in the situation', by which they meant Menilek's passing. The three signatories jointly agreed, in Article 3, that in such an eventuality they would maintain a policy of neutrality, and refrain from military intervention, except to protect their legations and foreign nationals, and that not one of the three powers would take any military action in the country except in agreement with the other two.

To ensure their respective interests they agreed, however, in Article 4, to partition the country into three spheres of influence. These were defined as a British, and Egyptian, interest in the Nile basin, and in particular in the regulation of the Nile waters; an Italian interest in the 'hinterland' of the Italian colonies of Eritrea and Somalia, and in their linkage west of Addis Ababa; and a French interest in the 'hinterland' of the French Somali Protectorate, and in the territory along which the railway from Addis Ababa to Jibuti was then already partially built.

The three signatories further agreed, in Article 10, that their representatives in Addis Ababa would keep each other mutually informed, and would cooperate in protecting their respective

---

[4] Rosenfeld, 1978.

interests. If they were, for one reason or other, unable to do so, they were to inform their respective governments.

This agreement was concluded, significantly enough, without consulting the emperor. When he was afterwards presented with a copy he ironically thanked the representatives of the three powers for acquainting him with their governments' desire, as the treaty put it, to 'consolidate and maintain' the independence of his realm. He observed, however, that the convention was 'subordinate' to his authority, and could not 'in any way' bind his decisions.[5]

The British representative in Addis Ababa, John Harrington, one of the drafters and keenest supporters of the convention, was insistent that he and his French and Italian colleagues should abide closely by it. He urged the Foreign Office, most forcefully, in February 1907, that all three representatives should receive 'strict orders to follow a policy in the interests of whites against blacks', and that if any of them were 'not in accord about any particular point, they should not disclose their difference of opinion to King Menelik, but refer the question to their respective Governments'.[6]

Despite his displeasure with the Convention, Menilek entered into a Treaty of Friendship and Commerce with France, on 10 January 1908. Signed by Antony Klobukowski, the French Minister in Addis Ababa, and generally referred to by his name, it laid down, in Article 5, that Ethiopia had the right freely to import firearms. This important proviso was intended to legalize the entry of weapons through Jibuti and the French Somaliland Protectorate. Menilek in return accepted a measure of French extra-territorial privilege. Article 7 specified that French subjects in Ethiopia involved in legal cases had to be tried according to French law, and, if detained, placed in the custody of the French Consul.[7]

The Appointment of Ministers and the Rise and Fall of Iyasu

Failing health, the increasing complexity of government, the danger to national independence inherent in the Tripartite Conven-

[5] Rossetti, 1910, pp. 319–25, 331.
[6] P.R.O., Foreign Office, 401/10, Harrington, 18. 1907.
[7] Rossetti, 1910, pp. 386–7.

tion, and the need to take account of the question of succession, caused the emperor to decide on the establishment of the country's first cabinet. Established in October 1907 it consisted initially of nine trusted noblemen. They were respectively responsaible for justice, war, the interior, trade and foreign affairs, finance, agriculture, 'writing', i.e. of diplomatic correspondence and the royal chronicle, public works, and the palace. Their appointment stemmed, according to his chronicler, Gabra Sellasé, from Menilek's desire to 'implant European customs'.[8]

Menilek also attempted to solve the succession question more directly. By then largely incapacitated by several strokes, he took the decisive step of designating a successor in May 1909. In a remarkable proclamation he reminded his subjects of the political difficulties which had followed the deaths of his predecessors Téwodros and Yohannes, and announced that his twelve-year-old grandson Lej Iyasu, the son of his daughter Shawaragga by Ras Mika'él, the Oromo and former Muslim ruler of Wallo, was his chosen heir.[9]

Despite Iyasu's nomination as heir, power was soon usurped by the dying monarch's formidable wife Empress Taytu, who claimed to be acting in accordance with her incapacitated husband's wishes. She succeeded in ousting some of her principal opponents, as well as in arranging a number of politically advantageous marriages. Her influence was, however, resented by many of the Shawan nobles, who feared that she, as a woman of Gondar, was bent on destroying their own political power. They rallied against her, and with the help of Abuna Matéwos, and of the *mahal safari*, or palace guards, banished her from the capital. The government was then entrusted to one of Menilek's loyal chiefs, Ras Tassama Nadew. He was appointed as Lej Iyasu's regent, but soon afterwards fell ill, and died in April 1911. Two and a half years later Menilek himself finally passed away, on 13 December 1913.[10]

On the death of Ras Tassama the Council of Ministers proposed

---

[8] Guèbrè Sellassié, 1931–2, II, pp. 527–8.
[9] Ibid., II, pp. 541–2; Molvaer, 1994, pp. 307–11; Bahru Zewde, 1991, pp. 116–17. On Iyasu's life see Molvaer, 1994.
[10] Guèbrè Sellassié, 1931–2, II, pp. 520–30; Molvaer, 1994, p. 320. On the power struggles and political changes of this period see also Mérab, 1922, II, pp. 225–78, and Guèbrè Sellassié, 1931–2, II, pp. 620–30.

appointing a new regent, but Iyasu, who had begun to enjoy his freedom, refused to accept one. Brushing aside the ministers, he impetuously declared, 'My father Menilek gave me a regent, but God took him away!' Thus asserting his independence he took control of the government and toured the country. Returning to Addis Ababa he tried to remove his dying grandfather from the palace, but was prevented by the latter's wife, Taytu, and daughter, Zawditu, supported by the palace guards. When eventually Menilek died Iyasu insisted on keeping the news secret, and offended many of his subjects by forbidding public mourning. He later became increasingly disrespectful to Menilek's old nobles, and sneered at them that they had 'grown old, and fat'. Not long after this he exiled both Taytu and Zawditu from the capital. The vested interests of Shawa retaliated by using his youth as a pretext for preventing him from being crowned.[11]

Iyasu, a child of the twentieth century, and son of Ras Mika'él, a former Muslim, had a significantly different attitude to religion from that of previous Ethiopian monarchs. Extending the secularist attitude of his grandfather, Menilek, who had permitted the practice of smoking, hitherto banned by the Church, he tried to treat followers of the country's two main religions, Christianity and Islam, on a more or less equal footing. This was doubtless easier for him than for many members of the royal family, in that Wallo, his father's homeland, was a province in which members of a single family often included members of both faiths. He was at the same time strongly opposed, like Emperor Yohannes before him, to foreign missionaries.[12]

Determined to weld the country together by dynastic marriages he followed the custom of earlier rulers by marrying into several of the country's most important families, both Christian and Muslim. His wives, acquired within a span of only a few years, thus included Wayzero Astér, daughter of Ras Mangasha Seyum of Tegray, Wayzero Sabla Wangél, daughter of Ras Haylu Takla Haymanot of Gojjam, and Wayzero Dasshé, later called Sehin, daughter of Dajazmach Kumsa of Wallaga. He was also married to daughters of King Abba Jifar of Jemma, Dajazmach Joté of Wallaga-Nakemté, Nagadras Abbokar of Chenno in Yefat, an

[11] Ullendorff, 1976, p. 49; Molvaer, 1994, pp. 321–50.
[12] Molvaer, 1994, pp. 326, 341.

Adai chief of Muhammad Yayyu's family, and two further Oromo chiefs, one of the Swalih family of Karra Qire in Yefat, the other of the Warra Sah clan of Yajju.[13]

Iyasu actively attempted to accomodate both faiths. As a Christian, he attended Church services, founded the church of Madhané Alam at Qachané, in Addis Ababa, and inaugurated that of St George, also in the capital. On the other hand, he also built a mosque, at Harar, and toured the Muslim provinces, where he consorted with Muslim chiefs, and too often, critics complained, with their nubile daughters. These travels, though in the tradition of Ethiopia's old rulers, weakened his already tenuous position by taking him away from the capital, which had by then, due to the coming of the telegraph and telephone, become the country's real centre of political power. His visits to the Muslim periphery also displeased the country's Christian establishment. The nobles of Shawa did not take kindly to the young man's attitude and policies. They were particularly incensed when the prince, declaring that he could not become emperor while his father Mika'él was only a Ras, promoted the latter to the title of Negus, or King, of Wallo and Tegray. This was resented in that it gave him precedence over all Menilek's former courtiers, many of whom had previously regarded him, an Oromo and a convert from Islam, as their political and social inferior.[14]

Notwithstanding growing opposition from both the Shawan nobility, and from the Church, Iyasu and his counsellors continued Menilek's reforming policies. They attempted to improve the system of land ownership and taxation, established a system of government auditing, abolished the traditional system by which plaintiffs and defenders were chained together, banned the traditional institution of *lebeshay*, or magical thief-catchers, and set up Addis Ababa's first police force. Iyasu also tended to give his support to populations on the country's periphery, in many cases oppressed by Amhara settlers or administrators appointed by the central state. In this way for example he reconciled the Yefat and Adal peoples, and others who had long been hostile to the Addis Ababa administration. His rule was on the other hand by no means fully benevolent. It was marred in particular by his partici-

[13] Ibid., 358–9.
[14] Ullendorff, 1976, p. 44; Molvaer, 1994, 321, 325–7, 346, 352.

pation in an inhuman slave hunt against the 'Shanqella' people of Gimirra.[15]

Iyasu's difficulties, which owed much to his youth, inexperience, and over-confidence resulting from his royal descent, were compounded by the outbreak, in August 1914, of World War I, a cataclysmic event from which it was difficult for Ethiopia to isolate herself. The country, after Italy's tardy entry into the war in 1915, was entirely surrounded, and in a sense encircled, by territories under Allied rule. Italy's involvement in the conflict had moreover a direct bearing on Ethiopia. The British, French and Italian Governments at that time signed the London Treaty of 26 April 1915, which laid down that 'in the event of France and Great Britain increasing their colonial territory in Africa at the expence of Germany, these two Powers agree in principle that Italy may claim some equitable compensation, particularly as regards the settlement in her favour of questions relative to the frontiers of the Italian colonies of Eritrea, Somaliland and Libya and the neighbouring colonies belonging to France and Great Britain'. The significance for Ethiopia of this agreement was later noted by the American author Ernest Work. 'There could have been no other possible place for Italy to expand from Eritrea and Somaliland than into Ethiopia', he wrote, 'except at the expense of England and France and no one would accuse these nations of having that in mind when they agreed that Italy might expand in Africa'.[16]

Iyasu, faced with the opening of hostilities, adopted an official policy of neutrality, but showed himself distinctly favourable to the Central Powers, Germany and Austria, and to their ally, the Ottoman Empire. There were two main reasons for this. Firstly, he was unsympathetic to the Allied Powers, i.e. to the Italian, British and French, with which his grandfather, Menilek, had earlier been obliged to contend. They had partitioned his country by the Tripartite Convention of 1906 into spheres of influence, and the existence of their colonies or protectorates on the coast prevented his access to the sea. The Germans, by contrast, rejected the Convention, and spoke of their wish to maintain Ethiopia's political integrity.[17] Secondly, he had allied himself to his country's

[15] Molvaer, 1994, pp. 328–32, 335, 342; Bahru Zewde, 1991, pp. 121–2.
[16] Work, 1936, pp. 33–4.
[17] Bairu Tafla, 1981, p. 131.

Muslim population, in the Ogaden, Jemma, and elsewhere, which for reasons of religious solidarity tended to be pro-Turkish. To manifest these sympathies he reportedly crossed in secret into British and/or Italian Somali territory. He also displayed support for the Somali nationalist leader, Muhammad Adbille Hasan, the so-called Mad Mullah, who had for over a decade challenged British and Italian colonial rule. Iyasu also made friendly contact with the authorities in German East Africa, later Tanganyika, to whom he despatched at least one good-will mission.[18]

All this angered the British, Italians and French, who reverting to a nineteenth-century policy of the colonial powers, prevented him from importing firearms. The Legations of the three powers later acted even more forcibly. They warned the Ethiopian Ministers, on 12 September 1916, that if their young master continued to support their enemies they would intervene militarily.

This threat, which recalled the British expedition against Emperor Téwodros fifty years earlier, caused a number of the nobles finally to decide on rebellion against their still uncrowned monarch. They were helped in this by Iyasu's reportedly pro-Muslim affinities, which eventually caused Abuna Matéwos to free them from their oath of allegiance. On 27 September, which was symbolically Masqal, or the Feast of the Cross, they announced that Iyasu, who was then in the Harar area, had been deposed, for the crime of abjuring the Christian faith. Menilek's daughter Zawditu was thereupon proclaimed empress. She was, it is said, the first Ethiopian woman since the Queen of Sheba to rule in her own right. Ras Makonnen's son Dajazmach Tafari, who had been one of the principal nobles working against Iyasu, was at the same time promoted to the rank of Ras, and designated Heir to the Throne. The latter was a previously unknown title, and gave him considerable powers. These were shortly afterwards formalized, and strengthened, when he assumed the rank of regent.[19]

Iyasu, on hearing news of the *coup d'état*, tried to hasten back to the capital, but was defeated at Miesso, half way from Dire Dawa. His father, Negus Mika'él, meanwhile marched south in an

---

[18] Molvaer, 1994, p. 341.
[19] Tafari writes in his Autobiography (Ullendorff, 1976, pp. 50, 57, 63, 65) that he became Regent Plenipotentiary at the time of Lij Iyasu's deposition, on 27 September 1916, but this appointment was not. Empress Zawditu's chronicle (Molvaer, 1994, p. 425) claims that this appointment was made only on 19 December 1922.

attempt to re-establish his son's rule. Two major engagements ensued. The first was at Toro Mask, near Ankobar, where the Wallo army was victorious. The second, and more decisive, was at Sagalé, north of Addis Ababa, on 27 October 1916, when the Shawan army, deployed by Ras Tafari, captured Mikaʿél, and thus brought the struggle to an end. Iyasu had little option but to flee into the Afar lowlands, where, refusing, it is said, to seek asylum abroad, he roamed among a friendly population for the next half decade. He was eventually captured, in 1921, after which he remained in close confinement at Garamulata, in the east of the country, until his death in the autumn of 1936.[20]

Zawditu and Tafari

The political settlement of 1916, which divided power between the Empress, Zawditu, and the Regent and Heir to the Throne, Tafari, inaugurated a difficult, and unprecedented, period of dual government. Power become further polarized in 1918, when Menilek's old ministers were dismissed as a result of popular agitation, in which the palace guards, played a major role.[21]

The two rulers had two separate palaces, groups of followers, and policies. Zawditu, who had received only a modicum of Ethiopian church education, and was innocent of foreign languages, represented patriotic, somewhat xenophobic, conservatism, earlier personified in Empress Taytu. Tafari, the son of the widely travelled Ras Makonnen, had by contrast been brought up in Harar, a city with outside contacts, and had received something of a modern education. He had studied with French missionaries, most notably Father André Jarosseau, known in Ethiopia as Abba Endreyas, and had attended the country's first modern educational establishment, the Menilek School. He was, doubtless for these reasons, more aware than Zawditu of the need for modernization, and of the necessity of taking the outside world seriously into account. He thus emerged as a protagonist of reform in the tradition of Téwodros and Menilek, and gathered around him a small, but increasing, number of foreign-educated young men, not

---

[20] Ullendorff, 1976, p. 55; Molvaer, 1994, pp. 365–73.
[21] Molvaer, 1994, p. 391. For a useful overall account of the country in this period see Rey, 1923.

Plate 22 Empress Zawditu, with her royal attendants. Photo: Collection of Denis Gérard.

a few of whom he had himself despatched for study abroad. One other difference between the two leaders deserves mention: Zawditu owed her position almost entirely to her royal birth. Tafari, though the grandson of King Sahla Sellasé, and hence, as he increasingly insisted, of imperial descent, had risen largely through his own efforts and ability. He had moreover administrative experience, having been governor of Harar and Sidamo successively.

Though Zawditu, as empress, held sovereign power, Tafari, was doubtless the more able leader. Younger than the empress by almost twenty years he soon emerged as the more active political figure. He was in particular in charge of foreign affairs, and matters connected with foreigners. The latter, on visiting Ethiopia, were graciously received by him, and tended to give him their admiration and support. They welcomed him as the first ruler of his country, at least since Aksumite times, to speak a European language: French. They were pleased moreover that he saw a role for Europeans in the development of his country. One of his first steps, on gaining power in 1916, was to recruit a number of White Russian officers to train his troops. In the following year he established an Imperial Bodyguard, a modern force composed largely of Ethiopians who had served with the British in Kenya or the Italians in Libya.[22]

Anxious to win friends abroad, and to make clear Ethiopia's abandonment of Lej Iyasu's pro-German stance, he despatched diplomatic missions, at the end of World War I, to the victorious Allies in Europe and to the United States, congratulating them on their military triumph. To improve his country's international image, which was then being severely criticized on account of its age-old institution of slavery, and faced the possibility of foreign intervention on that account, he that same year promulgated a symbolic decree, abolishing the practice. With a view to improving the system of government he also extended the ministerial system, earlier established by Menilek, by setting up a Ministry of Commerce and a Public Works Department, both in 1922. A certain amount of road-building also took place at this time, in Addis Ababa, as well as in the provinces, where Goré and other western towns were in particular linked with the inland port of Gambéla. Internal customs posts, a vexatious institution and a major hindrance to trade since time immemorial, were likewise gradually removed.

Entry to the League of Nations and Tafari's European Tour

Tafari's most spectacular achievement came in the field of foreign affairs. On 28 September 1923 he succeeded in gaining Ethiopia's entry into the League of Nations, which had been founded only four years earlier, in 1919. Admission to the international body was a notable step in overcoming the country's age-old isolation, and was potentially important in withstanding pressures from Italy and other neighbouring colonial powers. An Ethiopian diplo-

---

[22] On Tafari's early life and his subsequent reign as Emperor, see his autobiography (cited above) translated by Ullendorff; also Sandford, 1955; Mosley, 1964; Lockot, 1989; and, the most scholarly, Marcus, 1987.

matic corps came into existence at about this time, and was later issued with decorative official uniforms. In 1924, Tafari began to grapple, more effectively than before, with the question of slavery. He had a first practical decree enacted for the gradual eradication of slavery, and established a bureau, and a school, for freed slaves. This edict, like the earlier proclamation, served to counter foreign criticism, and thus to rehabilitate the country's international image.[23]

Later that year Tafari embarked, with Ras Haylu Takla Haymanot of Gojjam and several other nobles, on a major tour of Europe. This took them, via Egypt and Palestine, to nine European countries, France, Belgium, Holland, Luxembourg, Sweden, Italy, England, Switzerland and Greece. While in Paris, Rome and London, the Regent attempted to acquire Ethiopian access to the sea, or at least a free port on the coast of one or other of the neighbouring colonial territories. His requests were, however, turned down, in one way or another, by the three powers concerned. Despite this failure, his visit was important. Sometimes compared to that of Peter the Great to western Europe two centuries earlier, it encouraged Ethiopian society to become aware of the rest of the world, as well as to adopt foreign inventions. Tafari and Haylu both acquired a number of motor cars, besides sundry European gadgets. Tafari was also presented, on Zawditu's behalf, with one Emperor Téwodros's crowns, which the British had looted from Maqdala fifty-six years earlier.[24]

Modernization in the 1920s

Tafari also emerged as a modernizer in other fields. In 1923 he founded a modern printing press, the Berhanenna Salam, i.e. Light and Peace. It printed an Amharic newspaper with the same title, which carried articles popularizing the cause of reform, which some Ethiopian intellectuals of the time believed should follow the Japanese model. A steady flow of literary, religious, and educational books in Amharic were also published. Zawditu meanwhile

[23] Ullendorff, 1976, pp. 74, 76–7.
[24] Ibid., pp. 81–119.

established a scriptorium, with a staff of about 250 men, for the copying of Ge'ez religious texts. Since the institution of the *lebeshay*, earlier banned by Lej Iyasu, had not yet been eradicated, further action against it was also taken.[25]

Other institutions established at this time included a modern hospital, the Bét Sayda, founded in 1924, and a new secondary school, the Tafari Makonnen, in 1925. On the opening of that establishment, which taught in English as well as in French, Tafari urged his fellow nobles to fellow his example by founding schools. Later, in 1928, he decreed symbolic fines for parents who left their children illiterate. The number of students abroad for study meanwhile was substantially increased. Several hundred were sent to France, Egypt, Lebanon, Great Britain, and the United States.[26]

The first aeroplane, a Potez, purchased by the Ethiopian Government in France, arrived in Addis Ababa, in August 1929. A German Junkers followed a month later. The first was christened Regeb Tafari, or Dove of Tafari, and the latter Neser Tafari, or Eagle of Tafari.

Relations with Britain, Italy and France

Ethiopia's international position meanwhile was once more endangered by the British and Italian Governments. Reverting to a policy dating back to the late nineteenth century, they persuaded the League of Nations to ban the export of firearms by member states to much of Africa, including Ethiopia. The prohibition on Ethiopian arms imports was rigidly enforced by the two colonial powers, which between them controlled most of the territory on Ethiopia's borders. Tafari, however, opposed this arms restriction. He contended that it was incompatible with his country's League membership. He had, very conveniently, the support of the French Government, which wished to keep the port of Jibuti open to the arms trade. This was partly because this commerce was lucrative,

[25] Ibid., pp. 67; Molvaer, 1994, pp. 456–7, 462, 477–9.
[26] See also Molvaer, 1994, p. 576. For a glimpse of educational and other progress of the time see Rey, 1927, pp. 28–31; Molvaer, 1994, p. 418; and, more generally, Pankhurst, 1962, pp. 241–90.

and partly because it was considered a means of winning Ethiopia's friendship. French opposition to the arms ban proved decisive, and the League finally agreed, in 1925, to exclude Ethiopia from the restriction zone.[27]

A further diplomatic crisis between Ethiopia and the British and Italian Governments erupted shortly afterwards, in 1926. The two colonial powers, cooperating together in the spirit of the Tripartite Convention of 1906, agreed to put joint pressure on the Ethiopian Government, to grant them concessions in two areas of the country in which each was interested. The British thus supported Italy's demand to construct a railway to link the Italian colonies of Eritrea and Somalia, west of Addis Ababa, while the Italians reciprocated by backing Britain's ambition to build a dam on Lake Tana. Tafari, who, on account of his country's membership of the League, was in a stronger diplomatic position than Menilek twenty years earlier, immediately protested to the international organization. He declared, once again with the support of France, that the Anglo-Italian agreement, entered into without consulting Ethiopia, a fellow member of the League, was incompatible with the principles of that body. He pithily inquired whether members of the League desired 'means of coercion' to be applied against Ethiopia 'which they would undoubtedly dislike if applied against themselves'. The British and Italians, embarrassed by this strongly worded reaction, protested their innocence of trying to exert undue pressure on Ethiopia, and were obliged, at least ostensibly, to abandon their policy.[28]

In the following year, during a visit to Addis Ababa of the King of Italy's cousin, the Duke of Abruzzi, the Italian Government reopened the question of Ethiopia's request for access to the sea. They proposed making Asab a free port, and building a motor road to link it with Dasé, which, it was assumed, would be connected by a road to Addis Ababa. A twenty-year Treaty of Friendship and Arbitration between the two countries was duly signed, on 2 August 1928. Evidence of Italian intrigue and fear of future Italian intervention, however, prevented the Ethiopian Government from permitting the building of the road, and the free port of Asab was never established.[29]

[27] Ullendorff, 1976, p. 109.
[28] Ibid., pp. 124–45.
[29] Ibid., pp. 145–51.

Contacts between Ethiopia and the outside world were nevertheless strengthened by the establishment of an Ethiopian Ministry of Foreign Affairs, and by the setting up of Ethiopian Legations in Paris, Rome and London. Talks with the Japanese Government were opened in 1926, and led to the conclusion of a potentially important Treaty of Friendship between the two countries in the following year. Negotiations with the Coptic Church of Egypt were also initiated, with a view to reducing Ethiopia's age-old subordination to the Church of Alexandria. The Egyptians insisted that Ethiopia should continue to have an Egyptian Abun, but agreed, in 1929, to the appointment of five Ethiopian bishops. This was two more than Emperor Yohannes had succeeeded in procuring half a century earlier, but two less than the Zagwé King Harbé had unsuccessfully tried to obtain in earlier medieval times.[30]

Reforms were also undertaken in several other fields. The soldiers' requisitioning, or looting, of supplies from the peasantry was forbidden. The practice whereby a murderer would be handed over to his victim's family for punishment was abolished, and replaced by the institution of government executioners. Usurious rates of interest were forbidden.[31]

Tafari, throughout this period, was steadily outmanoeuvring his rivals, for the most part Menilek's courtiers, who were by then becoming weak and elderly men. The regent's enhanced position was recognized by Empress Zawditu, on 6 October 1928, when she accorded him the prestigious title of Negus. In the following year he established an Ethiopian airforce. This helped him further consolidate his power, and that of the central government, over the provinces, and their potentially rebellious lords. Aviation was in particular decisive at the battle of Anchém, in March 1930. In that engagement Zawditu's ex-husband, Ras Gugsa Walé, the ruler of Bagémder, from whom she had been parted when she assumed the imperial throne, was defeated and killed. Only a few days later the empress, a sick woman, herself passed away. Tafari thereupon assumed the imperial throne, as Emperor Haile Sellassie I.[32]

[30]   Molvaer, 1994, pp. 526–32.
[31]   Ullendorff, 1976, pp. 66, 68, 73.
[32]   Ibid., pp. 68, 115, 151–6, 171–7.

Haile Sellassie's Coronation and Programme of Reforms

The new emperor's first success, after his accession, was the conclusion of an arms agreement, with Britain, France, and Italy. Signed on 29 August 1930, it proclaimed the need to ensure 'efficient supervision over the trade in arms and munitions in Ethiopia', but specified that the emperor should be 'allowed to obtain all the arms and munitions necessary for the defence of his territiories from external aggression and the preservation of internal order'.

Haile Sellassie's subsequent coronation, on 2 November 1930, was a colourful event, for which Addis Ababa was considerably beautified, and some street lighting installed. The ceremony was attended by the Duke of Gloucester for Britain, the Prince of Udine for Italy, and Marshal Franchet d'Esperey for France. Representatives also came from Sweden, Holland, Belgium, Germany, Poland, Greece, Turkey, Egypt, the United States, and Japan. The celebrations attracted considerable international media coverage, for both the monarch and the country. One of those attending was the British novelist, Evelyn Waugh, who described the event in a journalistic account, and later also wrote a satirical novel, *Black Mischief*, set in Ethiopia of the time.[33]

The world-wide publicity accorded to the coronation, and in particular to Ras Tafari's assumption of the imperial title of Haile Sellassie, had no small international ramifications. Ethiopia, through the popular media, became far-better known than ever before, above all in Africa, where many regarded the country as an island of independence in a sea of colonialism. Many in far-off Jamaica, where Marcus Garvey's 'return to Africa movement' was by then well established, saw the coronation as no less than the realization of the biblical prophesy that 'Kings would come out of Africa'. Identifying themselves passionately with the new Ethiopian monarch, as well as with Ethiopia's status as an independent African state they rejected traditional European missionary-based Christianity, and created a new religion of their own. In it they accorded the emperor the rank of divinity, the Messiah of African

[33] Ibid., pp. 171–7. For a journalistic account see Waugh, 1931.

redemption.[34] This gave birth to the Ras Tafarian movement, a new faith which lies beyond the scope of the present work.

In Ethiopia meanwhile, the emperor, in the following year 1931, introduced his country's first written constitution. It was drafted after study of those of many other countries, including Japan, and was based on considerable debate between the nobles and the bureaucracy, which consisted largely of commoners. The Constitution was promulgated on 16 July 1931. In it the monarch, who was officially described as a descendant of King Solomon and the Ethiopian Queen of Sheba, was accorded virtually absolute powers, and his body was declared sacred. A two-house Parliament was established as a kind of political sounding board. It consisted of a Senate, nominated by the emperor from among the princes and nobles, and a Chamber of Deputies to be elected on the basis of fairly restrictive property qualifications. A line of imperial succession was also, for the first time, laid down, sovereignty being, it was stated, permanently based on descent from Haile Sellassie.[35]

The emperor that year also promulgated a second, anti-slavery decree. More comprehensive than its predecessor, it provided for the gradual, but systematic, emancipation of slaves. No less than 62 anti-slavery offices were set up in various parts of the country. Decrees were likewise issued for the curtailment of labour service, and for the reform, and monetarization, or land taxes. Menilek's old Bank of Abyssinia, a private institution, was nationalized, also in 1931, and replaced by a state institution, the Bank of Ethiopia. A new national currency, bearing the effigy of the new monarch, was established, and supplemented by a sizable issue of gold-backed paper money. New postage stamps were likewise inaugurated. An embassy was despatched to Japan to strengthen ties between the two countries.

Other developments, no less important from the point of view of state building, also took place. Ras Haylu Takla Haymanot, the traditional ruler of Gojjam, was fined for tax evasion and other offences, and arrested in 1932, for conspiring to assist Lej Iyasu's escape from detention. The semi-autonomous status of Jemma was terminated in the following year. Parts of Charchar and Balé were established as areas of model administration. As a result of

---

[34]   Barrett, 1977, p. 81.
[35]   Ullendorff, 1976, pp. 178–201; Bahru Zewde, 1991, pp. 140–2.

such acts, some dating back to the period of Tafari's regency, most of the country was brought under centralized rule, perhaps for the first time since the reign of Emperoz Zar'a Ya'qob.

The process of creating ministries meanwhile continued, with the establishment of a Ministry of Education, in 1930, and a Ministry of Public Works in the following year. A number of modern schools and hospitals were likewise established. The former included the first girls' school, founded in Addis Ababa by, and named after, Haile Sellassie's consort, Empress Manan, opened in 1931. Ethiopian women, as a result, began for the first time to be prepared for the professions. A number of schools in the provinces were also inaugurated. Some, situated near British possessions, gave instruction in English; the others in French. The Empress Zawditu Memorial Hospital, ran by Seventh Day Adventist missionaries, was set up in Addis Ababa in 1934. Further students were sent for study abroad, in the Middle East, Europe, and America. Several of them became military cadets.

Road-building continued, with the result that Addis Ababa became the nub of a not unimpressive embryonic road network. A road to the north led as far as Dasé, in Wallo, with an extension under construction to Addegrat, in Tegray. There were also three roads to the west. One went to Dabra Libanos, with work in progress as far as Dabra Marqos, in Gojjam; the second ran up to the Gibé river, with construction going on as far as Naqamté, in Wallaga; the third extended to Jemma. To the east and south of the capital a track led to the railway town of Mojjo, and thence southwards, through the Rift Valley, to Yergalam, far away in Sidamo.

Ethiopia by 1935 possessed around a dozen aeroplances. Almost half of them were Potezs, but there were also three Fokkers, two Farmans, a Breda, a Fiat, and a Beech. A rudimentary airport had been established in the capital at Jan Hoy Méda, with airfields also at Aqaqi, Dasé, Dire Dawa, Jigjiga, Dabra Marqos, Soddo, and Balé.

The emperor throughout this time employed, and made effective use of, a number of foreign advisors. Several of them played a notable role in policy making. The three most important comprized a Swede, Eric Virgin, in the Ministry of Foreign Affairs; a Swiss, Jacques Auberson, in the Ministry of Justice; and an American, E. A. Colson, in the Ministry of Finance. Three other advisors may also be noted: C. S. Collier, a Canadian, who served

as governor of the Bank of Ethiopia; Ernest Work, a black American, in the Ministry of Education; and Frank de Halpert, an
Englishman, who was employed to advise with the abolition of
slavery, in the Ministry of the Interior. With the exception of the
latter, who was appointed mainly to appease British complaints
about slavery, and had virtually no influence, none of the advisors
came from the neighbouring colonial powers, Britain, France or
Italy.

The last years of Ethiopian independence prior to the Italian
fascist invasion also witnessed several other significant developments. The country's first radio station was established, in 1931,
and later replaced by more powerful installations, which enabled
the emperor to address a 'message to the world' in January 1935.
Military reorganization was also intensified. A Belgian military
mission arrived, in 1930, to train the Imperial Bodyguard, and a
Swedish mission, in 1934, to establish a Military College. It was
situated at Holata, west of the capital, in one of Menilek's former
palaces. The first cadets, however, had not graduated before the
country was engulfed in an invasion of unprecedented ferocity.[36]

---

[36]   For data on modernization in the period see Zervos 1936, and Farago, 1935.

11

Invasion, Occupation and Liberation

Ethiopia, the victor of the battle of Adwa in 1896, was by the early twentieth century the only state in Africa to have survived the European scramble for the continent. The country was, however, dangerously situated between two Italian coastal colonies, Eritrea and Somalia. These territories could scarcely be developed in isolation from the Ethiopian hinterland, or expanded other than at Ethiopia's expense.

Adwa had been a turning point in the history of Ethio-Italian relations. Italy, prior to the battle, had sought to gain control of Ethiopia, first through Article 17 of the Wechalé Treaty, and later through military action. After the battle the Italians turned, no less assiduously, to economic penetration. Such Italian ambitions had been accepted, as we have seen, by Ethiopia's two colonial neighbours, Britain and France, who, by the Tripartite Convention of 1906, had recognized an Italian economic sphere of influence linking Eritrea and Somalia, west of Addis Ababa. The French, who regarded Ethiopia as important for the prosperity of their Somaliland protectorate, and wished to be in good relations with Ethiopia's ruler, later veered away from the 1906 formula as far as Italy's sphere of influence was concerned. The British, on the other hand, continued as late as 1925 to accept the principle of an Italian sphere of influence over most of Ethiopia in exchange for Italy's support for a proposed British dam at Lake Tana.

The Rise of Fascism and Italian Preparations for War

Italy's colonial ambitions in Africa were almost inevitably affected by Benito Mussolini's seizure of power in 1922, and the resultant emergence in Rome of a militaristic, and intensely chauvinist, regime. It was only a matter of time before the fascist state would shift Italian policy once more from economic to military penetration, and call on the people of Italy to 'revenge Adwa', by embarking on a new war of conquest.

Relations between the two countries were, however, at first superficially cordial. When Ras Tafari visited Rome in 1924 he was warmly welcomed by Mussolini. The fascist dictator, as his wife Donna Rachele recalls, then foresaw a 'great future for Italy in Abyssinia', and conceived the idea of 'developing Abyssinia with Italian labour'.

He found his Ethiopian visitor 'a clever and cultured man' with whom he believed he could 'get on very well'.[1] With this in mind the Duce sponsored the 1928 Treaty of Friendship and Arbitration in the hope of achieving rapid Italian economic penetration through the port of Asab and a proposed Italian road to Dasé. When, however, it became apparent that the Ethiopian Government would not accept any infringement of its sovereignty the Italian fascists turned their thoughts from peaceful pressure to outright war.

The first steps for the new invasion were taken by Marshal Emilio De Bono, an elderly fascist holding the post of Minister of the Colonies. On 22 January 1930 he wrote a confidential letter to the president of the Italian Council of Ministers, asking for a major increase in the budget for the Italian colonies bordering Ethiopia. It would be 'harmful to embark on large expenditure', and 'ridiculous to speak of the Romanity of the Empire', he added, 'if *expansion* [his emphasis] beyond the confines of the Fatherland was not considered possible'.[2]

The idea of a military operation was warmly accepted by Mussolini, who argued that war could rejuvenate the Italian people, and be an objective in itself. Accordingly, in the Spring of 1932, he despatched De Bono to Eritrea 'to see how matters stood there'. On the minister's return the two fascist leaders agreed that their country's 'colonial future must be sought in east Africa', where Italy had a 'hinterland', i.e. Ethiopia, 'which could be profitably exploited'. De Bono thereupon drew up a definite programme' in relation to the 'possibilities of war', which, he later recalled, 'had

[1]   Mussolini, 1959, p. 68.
[2]   PRO, *Captured Italian Documents*, No. 112809.

to be regarded not only as possible, but as always increasingly probable'.[3]

De Bono, in 1932–3, wrote memorandum after memorandum requesting increased military personnel and supplies for Eritrea and Somalia, and had several secret conversations on Ethiopia with his fascist master. Discussing his own attitude in 1933, he recalls:

It had been my proudest dream to end my public career as a soldier on public service. Of course, it was not yet possible to say in 1933 – the year in which we began to consider what practical steps must be taken in the event of war with Ethiopia whether there would or would not be a war in that country; but I made up my mind to lose no time, and one day I said to the Duce: 'Listen: if there is to be a war down there – and you think me worthy of it, and capable – you ought to grant me the honour of conducting the campaign.' The Duce looked at me hard, and at once replied 'Surely!' 'You don't think me too old', I added. 'No', he replied, 'because we mustn't lose time'.

From that moment, the Duce was definitely of the opinion that the matter would have to be settled no later than 1936, and he told me as much. I confined myself to replying: 'Very good!' – *without expressing the faintest doubt as to the possibility that this could be achieved* [De Bono's emphasis] . . .

It was the autumn of 1933. The Duce had spoken to no one of the coming operations in East Africa; *only he and I knew what was going to happen,* and no indiscretion occurred by which the news could reach the public.

Fascist strategy from 1933 onwards was based, De Bono explains, very largely on political subversion in Ethiopia, designed at achieving the country's complete disintegration. He informed the Duce that this would 'not be a very difficult task', provided they worked 'well on political lines', and that disintegration 'could be regarded as certain after a military victory on our part'. Mussolini, he adds, 'thought as I did, and ordered me "to go full speed ahead". I must be ready as soon as possible'.

[3] De Bono, 1937, pp. 5–6.

'Money [De Bono said] will be needed, Chief; lost of money'.
'There will be no lack of money', the Duce replied.[4]

Italian agents were thereafter actively engaged in the attempted subversion of Ethiopian chiefs, and nobles, who were given lavish bribes.[5] Action was also taken to foment ethnic tension, particularly in militarily strategic areas in the north and south of the country, notably in eastern Wallo, Ogaden and Hararg. Emperor Haile Sellassie commented at the time that he knew that many of his chiefs were accepting Italian money, but was confident that when the testing time came they would not betray Ethiopia. Later he declared, with unusual bitterness, in his autobiography, that the Italians had 'always been the bane of the Ethiopian people'.[6]

The Changing Stance of France

The rise of Hitler and nazi Germany's attempt to overturn the paramount world position of Britain and France, the victors or World War I, or 'satisfied powers' as he called them, had important implications for Ethiopia. The French, and to a lesser extent the British, came to see 'dissatisfied' nazi Germany as a potential threat to their hegemony. They therefore become increasingly reluctant to take any stand against Mussolini, lest it drove him into the hands of the Germans, to whom he was, however, already linked by a common militaristic, and 'fascist' doctrine.

Such thinking led to a major re-orientation on the part of France. Hitherto, as we have seen, she had regarded Ethiopia as a valuable 'hinterland' for Jibuti, and had supported Ethiopian independence against the predatory pressures of Italy, and to a lesser extent Britian. The French Government, becoming increasingly concerned with the situation in Europe, now, however, changed its policy. To please Mussolini, it began to withdraw opposition to

---

[4]   Ibid., pp. 12–13, 15.
[5]   Ullendorff, 1976, pp. 156–63, 202–6. On the funding of extensive Italian espionage and political disruption, see Pankhurst, 'Reminiscences of Banking in Ethiopia on the Eve and Beginning of the Italian Fascist Invasion', in Bahru Zewde et al., 1994, I, p. 233.
[6]   Ullendorff, 1976, p. 158.

Italian expansion in Ethiopia, and proposed that Italy in return should waive its interests in the French colony of Tunisia.[7]

The Wal Wal Incident and Anglo-French Relations

Fascist Italy, aware that there would no longer be any significant French opposition to an invasion, then embarked on massive war preparations, both in Italy and its east African colonies. Activity in Eritrea was personally supervized by De Bono, first as Minister of the Colonies, and, after January 1935, as the colony's High Commissioner. Massawa harbour installations were vastly expanded to handle the arrival of troops and war material. The road from the port to Asmara was broadened, and those to the Ethiopian frontier rendered suitable for the passage of soldiers and military supplies. Airports were constructed or expanded for the use of fighter and bombing planes, and hospitals built to cater for the probable wounded.

The Italian pretext for invasion came with the Wal Wal incident which took place little more than a year after Mussolini's above-mentioned talks with De Bono. On 23 November 1934 an Anglo-Ethiopian boundary commission, which had been surveying the frontier between British Somaliland and Ethiopia, arrived at Wal Wal, 100 kilometres within Ethiopia. There they were confronted by an Italian force, which had earlier arrived from Somalia. The British members of the commission protested at the Italian presence, but then withdrew to avoid an 'international incident'. The Ethiopians on the other hand faced the Italians for about a fortnight, until a shot of indeterminate, but probably Italian, origin, precipitated a clash.

The Italians responded by despatching an ultimatum to Ethiopia. They demanded the equivalent of £20,000 in damages, a formal apology, a salute to the Italian flag, and the punishment of the Ethiopian troops involved.[8] These terms, which would have constituted recognition of Italian sovereignty over Wal Wal, were considered unacceptable by the Ethiopian Government. Haile Sellassie therefore sought arbitration in accordance with the Ethio-

[7] For the development of French policy see, for example, Marcus, 1987, pp. 74–5, 128–30, 149–50.
[8] Baer, 1947, pp. 45–61.

Italian Treaty of 1928. Mussolini rejected this proposal. The emperor thereupon took the matter to the League of Nations, which spent the next eleven months in fruitless discussion, during which fascist Italy accelerated its preparations for war.

During the critical months prior to the opening of hostilities the French and British Governments carefully reviewed their interests in relation to the forthcoming conflict. In the evening of 6 January 1935 the French premier, Pierre Laval, held a conversation with Mussolini in which he gave the dictator the encouraging information that France was from the economic point of view 'disinterested' in Ethiopia.[9] Five months later, in June, a British Government committee, headed by Sir John Maffey, came to the conclusion in a secret report, leaked to the Italian press, that there were 'no vital British interests in Abyssinia or adjacent countries such as to necessitate British resistance to an Italian conquest of Abyssinia'. The report added that, 'in general as far as local British interests' were concerned, 'it would be a matter of indifference whether Abyssinia remained independent or was absorbed by Italy'.[10]

The French and British Governments, having thus formulated similar attitudes of 'disinterest' towards the projected invasion, decided on a joint policy of 'neutrality'. To this end they decided to ban arms exports to both potential belligerents.[11] This restriction ran counter to the international arms agreement of August 1930, in which both powers, as well as Italy, had agreed that the emperor had the right to import arms and ammunition for purposes of defence. The obvious unfairness of the new Anglo-French move was noted by Haile Sellassie, who exclaimed in an interview with the London *Sunday Times*:

> Italy is a great manufacturing country working day and night to equip her soldiers with modern weapons and modern machines. We are a pastoral and agricultural people without resources and cannot do more than purchase abroad a few rifles and guns to prevent our soldiers from entering battle with swords and spears only.[12]

[9]   Marcus, 1987, pp. 148–50.
[10] Barker, 1968, pp. 79–80.
[11] Ullendorff, 1976, pp. 256–8.
[12] Salvemini, 1953, see especially, pp. 271–2.

Notwithstanding the manifest logic of these remarks the United States likewise passed a Neutrality Act, on 24 August, which placed an embargo on the supply of arms to either side. The French and British Governments also developed identical views on how to react to the opening of hostilities. Laval met the British Foreign Secretary, Sir Samuel Hoare, on 10 September 1935 to discuss the matter secretly. He later told the French Chamber of Deputies that he and his British opposite number found themselves:

> instantaneously in agreement upon ruling out military sanctions, not adopting any measure of a naval blockade, and never contemplating the closure of the Suez Canal – in a word, ruling out everything that might lead to war.[13]

Publicly, however, Sir Samuel spoke in a very different vein. On the day after his talks with Laval, he declared, in an address to the League of Nations Assembly:

> His Majesty's Government and the British people maintain their support of the League and its ideals as the most effective way of ensuring peace . . . this belief in the necessity of preserving the League is our sole interest in the present controversy . . . The ideals enshrined in the Covenant, and in particular the aspiration to establish the rule of law in international affairs, have appealed . . . with growing force to the strain of idealism which has its place in our national character, and they have become part of our national conscience . . . The League stands, and my country stands with it, for the collective maintenance of the Covenant [of the League] in its entirety, and particularly for steady and collective resistance to all acts of unprovoked aggression . . . This is no variable and unreliable sentiment, but a principle of international conduct to which they [the British people] and their Government hold with firm, enduring and universal persistence.[14]

The Italian anti-fascist historian Gaetano Salvemini later commented that, if the secret agreement of 10 September between Laval and Hoare had been known, the latter's speech 'would have

---

[13]   Harris, 1964, p. 66.
[14]   Salvemini, 1953, p. 296.

been greeted with a tempest of boos and hisses', but, not being known. 'met with an immense ovation'.[15]

In sharp contrast to the position of the British and French democracies was that of nazi Germany. Hitler, its dictator, had adopted an ideology akin to that of fascist Italy. He saw that Mussolini was, however, unwilling to countenance a German annexation of Austria, which would have brought the nazi state to the Brenner pass, on the very borders of Italy. The German dictator, who was determined on expanding southwards into Austria, his birthland, reasoned that Mussolini, if victorious in Ethiopia, would be in a strong position to oppose Germany's ambitions, but would be unable to do so as long as his army was embroiled in an African war. The nazi ruler was therefore only too anxious to stiffen Ethiopian resistance. He responded favourably to German requests for aid, brought mainly by David Hall, an envoy of Ethio-German origin. Nazi Germany was thus virtually the only country to come to Ethiopia's assistance, and without Mussolini knowing, supplied Haile Sellassie's army with three aeroplanes, over sixty cannon, 10,000 Mauser rifles, and ten million cartridges.[16]

The Invasion and League of Nations Sanctions

Mussolini, aware that he would encounter no significant opposition from either Britain or France, and in the dark about the secret position of Hitler, adopted a bold posture. In an histrionic speech, on 2 October 1935, he cried out, 'To sanctions of an economic character, we will reply with our disclipine, with our frugality and with our spirit of sacrifice. To military sanctions, we will reply with military measures. To acts of war, we will reply with acts of war.'[17]

On the following day the fascist army began its long-expected invasion, without any formal declaration of war. That same day Italian airmen bombed Adwa, in symbolic revenge for their compatriots' defeat there forty years earlier. The invading army was five times larger than that employed by the Italians in the previous war, and now, for the first time, enjoyed overwhelming superiority of armament, as well as complete control of the air.

[15] Ibid., p. 297.
[16] Funke, 1970, p. 44.
[17] Head, 1937, II, pp. 170–1.

Confronted with the long-anticipated act of invasion the League of Nations met, on 5 October, and, six days later, ruled that the Italian Government was guilty of having resorted to war in disregard of the League Covenant. This decision was reached by fifty votes to one (Italy), with three abstentions: Albania, Austria and Hungary. All three were either dependent on Italy or ideologically allied to her fascist government. On the same day the League established a committee to consider the imposition of sanctions against the aggressor. The committee duly proposed four prohibitions, which became effective on 18 November. These comprised:

(1) An embargo on the exportation, re-exportation, or transit of arms, ammunition, and implements of war to Italy and the Italian colonies.

(2) An embargo on loans and credits to the Italian Government or to public authorities, persons or corporations in Italian territory, either directly or indirectly.

(3) An embargo on the importation or goods grown, produced, or manufactured in Italy or Italian possessions, or consigned therefrom.

(4) An embargo on the exportation or re-exportation to Italy or Italian possessions of transport animals, rubber, bauxite, aluminium, iron ore, scrap iron, chromium, manganese, nickel, titanium, tungsten, vanadium, their ores and ferro-alloys, tin and tin ore.[18]

These prohibitions, which were described by the British economist, Lord Keynes, as 'comparatively mild' economic sanctions,[19] contained several major omissions, which, as many commentators have observed, rendered the whole scheme nugatory, Prohibition 1, on arms, thus 'hardly restricted Italy which could manufacture its own armaments'.[20] Prohibitions 2 and 3, on loans to Italy and imports therefrom, could be only of long-term significance, and 'would have been effective only if the war was prolonged until Italian gold reserves were exhausted.'

Prohibition 4, on exports to Italy, proved, however, the greatest disappointment to the sanctionist cause, for it excluded several strategic commodities on the ground that Italy could obtain them

[18] Ibid., II, pp. 193–4, 203–7.
[19] *New Statesman and Nation*, 28 November 1935.
[20] Harris, 1964, p. 71.

from countries outside the League, notably the United States. Crucially important commodities excluded from the embargo included steel, pig iron, copper, cotton and above all oil. The absurdity of these exclusions was later noted by Winston Churchill, who commented: 'The export of aluminium into Italy was strictly forbidden; but aluminium was almost the only metal that Italy produced in quantities beyond her own needs. The importation of scrap iron and iron ore into Italy was sternly vetoed in the name of public justice. But the Italian metallurgical industry made but little use of them, and as steel billets and pig iron were not interfered with, Italy suffered no hindrance'. The League's sanctions, Churchill concluded, were therefore 'not real sanctions to paralyze the aggressor, but merely such half-hearted sanctions as the aggressor would tolerate'.[21]

Disillusion with the League's action was also captured by the British cartoonist David Low. He depicted Sir Samuel Hoare and Anthony Eden, the British Minister for League Affairs, asking Laval whether it was not time to lock the stable door. The French leader archly replies, 'But no, the horse, he is not yet flown'.[22]

Sanctions, though unable to halt the aggression, were not without considerable effect on the Italian economy. The Banca d'Italia's gold reserves, which had stood on 31 December 1934, a few days after the Wal Wal incident, at 5.8 billion lire, soon began to drop. In an attempt to save the situation the Italian Government took over all private gold deposits, but the bank's reserves by 20 October 1935, a fortnight after the beginning of hostilities, had fallen to 3.9 billion. A decree was thereupon issued to prohibit the continued publication of information on gold holdings. The Queen of Italy soon afterwards led a campaign, initiated on 18 December, for her women compatriots to surrender their gold wedding rings to the State. Despite this much publicized event, the bank's reserves, we now know, fell by August 1936 to only 2.2 billion.

The value of the lira, which Mussolini had long sought to defend, had accordingly to be devalued, on 5 October 1936, by no less than 59 per cent.

[21]   Churchill, 1948, pp. 172–3, 176.
[22]   *Evening Standard*, 28 October 1935.

Military Operations and the Use of Mustard Gas

The main Italian invasion, launched from the colony of Eritrea, was at first directed by De Bono. He initially encountered no resistance. The emperor had ordered his troops to pull back from the frontier area, to squash any pretence that Ethiopia was the aggressor, as well as perhaps to extend the enemy's lines of communication. Ethiopian resistance was moreover weakened at the beginning of the campaign by the defection of the emperor's disaffected ex-son-in-law, Dajazmach Hayla Sellasé Gugsa, governor of eastern Tegray.

From the opening of the campaign De Bono was under strong pressure from Mussolini to achieve a speedy victory, so as to capture Addis Ababa before the rainy season, expected to begin toward the end of June 1936. This was essential, as the Duce saw it, both to boost Italian morale, which would otherwise soon have flagged, and to forestall any possible extension of sanctions. De Bono on the other hand feared that too rapid an advance would dangerously extend his lines of communication. He revealed this in the secrecy of his diary, where he observes that 'the cat that was in a hurry made blind kittens'. As a result of his cautious policy, and stiff Ethiopian resistance, the Italian advance ground almost to a halt. De Bono had seized Aksum, forty miles within Ethiopia, on 15 October 1935, but it took him over three weeks, until 8 November, to capture Maqalé, little more than 60 kilometres further south. The Duce, frustrated by this painfully slow progress, three days later commanded him to advance 'without hesitation'. The harassed commander replied that greater speed was virtually impossible, and that 'the military situation should have precedence over any other consideration'.[23]

Mussolini, infuriated by this response, dismissed De Bono, on 14 November, and replaced him by an Italian career general, Pietro Badoglio, whom he authorized, on 28 December, 'to use, even on a vast scale, any kind of gas and flame-throwers'. Aware that these instructions flouted the Geneva Convention of 1926 banning the use of gas, the dictator cynically countermanded his instructions, on 5 January 1936. 'Suspend the use of gas', he

[23] Del Boca, 1968.

telegraphed, 'until the Geneva meetings unless it becomes necessary for supreme offensive or defensive necessity. I will give you further instructions with regard to this'. The said instructions came a fortnight later when Mussolini once more telegraphed, 'I authorize Your Excellency to use all means of war – I say all, both from the air and from the ground'.[24]

The emperor meanwhile was endeavouring to organize Ethiopian resistance in the face of overwhelming odds. On 11 November, he flew to Jigjiga, in Ogaden, and drove thence to Daggabur, to strengthen resistance on the south-eastern frontier, facing Italian Somalia. Then, at the end of the month, he proceeded to Dasé, in Wallo, which, despite heavy enemy bombing, was to be his headquarters for the remainder of the campaign.

The Hoare–Laval Proposals

Mussolini throughout this time was 'extremely nervous', as his representative to the League, Count Aloisi, later admitted, that sanctions might be extended to include oil. The dictator went so far as to warn Laval, at the end of November, that Italy would regard this as 'an unfriendly act', and later admitted to Hitler that if an oil sanction had been imposed he would have had to 'withdraw from Abyssinia within a week'.[25]

The British and French foreign ministries, which also had no desire to see the imposition of an oil sanction, strove meanwhile to devize a compromize which would render it unnecessary to impose one. Proposals were duly formulated, after which Hoare went to Paris, on 7 December, to finalize them. Their terms were then submitted to both Rome and Addis Ababa. They were also leaked to the French press, and thus almost immediately became known to the entire world.

The Hoare-Laval plan, which from the geographical point of view was strikingly reminiscent of the Tripartite Convention of 1906, proposed that Ethiopia should cede to Italy more or less all the areas then occupied by the Italians, i.e. Tegray and Ogaden, and that Italy should be given 'economic rights' over most of

[24]   Ibid.
[25]   Aloisi, 1957, p. 324.

southern Ethiopia, except the very far west, which had earlier been considered a British sphere of influence. Ethiopia in return was to be offered an outlet to the sea at Asab, and a corridor through the Afar desert leading thereto, i.e. the very same arrangement which Ethiopia had found unsatisfactory when proposed by Italy seven years earlier, in 1928.

These proposals, which the emperor described as 'a prize offering to the aggressors', led to a storm of indignation, in Britain and to a lesser extent throughout the world. Hoare was obliged to resign, and was replaced by Anthony Eden. In the general excitement public opinion, however, largely forgot about the question of an oil sanction. The British and French governments were thus able to continue their opposition thereto almost without debate. The policy of the new Foreign Secretary, it soon transpired, differed little from that of his predecessor. He thus claimed in the House of Commons, on 24 February 1936, that the limited sanctions then in force would 'ultimately have an important influence', and that there was therefore no need to extend them to oil, which, he declared, was merely 'a sanction like any other'. This inane remark carried the day, even though it was regarded with incredulity in some opposition quarters. The British liberal newspaper, the *Manchester Guardian*, for example commented, 'The half-naked Abyssinian meeting a "mechanized" enemy could tell him otherwise'.

The British and French Governments remained also unwilling to contemplate closing the Suez Canal, which would almost certainly have brought the invasion to a halt. This was later recognized by the American President, Franklin Roosevelt, who observed, 'if Great Britain had closed the Suez Canal, Italy would have been balked in respect to Abyssinia'.[26]

Failure to impose the oil sanction, or to close the canal, resulted, in the last analysis, from the fact that the British and French Governments saw no interest in halting Mussolini's invasion. They were reluctant to see the Duce humiliated, and threatened by rebellion, let alone provoked into a hostile show of force, and driven into a closer military alliance with his ideological partner Hitler. Hugh Wilson, the American representative in Geneva, recalls, 'Time and again, I was told that sanctions applied to Italy must be such as not to drive that nation to desperation, not to

[26]   Ickes, 1955, p. 84.

push it to a point where it would assault the States applying the pressure'.[27]

The Later Course of the Campaign

The Ethiopian army, though faced by a much more powerful foe in full command of the air, succeeded at the end of 1935 in launching a major counter-offensive, aimed at isolating the Italian position at Maqalé. This operation was carried out by forces under three separate commands: On the western flank, Gojjam and Bagémder soldiers commanded by Ras Emru Hayla Sellasé. In the centre, Ras Kasa, the overall commander of the northern front, with his three sons, Asfa Wassan, Abarra, and Wandwassan, and Ras Seyum Mangasha, with their men, composed respectively of Amharas and Tegrays. On the eastern wing, the soldiers of Ras Mulugéta Yeggazu, a veteran of the Adwa war and nominal Minister of War. These four main commanders, like their Italian opposite numbers at Adwa forty years earlier, had relatively little contact between each other. This, however, was not entirely a disadvantage, for the invaders broke the Ethiopian code, and were therefore informed as to Ethiopian radio and telegraph messages.

The Ethiopian Christmas Offensive, as it was sometimes called, drove the enemy back from the Takkazé River, out of much of the territory De Bono had captured. This enabled Ras Emru, the most successful of the three principal Rases, to defeat a force of Italian colonial troops at the pass of Dambagwina, and advance at several points as far as the Eritrean frontier. Some Italian observers described this as a 'black period' for fascist arms. The invaders, however, threw all their forces into the struggle, and made extensive use of artillery, tanks, bombing, and, on Emru's front, mustard gas. The Ethiopian advance was halted, and decisively defeated, between 20 and 24 January 1936.

The Italian victory in the above fighting, which came to be called the First Battle of Tambén, opened the way for a powerful new fascist offensive. This was at first directed against Ras Mulugéta and the imperial troops, who were stationed on the natural fortress of Amba Aradam, south of Maqalé. The Italians

---

[27]   Wilson, 1941, pp. 330–1.

employed 170 aeroplanes and 280 cannon, and at one point dropped no less than forty tons of bombs in five hours, besides a vast quantity of mustard gas. Massed artillery fire, reminiscent of that of World War I, was also used. Ethiopian casualties were considerable, and included the aged Ras himself.[28]

The Italians then turned their assault on Kasa and Seyum, whose forces were vastly inferior in numbers, let alone fire-power. The defenders inflicted heavy casualties on the enemy, but were fairly easily crushed, between 27 and 29 February, in the Second Battle of Tambén. The eastern and central Ethiopian fronts had thus both been broken, and the two Rases, to escape Italian encirclement, were obliged to withdraw precipitously, with what was left of their army, to join the emperor at Qoram, is southern Tegray.

One of the effects of this retreat was that Ras Emru's army, though still undefeated, was obliged to undertake a strategic withdrawal, across the Takkazé River, to avoid encirclement. This operation was rendered the more difficult by the fact that Dajazmach Ayalaw Berru, the ruler of Samén, and some of the Gojjam troops, had been in secret contact with the enemy, and were uninterested in continuing the struggle. Emru's retreat, known as the Battle of Sheré, took place at the end of February and first days of March, and involved some of the fiercest fighting of the war. The invaders dropped as much as eighty tons of bombs on Emru's army, set the surrounding countryside on fire with incendiary devices, and made extensive use of mustard gas. The Ras later recalled that his men held firm against bombs, and put enemy tanks out of order with their bare hands, but could do nothing against gas; they could not 'kill' such rain.[29]

The Royal Italian Air Force was meanwhile also engaged in the systematic bombing of British, Swedish, Egyptian and other international Red Cross hospitals and ambulances in Ethiopia. Attacks were so severe that virtually all foreign personnel were driven from the field. Dr John Melly, head of the British Red Cross unit, wrote, on 13 April, 'This isn't a war – it isn't even a slaughter – it's the

---

[28] Gentizon, 1936, pp. 126–8; Del Boca, 1965, pp. 126–8; Burgoyne, 1967, pp. 249–326. On the war in general, see also a good contemporary journalistic account in Steer 1936, and Mockler's subsequent monograph, 1984, which likewise covers the subsequent Ethiopian liberation campaign of 1941.
[29] Del Boca, 1965, p. 156.

torture of tens of thousands of defenceless men, women, and children, with bombs and poison gas. They're using gas incessantly, and we've treated hundreds of cases, including infants in arms'.[30]

It may be noted in passing that the fascist use of gas, as well as of the bombing of the Red Cross, is fully substantiated, and was known indeed at the time throughout the world. Any mention of this action was, however, strictly excluded from the Italian press, which was highly censored. The use of gas, and the bombing of Red Cross units, is likewise entirely concealed in all the subsequent writings of Badoglio, Graziani and other Italian officers, which therefore give a manifestly incorrect picture of the war. The Italian Ministry of Defence, even more remarkably, refused, for almost sixty years, to admit that gas had been used in Ethiopia, until forced to do so in 1995, largely through the persistant efforts of an Italian professor Angelo Del Boca.[31]

Meanwhile, towards the end of March 1936, the emperor, whose army had not yet been engaged in the battle, decided on a final counter-attack, aimed at driving the invaders back from May Chaw in southern Tegray. This move ran counter to his general advice to the chiefs that they should avoid a direct engagement with the enemy, and instead organize guerrilla resistance. The attack was delayed for over a week, until 31 March, which gave the Italians time to entrench themselves. The emperor's men, and his bodyguard in particular, attacked with great determination, but were unable to breech the Italian defences, the more so as they were soon subjected to heavy bombing and extensive mustard gas attacks from the air.

The Ethiopian army, after thirteen hours of fighting, was obliged to abandon its offensive, after which it was attacked by the Rayya and Azabo people, whom the Italians had encouraged to rebel. The emperor's soldiers, forced to retreat, made their way southwards towards the Ashangi plain, where they were once more subjected to heavy bombing.[32] Cesco Tomasselli, an Italian observer, wrote: 'Wave after wave of bombers with full loads hammered their main objective, the Ethiopian columns making for

[30]   Nelson and Sullivan, 1937, p. 240.
[31]   Del Boca, 1996.
[32]   Ullendorff, 1976, pp. 280–90.

the east shore . . . the bombs exploded among the dense mass of fugitives'.[33] Mustard gas was also extensively used. 'Of all the massacres of the terrible and pitiless war', the emperor later recalled, 'this was the worst. Men, women, pack animals were blown to pieces or fatally burned by mustard gas. The dying, the wounded, screamed with agony. Those who escaped the bombs, fell victim to the deadly rain. The gas finished off the carnage the bombs had begun. We could do nothing to protect ourselves against it'.[34] After the defeat at May Chaw the Ethiopian northern army disintegrated. The emperor, a broken man, made his way back to his capital, halting only for a brief stay to pray at Lalibala.

Badoglio meanwhile continued his southward advance towards Addis Ababa. This, in the absence of good roads, took him a little over a month, and led to his occupation of the Ethiopian capital on 5 May 1936.

Although the war was decided on Ethiopia's northern front, considerable fighting also took place to the south and south-east of the country. The invading forces there were, however, far less numerous than those in the north. They were commanded by one of fascist Italy's most ruthless colonial generals: Rodolfo Graziani, who had earlier served in Italian North Africa, where he had earned the nickname, 'hyena of Libya'. He was opposed in the south by two of the emperor's sons-in-law, Ras Dasta Damtaw and Dajazmach Bayana Mared, and in the south-east by the governor of Harar, Dajazmach Nasibu Za-Emanu'él. Unlike the traditional Rases in command of the northern front, they were all three members of Ethiopia's younger generation.

Graziani, lacking anything like the men and material available to Badogio, played, to his disgust, a subordinate role in the campaign. Some of the fiercest fighting was at Qorahé, referred to by the Italians as Gorahai, a strategic Ethiopian post in southern Ogaden. One of the most heroic acts on the Ethiopian side was played by Grazmach (posthumously Dajazmach) Afawarq Walda Samayat, who personally operated one of the Ethiopian army's few anti-aircraft guns. Faced by repeated enemy bombing, he was seriously wounded, but, determined to maintain the morale of his

[33] Tomasselli, 1936, pp. 218–19.
[34] Griaule, 1936, pp. 45–9.

men, refused to abandon his anti-aircraft gun. He died of a gangre-
nous leg, which could almost certainly have been cured had he
agreed to leave his post for hospital treatment.[35]

After Afawarq's death, Qorahé soon fell, on 7 November – the
day before De Bono's occupation of Maqalé. Italian forces then
proceeded to capture Negelli, and later several posts in Ogaden.
Graziani failed, however, to reach Harar until after Badoglio's
capture of Addis Ababa.[36]

The Emperor's Departure for Europe and the Proclamation of the Fascist Empire

The emperor, who had returned to Addis Ababa on 30 April 1936,
left the city almost immediately afterwards, on 2 May, to escape
the invader, as well as to lay the cause of Ethiopia before the
world. He was accompanied by his family and several of his
closest associates.

Haile Sellassie's departure, which shocked many of his subjects,
was followed by a break-down of public order in the capital, and
extensive looting. This is believed to have been started by several
patriotic individuals, who sought to deny Addis Ababa to the
invader, as the Russians had burnt Moscow prior to the advent of
Napoleon's army in 1812. Much of the destruction resulted, however, from mob violence, directed mainly against the business
quarter by the destitute section of the population. The Italians, on
reaching the capital, on 5 May therefore found Addis Ababa a city
of ruins, with many foreigners seeking refuge in their legations.
Four days later Mussolini proclaimed the successful end of the
war, and triumphantly declared: 'Ethiopia is Italian'. Ethiopians
continuing to resist were thereafter regarded as rebels, and, as
such, were liable to immediate execution, without trial, even
after surrender. Those so killed included two of the emperor's
sons-in-law, Ras Dasta Damtaw and Dajazmach Bayana Mared,
and three of Ras Kasa's sons, Abarra, Asfa Wassan and Wand
Wassan.

The emperor and his party had meanwhile travelled by train to
Jibuti. He sailed thence, under British protection, to Haifa, and

[35] Ullendorff, 1976, pp. 239–40.
[36] Del Boca, 1965, pp. 112–23, 186, 198.

Plate 23   Emperor Haile Selassie, addressing the League of Nations, at Geneva, in the summer of 1936.

drove to Jerusalem, to pray in the Ethiopian church there. He then took a ship, through the Mediterranean, to England, where he was to be given discrete asylum in Bath, in the west of the country, for almost five years.[37]

On 30 June 1936 he made his way to Geneva to address the League of Nations. In his speech, one of the highlights of his career, he outlined, in coniderable detail, the 'crimes' committed by the invaders against his people, and asked the delegates the forceful question, 'What answer am I to take back to my people?' His quiet dignity, which contrasted with the boisterous behaviour of a group of Italian journalists who had to be removed from the hall, made a deep impact on international opinion. The League's answer was, however, to vote, on 4 July, for the ending of sanctions.

From the outset, Italy's unprovoked aggression, the dilatory

[37]   Ullendorff, 1976, pp. 293–7.

action, or non-action, of the League of Nations, and the fascist use of poison-gas had made a deep impact on international opinion. Societies dedicated to the support of Ethiopia were founded in Britain, the United States, Holland, and a number of other democratic countries. Two pro-Ethiopian newspapers were established; *New Times and Ethiopia News*, edited by the former Suffragette Sylvia Pankhurst, in Britain, and the *Voice of Ethiopia*, by an Ethiopian medical doctor, Melaku Bayen, in the United States.

The invasion had a no less significant impact in Africa, and among people of African descent throughout the world. Not untypical was the reaction of Kwame Nkrumah, the future Ghana leader, who was then a student. He relates in his autobiography that he was in London, on the way to the United States, when he saw the newspaper poster, 'MUSSOLINI INVADES ABYSSINIA'. He was immediately seized by a violent emotion. 'At that moment', he writes, 'it was almost as if the whole of London had declared war on me personally. For the next few minutes I could do nothing but glare at each impassive face, wondering if these people could realize the wickedness of colonialism, and praying that the day might come when I could play my part in bringing about the downfall of such a system. My nationalism surged to the fore; I was ready to go through hell itself, it need be, in order to achieve my object'.[38]

Opposition to the invasion was also voiced by many Italian anti-fascists, among them Carlo Rosselli, an exile in France, who edited the emigré newspaper *Giustizia e Libertà*, He was later assassinated in Paris, on Mussolini's personal orders.

Despite widespread popular opposition Italy's 'conquest' of Ethiopia was recognized by most of the world, most notably by Britain in April 1938. Eden, who had opposed Prime Minister Chamberlain's policy of conciliation with Mussolini, had resigned two months earlier, the second British minister to leave office as a result of the Italo-Ethiopian war. A few countries meanwhile refused to recognize the 'conquest'. They were the United States, the Soviet Union, Mexico, New Zealand, and Haiti.

The Occupation

The Italian occupation led to important political and other changes. Italian-occupied Ethiopia was officially merged with

[38]   Nkrumah, 1957, p. 27.

Eritrea and Somalia, into an entirely new territory designated Africa Orientale Italiana (AOI), i.e. Italian East Africa. This for the first time brought the greater part of the Horn of Africa under a single administration. The area was divided into six constituent units: (1) Eritrea, including the former Ethiopian province of Tegray, with capital at Asmara; (2) Amhara, formed out of the old provinces of Bagémder, Gojjam, Wallo, and northern Shawa, with capital at Gondar; (3) Galla and Sidamo, comprizing lands to the south-west, occupied by people of that name, with capital at Jemma; (4) Addis Ababa, later renamed Shawa; (5) Harar, the town of that designation; and (6) Somalia, including Ogaden, with capital at Mogadishu. As a result of these arrangements Ethiopia ceased to be a legal entity.

Mussolini, from the outset, was determined to remove all symbols of Ethiopia's historic independence. He gave personal orders for the removal of two Addis Ababa's principal statues, one of Emperor Menilek, the victor of Adwa, and the other of the Lion of Judah. He later gave orders for the looting, and shipping to Rome, of one of the great obelisks of Aksum. The loot taken to Italy also included the aforesaid Lion of Judah monument, five Ethiopian royal or other crowns, and a number of historically interesting paintings which had adorned the Ethiopian parliament building.

Fascist Italy, which had to justify its invasion of Ethiopia both to itself and to the world, was motivated by dreams of economic grandeur. This objective had to be carried out in an extensive territory with a still very limited infrastructure, and in the face of strong on-going patriotic resistance. Mussolini, in this far from enviable position, was willing to invest far more capital and resources in his newly won empire than the older colonial powers, who had been concerned essentially with short term profits, had ever done. The Italian occupation was therefore accompanied by very considerable Italian state expenditure, much of it, however, unwisely, or corruptly, spent.

Immediate strategic interests, as well as long term economic considerations, necessitated heavy initial investment in road construction. In 1936–7 as many as 60,000 Italian workmen were employed on the roads, though this figure fell by 1939 to 12,000 Italians, assisted by 52,000 'native' labourers. The rudimentary pre-war Ethiopian road network centred on Addis Ababa, was in this way integrated into a more extensive grid based on the Italian colonial ports of Massawa and Mogadishu. The country's road milage was thus considerably expanded. Such road-building, though impressive, was achieved at the price of postponing, and seriously curtailing, investment in other, potentially more profitable, fields of economic activity.

The number of Italians in the empire as a whole was by 1939 a little over 130,000. This was far lower than the fascists had originally anticipated, but nevertheless led to the construction, in the principal towns, of a substantial number of European-type buildings, government offices, shops, flats and houses. Their location was based on rigid urban segregation between Europeans and 'natives'. Intermarriage, or even co-habitation, between the races was strictly prohibited, and transportation in buses and other vehicles was strictly segregated.

The greatest urban development took place, not surprisingly, in Addis Ababa. The city witnessed the establishment of two segregated Italian residential areas: Case INCIS, a quarter reserved for state officials, called after its managing corporation, the Istituto Nazionale per Case degli Impiegati dello Stato, and Case Popolare, or workers' flats. Some 20,000 Ethiopians were evicted and transferred to the west of the settlement, which was projected as 'native city'. The capital's market, located since Menilek's day in the centre of the town, near St George's cathedral, was moved westwards to this 'native' area.

The city's facilities, and particularly those of its white population, were substantially improved. An electric grid, ran by a para-statal company, the Compagnia Nazionale Imprese Elettriche, often referred to as CONIEL, was established, and the supply of water expanded by the construction of a dam at nearby Gafarsa.

Industrial development in the empire as a whole was, however, curtailed by fears that it would compete with establishments in the Italian 'motherland', and thus endanger Italian exports. Several small factories were, however, established, notably for cement and textiles at Dire Dawa, for hessian rope and sacks at Jemma, and for *pasta* and biscuits at Kalité, just outside Addis Ababa.

Trade made a poor showing, and in some sectors actually declined. There were three main reasons for this. Firstly, fascist xenophobia, which resulted in the expulsion of long-established Indian and other foreign merchants, most notably the major Indian from of Mohomedally and the French company, A. Besse.

Secondly, efforts to replace the old, and well-liked, silver Maria Theresa thaler by Italian paper money, the value of which declined during the occupation, and was almost unacceptable by the population at large. Thirdly, the establishment of top-heavy, bureaucratic, and at times corrupt, state trading corporations.

An important fascist objective, much publicized at the beginning of the invasion, was to win Italy a 'place in the sun', by settling hundreds of thousands, if not actually millions, of Italians in the empire, to solve what was officially described as Italy's 'surplus population'. Settlement schemes were accordingly attempted, at Bishoftu and Holata, on the outskirts of Addis Ababa, and in the provinces, at Wagara, Charchar and Jemma. Such projects, however, proved a dismal failure. Would-be settlers were discouraged by the difficulty of embarking on agricultural work in an unaccustomed environment, by lack of adequate infrastructure, by insecurity occasioned by Ethiopian patriotic resistance, and by shortage of Italian state funds, which had been allocated elsewhere. The result was that only a few thousand Italians were settled. The empire could not even feed its Italian population, and had to import substantial quantities of wheat from Italy.[39]

Social and welfare services were directed mainly to the Italian population. A number of small new hospitals were constructed, mainly for Europeans. An extensive inoculation programme for 'natives' was, however, instituted. Several pre-war Ethiopian schools were reopened for the instruction of Italian children. Education of 'native' youth was, however, strictly controlled, with the avowed aim of preventing the emergence of a 'native intelligentsia'. Many Ethiopians nevertheless obtained manual work on road or house-building, or service in the colonial army, and learnt at least some elements of the Italian language.

Italian fascism had little interest in race until the occupation of Addis Ababa, but the strictly controlled Italian press soon began to devote considerable attention to the issue. The *Gazzetto del Popolo* of 21 May 1936 thus proclaimed that 'the fascist empire must not be an empire of half-castes'. Many newspapers argued that to prevent such a possibility it was necessary to keep Italian

---

[39]   Smith, 1976; Haile M. Larebo, 1994.

colonists 'rigidly separate' from the 'natives'. The Italian media in ensuing months became ever more racially vociferous. A not un-typical article declared that fascism 'protected the race' and tried to 'keep it pure'. A speaker at a Congress of Colonial Studies, held in Florence in April 1937, asserted that Italians must affirm the 'dignity of race' in order to protect their 'prestige as rulers'. Such utterances served as a prelude to the enactment of a series of increasingly strict racial decrees. The first, signed by the Italian king, Vittorio Emanuele, on 19 April 1937, prohibited conjugal relations between Italians and 'natives' (but did not prevent the former from consorting with 'native' prostitutes). A number of ordinances establishing urban and other segregation were afterwards issued.

The racist influence of nazi Germany, which became increas-ingly apparent in the autumn of 1938, led to the founding, on 5 August, of a virulently racist Italian magazine, *La difesa della razza*, i.e. Defence of the Race. This was followed, on 5 Septem-ber, by an anti-Semitic royal decree, which *inter alia* rendered illegal the marriage of Italian Aryans and Jews. Further legislation was enacted, on 29 June, providing 'Penal Sanctions for the Defence of the Prestige of the [Italian] Race in face of the Natives of East Africa'. A later decree of 13 May 1940 reduced the status of 'half-castes' to that of the 'native' population. Racial laws, though firmly endorsed by the fascist party, ran counter to Italy's 'Latin temperament'. Many Italian men, who had come to Africa without wives, found ways of associating with Ethiopians of the opposite sex, and not a few were deported or otherwise punished for this offence.

The last years of the occupation were particularly difficult. The fascist authorities, anticipating the Duce's involvement in a Euro-pean war, embarked on a strict policy of autarchy, designed to make the empire as far as possible self-sufficient. Horse-drawn garries, or carts, were for example introduced as a substitute for cars making use of petrol.

Such difficulties notwithstanding, there can be no denying that the occupation had produced a major, and largely irreversible, impact on Ethiopian society. The old patriarchal social fabric had, in many parts of the country, been fragmented, and a vastly increased, and much more mobile, independent labour force had come into existence.

The Patriots' Resistance

Despite Ethiopia's military collapse in 1935–6, patriotic resistance continued throughout the occupation.[40] Many patriotic Ethiopians were from the outset determined to continue the struggle. The first to do so was Lej Hayla Maryam Mammo, of Dabra Berhan, 130 kilometres north of Addis Ababa, who on 4 May 1936 attacked a group of invading forces on the way to the capital. This action earned him the title the 'first *arbagna*', or, patriot, of Shawa. Other, more or less uncoordinated, attacks on the invaders followed.

In an attempt to crush such opposition Graziani, who had by then become the Italian viceroy, issued an edict in the middle of May, proclaiming that Italy was the 'absolute master of Ethiopia', and would 'remain so at whatever cost'. He threatened that he would use 'extreme severity' towards rebels, but the 'greatest generosity' to Ethiopians who submitted. Mussolini, agreed with this policy, and telegraphed, on 5 June, that 'all rebel prisoners must be shot'.

Undeterred by threats of vengeance numerous Ethiopian patriots determined to fight on. During the rains of 1936 several conceived the ambitious plan of re-capturing Addis Ababa. On 28 July one of the principal young Shawan chiefs, Dajazmach Abarra Kasa, son of Ras Kasa Haylu, attacked from the north-west, but was repulsed by Italian machine-gunning from the air. Almost a month later, on 26 August, one of Emperor Menilek's former commanders, Dajazmach Balcha, launched a further unsuccessful assault from the south-west, which was likewise defeated on account of Italian control of the air. After the rains the invaders resumed the offensive, carrying out extensive bombing, and poison gassing, in Shawa, Lasta, Charchar, Yergalam, and elsewhere.

An attempt on Graziani's life by two Eritreans, Abraha Daboch and Moges Asgadom, on 19 February 1937, opened a new phase of the struggle. The fascists, reacting violently to the attempted assassination of their leader, carried out a three-day massacre in Addis Ababa, in the course of which thousands of innocent Ethio-

[40] On their history see Pankhurst, 1970, pp. 40–56; Shirreff, 1995; and Sykes, 1959.

pians were killed. Many survivors fled the capital, and joined the patriots. Strengthened by this increase in their numbers patriot forces again took the offensive during the 1937 rains, in Lasta under Dajazmach Haylu Kabada, and in Gojjam under Dajazmach Mangasha and Belay Zalaka. Mussolini responded by ordering Graziani to 'use all measures, including gas'. The Viceroy intensified his reign of terror, but, unable to crush the rebellion in Shawa, opened abortive peace negotiations with the area's principal patriot leader, Ras Ababa Aragay.

The occupying forces took the offensive again after the rains, but the patriots did not lose hope. Well aware of the increasing political divergence between the 'totalitarian' and 'democratic' powers in Europe, they were confident that the latter would ultimately be embroiled in a European war and as a result be obliged to come to their assistance. Graziani frankly admitted as much when he observed, on 9 November 1937, that the 'rebels' were awaiting a European war. Some of the patriots at about this time also attempted to forge more integrated resistance, as indicated by the fact that three of the principal Shawan patriot leaders, Lej Zawdé Asfaw, Blatta Takala Walda Hawaryat, and Shalaqa Masfen Seleshi at about this time drew up a manifesto urging the Gojjam people to rally behind them. Graziani, however, continued to insist on repression. Referring to the Shawan patriots, he declared it necessary to 'eliminate them, eliminate them, eliminate them', as he had preached since assuming office.

The patriot movement was centred mainly in Shawa, Bagémder and Gojjam, but drew support from almost all parts of the country. Some of the most resolute fighters included Eritrean deserters from the Italian colonial army. There was also an active underground movement, in Addis Ababa and a few other towns, composed of *wust arbagna*, or 'insider' patriots. They helped to provide military, medical and other supplies to the patriots in the field, and to inform them of enemy movements. Many Ethiopian women, including one of the daughters of Ras Kasa and the renowned Shawaragga Gadlé, were also prominent, either in the field or as *wust* patriots.

Continued patriot resistance was one of the causes of the Viceroy's dismissal, and replacement, on 26 December 1937, by the Duke of Aosta, a member of the Italian royal family. The latter's chief-of-staff, Ugo Cavellero, subsequently admitted that 'large parts' of Shawa and Amhara were then in rebellion, and that 'pockets of resistance' also persisted in the south-west. He added that the 'rebels' enjoyed the 'full support' of the people, who were ready to join them. The extent of opposition to the invaders was confirmed by the exiled Emperor Haile Sellassie, who claimed that patriot resistance was then 'more extensive' than ever before. Menilek's great-grandson, Lej Yohannes Iyasu, himself a patriot, observed that the invader, though in control of the major towns, had been unable to conquer the country.

By 1939, the year of the outbreak of the European war, a stalemate had developed. The Italians had failed to crush the patriots, but the latter were unable to break into the well-guarded Italian forts. Mussolini's son-in-law, Count Ciano, nevertheless noted, on 1 January, 1940 that the Duce was 'very much dissatisfied', for Amhara was in 'complete revolt', and sixty-five Italian battalions were 'compelled' to live in forts. The situation was so serious that the Duke of Aosta advised Mussolini to avoid a European war 'which would bring on the high seas the task of pacifying the country and jeopardize the conquest itself'.[41]

A leading fascist, Arcanovaldo Bonacorsi, reported, in May, that throughout the empire there was 'a state of latent rebellion', which:

> would have its final and tragic denouement when war breaks out with our enemies. If at any point whatever, a detachment of English or French were to enter with banner unfurled they would need little or no troops for they would find the vast mass of the Abyssinian population would unite themselves to that flag to combat and eject our forces. In the case of such an emergency we should find ourselves unable to withstand our enemy given the state of unpreparedness and lack of equipment of our forces'.[42]

Mussolini's Entry into the European War

At the outbreak of the European war, on 3 September 1939, Mussolini refrained from involving himself in the war. He nevertheless declared that fascist Italy, a close ally of nazi Germany, was in a state of 'pre-belligerency'. By that he implied that he was committed to eventually participating in the struggle. By postpon-

[41] Ciano, 1947, pp. 3, 42.
[42] Steer, 1942, pp. 41–2.

ing his entry into the conflict he obviated having to fight with Italy's neighbour, France, and avoided any immediate Allied attack on the insecure Italian East African empire, where the Ethiopian patriots were still unbeaten. After Hitler's victory over France in the early summer of 1940, however, the Duce anticipated that Germany would rapidly win the war. Anxious to participate in an ensuing peace conference he declared war on Britain and France, on 10 June.

Italy's entry into the European war, for which the Ethiopian patriots had long been waiting, had important, and almost immediate consequences, making it a turning point in Ethiopian history. Britain, as a result of Mussolini's action, found itself obliged to modify, if not entirely to abandon, its long-established, pro-colonial, attitude to Italo-Ethiopian relations. The British Government, it will be recalled, had for half a century favoured Italian expansion in Ethiopia. Britain had supported Italy's occupation of Massawa in 1885, and had thereafter consistently sought to accommodate Italian colonial ambitions; by despatching the Portal mission to help the Italians after Ras Alula's victory at Dogali in 1887, by recognizing Italy's Protectorate claim in 1890, by signing the Tripartite Treaty of 1906, by offering Italy a revision of colonial frontiers in 1915, and by participating in the Anglo-Italian démarche of 1925 against which Tafari Makonnen had protested to the League. Britain's policy of accommodation had continued into the immediate pre-war period, with the restriction of arms sales immediately prior to the fascist invasion, the limitation of sanctions against Italy and the Hoare–Laval plan of 1935, and, finally, the recognition of the Italian 'conquest' in 1938.

The opening of hostilities in the summer of 1940 necessarily changed the British perspective. The Italians in East Africa threatened Britain's important sea route to India, and were in a position to overrun three British or British-run territories: Kenya, British Somaliland, and Sudan. The Italians in Libya to the north and in East Africa to the south seemed furthermore poised to occupy Egypt and Sudan, in a pincer operation. This, if successful, would have severed what a contemporary official British publication aptly described as 'the wasp-waist of the British Empire'.[43]

---

[43]   HMSO, 1941. Other accounts of the Liberation campaign include Crosskill, 1980; Glover, 1987.

The Italians in East Africa, almost entirely cut off from metropolitan Italy, and gravely weakened by the activities of the patriots, were, however, in no position to exploit the situation in their favour.

The Liberation Campaign

The first, and easiest, British response to Italy's entry into the European war was to offer assistance to the Ethiopian patriots on the borders of Sudan. The British District Officer at Gedaref, on the Sudanese side of the frontier, immediately despatched twelve already prepared Amharic letters, written in the name of the British commander in Sudan, General Sir William Platt, to patriot chiefs of Gojjam, Armachaho, Walqayt, and Bagémder. These promised the patriots assistance in 'destroying the common enemy'.[44] On 23 June 1940, Emperor Haile Sellassie was flown from England, and shortly afterwards proclaimed, on 2 July that Great Britain would grant Ethiopia 'the aid of her incomparable might'. The promised assistance was, however, far less than the patriots expected. Haile Sellassie, in his autobiography, complained bitterly at its inadequacy, as well as its tardy arrival.

Despite such criticism British help proved of decisive importance. News of it, and of the emperor's arrival in Sudan, had an electrifying effect. Hundreds of Ethiopians trekked across the frontier into Sudan, while many Italian colonial troops deserted.

The British in the months which followed continued to woo the patriots. On 12 August, a British officer, Colonel Daniel Sandford, entered Gojjam, as head of a small Ethio-British mission, Mission 101, to make contact with the patriots, and to encourage them to join together in a common struggle. Several leaders, then torn by rivalry, shortly afterwards agreed to sign a unity pact. On 20 November a more senior British officer, Major-General Orde Wingate, arrived in Gojjam by plane, with promises of speedy, though limited, aid. The patriots, thrilled by his coming, spoke of it as a 'sign from the skies'. A dynamic, if at times controvertial, leader skilled in guerrilla warfare, he had earlier said to General Archibald Wavell, his superior in Cairo: 'Give me a small fighting force of first-class men, and from the core of Ethiopia I will eat

[44] HMSO, 1941, p. 56; Mosley, 1964, p. 249.

into the Italian apple and turn it so rotten that it will drop into our hands'.

Anglo-Ethiopian cooperation bore fruit in the second half of January 1941 when the British launched three major, almost simultaneous, attacks on Italian East Africa. The first began on 19 January, when British and Indian troops under General William Platt crossed the frontier at Kassala into Eritrea. They thus began an attack which took them, with unexpected speed, via Karan, site of a fierce battle, through Eritrea into northern Tegray. The second attack, almost five hundred kilometres to the south, opened on the following day, when a much smaller force of Ethiopians, Sudanese and Britons, led by the emperor, with Wingate and Sandford, raised the Ethiopian flag at the Ethiopian border village of Um Idla. Making contact with the patriots of Gojjam they began an advance to the Blue Nile on the road to Addis Ababa. The third attack, a thousand five hundred miles further south, started four days later, on 24 January, when British and South African soldiers, under the command of General Alan Cunningham, crossed from Kenya into Italian Somalia. They thus began an immense trek via Mogadishu and Harar to Addis Ababa, which they occupied, on 6 April. The advance to the Ethiopian capital, which had taken De Bono and Badoglio seven months in 1935–6, was thus accomplished by the Allies, with patriot help, in little more than three months.

The Victories of the Patriots

The Ethiopian patriots played a major, if at the time perhaps not always sufficiently recognized, role in the Liberation campaign. Throughout their previous four year struggle they had done much to isolate, tie down, and eventually weary, the enemy. On finally receiving British military assistance, they took the offensive and, when provided with British aerial support, swept across Gojjam to play a significant role in the capture of Buryé. The advance of the emperor's patriot army was so rapid that the British high command began to fear that Ethiopian forces might reach Addis Ababa before their British – and South African – allies, and thus endanger the safety of the city's Italian, i.e. fellow European, population. Royal Air Force support for the patriots was for that reason no longer forthcoming.

In Shawa meanwhile, the patriot leader Ras Ababa Aragay, who had fought virtually throughout the entire occupation, now strengthened his position. Addis Ababa, though guarded by Italian garrison troops protected by pill-boxes and barbed wire entanglements, was virtually surrounded by his and other patriot units. The Italians, terrified that the patriots would break into the capital, were seriously demoralized. Rather than fall into the hands of their Ethiopian enemies they hastened, on 4 April, to surrender to the South Africans, who entered the capital two days later. Central Italian resistance thus ended. Mussolini's once triumphant army was reduced to a number of isolated, and beleaguered garrisons.

The emperor, with the patriots, finally entered Addis Ababa, on 5 May 1941, exactly five years after Badogio's capture of the city in 1936. Patriot forces subsequently played an important role in finally 'mopping up' operations throughout Ethiopia, from April to November 1941. They were prominent in the capture of many towns, among them Dasé, Jemma, Goré, Dabra Tabor, and Naqamté. The patriots also took part in scaling the heights of Amba Alagé, where the Duke of Aosta surrendered, on 16 May. A South African soldier, recalling this operation, observed: 'When we, the mighty white conquerors, fell down exhausted, after climbing a few hundred feet', the patriots 'stared at us in amazement; that we were unable to walk unburdened while they ran with loads never failed to astonish them'. The last battle of the war was fought, once more with considerable patriot help, at Gondar, which succumbed to the Allies, on 27 November 1941.

12

Restoration and Revolution

The Italian Legacy

The collapse of fascist rule, the termination of Italian investment, upon which the empire had hitherto been based, the demobilization of colonial soldiers, many still in possession of their weapons, the disruption of the economy, the consequent drying-up of trade, and hence of government revenue, created major problems for newly liberated Ethiopia, in 1941. Neither the emperor, whose pre-war administration had been disbanded five years earlier, nor the British, who lacked any experience of the country, were well equipped to run an efficient post-liberation state. Ethiopian administration was further handicapped by the fact that a significant section of the educated class had died, in some cases massacred, during the occupation, and because education of 'natives' during that period of occupation had largely ceased.

Post-liberation problems were compounded by the Ethiopian Government's virtual inability to raise taxes, as well as by the presence in the country of 40,000 Italian civilians. The latter were enemy nationals, and hence a security risk, but were expected, in accordance with then contemporary racial values, to be provided, as Europeans, with food, and medical facilities, at the level to which they were accustomed.

The politics of the immediate post-liberation era were further complicated by the widespread diffusion of Italian arms, many in the possession of former colonial troops, and by the fragmentation of the Ethiopian elite into three different groups: the Returnees, who had been in exile with the emperor, and were therefore to some extent out of touch with the situation in Ethiopia; the

Collaborators, who had worked with the invaders, and were therefore better informed, but held in disrepute in patriotic circles; and the Patriots, who had played a major role in the liberation, but were generally unfamiliar with modern administration. All three groups expected, and to some extent received, posts in government service, as a reward for past services, or in recognition of their influence, or loyalty to the monarch.

Tensions between the central government and the provinces had to some extent been acerbated by fascist policy, which had tried to divide the 'native' population on both ethnic and religious lines. This disintegrative tendency had, however, been largely counterbalanced by other developments of the occupation period. These included the improvement of roads, and the installation of a public radio address system in the principal towns, as well as an awakened sense of Ethiopian patriotism. The political power of the centre was likewise much strengthened by the triumphant return of the emperor, and by the visible support he received from the British, who in the immediate post-war period enjoyed a virtual monopoly of military power. Like previous rulers he also exercised many forms of patronage, not only, as in the past, in respect of land and political appointment, but now also in the allocation of school places, and scholarships abroad.

Ethio-British Relations

The emperor, after his return to Ethiopia, was primarily preoccupied with relations with the British. The latter, who had entered the country as liberators, had in fact replaced the Italians as an occupying power. Relations between the Ethiopians and the British were from the outset ambiguous. British policy *vis-à-vis* Ethiopia was first enunciated, in general terms, by Foreign Secretary Eden, who told the House of Commons, on 4 February 1941, that his government 'would welcome the re-appearance of an independent Ethiopian State and recognize the claim of Emperor Haile Sellassie to the throne'. Official British policy was further clarified in high-level talks, held shortly afterwards in February and March. These were based, in accordance with Eden's statement, on the 'rejection of any idea of a protectorate', or of 'the provision of a strong western administration of the country'.

After the emperor's return to Addis Ababa, in May, there was, however, considerable tension between the Ethiopians and the British. The two parties differed greatly in their views on the country's future government. The Ethiopians expected to assume full sovereignty without delay, whereas the British considered the country's independence only as a long distance objective. A first clash on this question occurred as early as 11 May 1941, when the emperor appointed his first post-war cabinet. The British representative, Brigadier Maurice Lush, sternly informed him that such appointments could not be made 'until a peace treaty has been effected with Italy'. Haile Sellassie was, not surprisingly, indignant. A compromize was, however, duly effected, whereby the British accepted the appointment of the ministers, but 'chose to regard them as merely advisors' to the British military administration of the country.

Tension was further increased by the decision of the British military authorities to appropriate, and take out of the country, some of the principal factories earlier installed by the Italians, as well as weapons, and military and other transport. Ethiopia was thus very visibly empoverished by its liberators, who soon came to be popularly regarded as its looters. Friction was also created by the presence, in the Ethiopian capital, of white South African troops, who attempted to perpetuate the strict colour bar earlier instituted by the Italians.

British opinion in relation to Ethiopia's independence varied greatly. Sir Philip Mitchell, the chief British Political Officer in the Middle East, sought to impose particularly strong control over Ethiopia, but others in London took the view that Great Britain should demonstrate to the world that it could liberate a country without imposing political strings. Sir Philip, because of his official position, was nevertheless able to press the emperor to abide by British 'advice' in 'all important matters, internal and external, touching the government of the country'; to levy taxes and allocate expenditure only with 'prior approval' of the British Government; to grant British courts jurisdiction over foreigners; 'to raise no objection' if the British Commander-in-Chief 'found it necessary to resume military control over any part of Ethiopia'; and not to raise armed forces, or undertake military operations, 'except as agreed by His Majesty's Government's representative'. Taxation, expenditure, communications, and the jurisdiction of foreigners were to be under British control. In return for this extensive control he proposed that the emperor be offered a subsidy, British advisors, and the opportunity of discussing proposals for a treaty.[1]

Ethiopia, as a result of its liberation by the British troops, was at this time firmly under British economic as well as political control. The country was incorporated into the British-based Sterling Area, used British East African Shillings, was dependent on a British bank, Barclay's, and was served exclusively by the British Overseas Aviation Corporation (BOAC). Virtually all political power was likewise in the hands of the British military, who went so far as to censor the emperor's private correspondence. The local British officials were so bent on perpetuating their paramountcy that an American Government memorandum of June 1941 bluntly asserted that Britain was seeking to 'establish a protectorate over Abyssinia'.

Some British officials at this period, and for the next few years, moreover sought to partition the country. In the north there were plans to unite parts of Tegray with the adjacent highlands of Eritrea, to form a new state under British protection. In the southeast the British Government proposed incorporating the already British-occupied Ogaden with British-occupied Somalia, to create a Greater Somalia, under British trusteeship. British official thinking also for a time envisaged the partition of Eritrea, with the western portion annexed to the then Anglo-Egyptian Sudan.

Haile Sellassie was unwilling to acquiesce in British hegemony, or to accept the British political agenda. He succeeded in despatching a telegram to Prime Minister Winston Churchill, in London, inquiring why a treaty between Ethiopia and Britain had been so long delayed. The British Premier replied, by way of excuse, that this had been due to a desire to ensure that nothing remained in the draft agreement 'which could be interpreted as interfering with your sovereign rights or with the independence of Ethiopia'. The emperor, determined to spur the British to action, promptly had this reply broadcast on Addis Ababa radio. The Government in London, feeling that further delays were impermissible, thereupon summoned Sir Philip to England, where Churchill and Eden pressed him to come to a speedy agreement with the emperor.

After much bargaining an Anglo-Ethiopian Agreement and Military Convention were duly signed, on 31 January 1942. The treaty recognized Ethiopia as an independent state, and laid down

[1] Spencer, 1984, p. 97.

Restoration and Revolution

that the emperor was free to form a government. Britain's paramount position was, however, officially recognized, and many restrictions were imposed on Ethiopian sovereignty. The agreement thus specified that the British representative was to be *ex-officio* doyen of the diplomatic corps, followed in precedence by the British Commander-in-Chief, East Africa, or his representative. The emperor was obliged to appoint British advisors, a British Commissioner of Police, and British police officers, inspectors, judges, and magistrates. No other foreign advisor could be appointed without consultation with the British. The latter were to be responsible for policing Addis Ababa, and had the right to station their military wherever they deemed necessary.

The Military Convention went further. It permitted the British to assert military control over Addis Ababa and the country's principal towns, and to move their armed forces, and military aircraft, into, out of, and around the country at will. The British military were exempt from the jurisdiction of Ethiopian courts, and could use former Italian state property without payment. The emperor was obliged to requisition and hand over to the British military authorities whatever private property they might require. The radio station, the telephone system, and the railway were to remain under British control. The Ethiopian army was to be trained by a British military mission, and all prisoners-of-war were to be handed over to the British military, who were also to have sole jurisdiction over the repatriation of Italian civilians. The British were, finally, allowed to remain in control of Ogaden, the Somali-inhabited area adjacent to Italian Somalia, which occupied almost a third of the entire country, the Reserved Area, a smaller strip of land adjacent to British Somaliland, and the entire stretch of territory occupied by the Addis Ababa-Jibuti railway.

In return for these considerable concessions the British agreed to provide the emperor with an annual subsidy, amounting to one and a half million pounds Sterling for the first year, a million for the second, half a million for the third, and a quarter of a million for a fourth, if the agreement was still in force at that time.[2]

The emperor and his ministers were deeply concerned, not only at the restrictions on Ethiopian sovereignty, but also at the eco-

[2] Ibid., pp. 98–9; Aklilu Habtewold, 1994, pp. 22–3. For the text of the treaty, and its background as seen from a strictly British point of view, see Lord Rennell of Rodd, 1948, pp. 539–58. See also Mitchell, 1954, pp. 195–208; and compare with the Emperor's own account in Marcus, 1994, pp. 167–76.

nomic consequences thereof. The country was at that time export-
ing more than it imported, and was thus contributing more to the
Sterling area than it received therefrom. The British were thus
profiting from Ethiopian exports, and appropriating resources
which could otherwise have been used on Ethiopian development.
Notwithstanding this manifestly unfair situation the Ethiopian
Government was for several years reluctant to press the British for
any revision of the agreement. This was largely, according to their
American foreign affairs advisor, John Spencer, because they were
afraid that the British might retaliate by reoccupying parts of the
country. This, in the aftermath of the war, could well have led to
the government's political de-stabilization.[3]

Despite such fears the Ethiopian Government eventually decided, on 25 May 1944, to demand a new agreement. Receiving no
reply from the British by 16 August. It threatened to re-occupy
Ogaden and the Reserved Area. The British, towards the end of
September, accordingly despatched an envoy, Lord de la Warr, to
Addis Ababa. In the ensuing talks he stubbornly insisted on the
British retention of Ogaden and the Reserved Area. Tough negotiations followed. At one point he threatened to break off the
talks, and at another warned that the British, if balked in their
objectives, would reoccupy the entire country. A treaty was, however, eventually signed, on 19 December 1944.

In this second Anglo-Ethiopian Treaty the Ethiopians had little
option but to agree to British demands for the continued occupation of the Reserved Area and Ogaden. The emperor's negotiators
nevertheless persuaded the British to accept a reformulation of the
relevant article, Article 7, which accordingly declared:

> In order as an Ally to contribute to the effective prosecution of the
> war, and without prejudice to her underlying sovereignty, the Impe-
> rial Ethiopian Government hereby agree that, for the duration of
> the agreement, the territories designated as the Reserved Area and
> the Ogaden . . . shall be under British Military administration.

This formula, from the Ethiopian point of view, was more
cleverly devized than the British negotiators perhaps realized. The
use of the word 'ally' implied that the country could no longer be
treated as 'occupied enemy territory', that it was entitled to a seat
in any future peace conference, and that the British occupation of

---

[3] Spencer, 1984, pp. 141–4.

the two territories was only temporary, to last no more than the duration of the war. The reference to Ethiopia's 'underlying sovereignty' was also significant. It enabled the Ethiopian Government immediately to re-assert its rights by granting an American concern, the Sinclair Company, an oil concession over the area.

In the rest of the treaty the British waived their earlier insistence on diplomatic precedence, abandoned their extra-territorial military privileges, and relinquished their control over the Addis Ababa-Jibuti railway, and their monopoly over aviation. The treaty thus marked the full resumption of Ethiopian independence. It was, however, symbolic of the emperor's displeasure that he did not sign the agreement, but relegated this onerous task to his Prime Minister, Makonnen Endalkachew. Haile Sellassie also, significantly, rejected any further subsidy from Britain.[4]

Britain's motive in retaining Ogaden became apparent in the Spring of 1946, when the British Foreign Secretary, Ernest Bevin, proposed that the territory be joined to ex-Italian Somalia and placed, together with British Somaliland, under British trusteeship. His government further suggested that Ethiopia, bereft of Ogaden, should be given compensation in Eritrea. This Greater Somalia plan, as it was called, was immediately rejected by the Ethiopian Government, and ran into strong Soviet opposition. Soviet Foreign Minister Molotov declared that the scheme was designed to 'expand the British Empire at the expense of Italy and Ethiopia, and to consolidate the monopolistic position of Great Britain in the Mediterranean and the Red Sea'.[5]

Faced with such fierce opposition, Britain abandoned its hold on most of Ogaden in 1948, but retained the fertile grazing land of Haud until 1954, when the entire region was at last returned to Ethiopia. This was a full two decades after the region's first alienation by fascist Italy at the time of Wal Wal.

Post-War Reconstruction and Ties with the United States

The 1940s and early 1950s constituted an important period of post-war reconstruction. Decrees designed for the most part to

[4] Ibid., pp. 139–57.
[5] For documentation on evolving Soviet attitudes to Ethiopia see Darch 1980.

Plate 24   Modernization reaches the remote countryside: mules at a remote airstrip wait to take passengers the rest of their journey home. Note Ethiopian Airlines' plane in the background. Photo: Ethiopian Airlines.

bring the entire country under centralized, and standardized, administration, were issued as early as 10 March 1942. Dealing with a wide variety of subjects, including significantly enough taxation, they were from that date published regularly, in the *Negarit Gazeta*. They bore the signature of the Minister of the Pen, or official writer of proclamations, which gave them the stamp of imperial authority.

Developments, as the years went by, were based on steadily increasing American economic, military, and other assistance. Ethiopian ties with the United States were symbolized by a meeting between the emperor and President Roosevelt, held by the Suez Canal Bitter Lake at the beginning of 1945. The British Minister in Addis Ababa, Robert Howe, hearing the emperor's Egypt-bound aeroplane flying over his legation, before daylight, at once investigated the cause of the unusual noise. Ascertaining what this was, and perhaps fearing an Ethiopian opening to the United States, he commissioned a small plane to pursue the monarch to Egypt.[6]

Post-war Ethiopian contacts with the United States had in fact

[6]   Spencer, 1984, pp. 159–61.

started three years earlier. A new government bank, the State Bank of Ethiopia, established in 1942, was run at first by an American governor, George Blowers. A new national currency, inaugurated in 1945, owed its successful introduction to the United States. The latter provided the silver needed to mint 50 cent coins, whose intrinsic value ensured popular acceptance of the new paper money. The country's first national air services, Ethiopian Airlines, at first almost entirely American-manned, were set up in close collaboration with the American carrier Trans World Airlines, in 1946. American financial assistance made possible the establishment of an Imperial Highway Authority (IHA). Funded with assistance from the American-sponsored International Bank for Reconstruction and Development (IBRD) it restored the old, and built many new, roads.

An important landmark in Ethio-American relations was the signing by the two countries, on 22 May 1953, of a 25-year Treaty of Amity and Economic Relations. This provided *inter alia* for an American communications base, the Kagnew base as it was called, just outside Asmara, which was by then under Ethiopian rule. Training of Ethiopian soldiers, by a British Military Mission to Ethiopia (BMME), withdrawn in 1951, was carried out, after 1953, by an American Military Assistance Advisory Group (MAAG). American staff, including deans, were prominent in the country's institution of higher learning, Haile Sellassie I University, in educational development and planning, through the United States Point Four Program, and in secondary school teaching, through the US Peace Corps. The majority of Ethiopian students studying abroad, including many members of the military, went to the United States, and Ethiopian soldiers fought, under American command, in the Korean War, of 1950–3.

Continuing, though perhaps less consistently than in Menilek's day, Ethiopia's old policy of avoiding dependence on any one foreign power, Haile Sellassie's government also made use of foreign assistance, and expertize, from other lands. The Air Force, the Imperial Bodyguard, telecommunications, and school-building, were thus entrusted to Swedes, the police to Germans and Israelis, planning to Yugoslavs, and the country's principal Military Academy, at Harar, to Indians. Teachers from the sub-continent were also extensively employed, particularly in the provinces.

This period witnessed many promising developments in the

educational sector. These included the re-opening of pre-war schools, and the establishment of many new ones. The most prestigious schools in the capital were the Haile Sellassie I Secondary School, founded in 1943, and the General Orde Wingate Secondary School, in 1946. Useful teaching was also given at vocational schools, for commerce, handicrafts, and technology. Education, contrary to the situation prior to the war, was now extremely popular. Almost every school had a waiting list for new student intake. The emperor, when driving in his car, was frequently mobbed by children crying, 'School! school!' Increasing numbers of students were sent for study abroad, mainly to English speaking countries; first to Britain, and later to the United States, Canada, and India. The growth of secondary education made possible the establishment, in 1950, of the country's first institution of higher learning, the University College of Addis Ababa. This educational establishment was later merged with other colleges, specializing in agriculture, building, commerce, engineering, public health, technology, and theology, to form the nucleus of Haile Sellassie I University, established in 1961 (later renamed Addis Ababa University). It subsequently also comprised colleges of business administration, education, law, and medicine, a school of social work, and Institutes of Ethiopian Studies, Patho-Biology, and Development Research. The University's administration, and some of the faculties, were housed in the former Imperial Palace, and its well-kept grounds, which the emperor donated for the purpose.

A number of new hospitals were also established. The most prestigious was the country's first modern teaching hospital, named after the emperor's daughter, Princess Tsahay, who had served as a nurse in Britain in 1940, during the London blitz. This institution, founded in 1951, was funded by international subscription, mainly in Britain.[7] A Russian Red Cross hospital was also set up, named after Dajazmach Balcha, who had fought at Adwa, and later in the patriotic resistance to the fascist occupation.

This period witnessed steady, though far from rapid, economic growth, mainly, however, in the capital, and, to a much lesser extent, in a few other towns. Light industries, notably cotton,

[7] On the achievements of this period, see the sympathetic accounts in Sandford, 1946; Sandford, 1955; Talbot, 1955; and Atnafu Makonnen, 1960. Compare the later, more critical, judgement of Addis Hiwet, 1974.

sugar, cement, leather, and printing factories, were established; road, air, and shipping, as well banking and insurance services, were expanded; many hotels and restaurants, shops and trading companies, were established. Commercial agriculture was also developed, mainly in the Arsi province, and in the vicinity of the Jibuti railway. All this led to an unprecedented growth in paid employment, and thereby encouraged urbanization. These developments, coupled with the considerable increase in the number of school and college graduates, brought about a significant change in the country's hitherto largely patriarchal social structure.

International Consideration of the Future of Eritrea

Ethiopian foreign policy, during the post-war years, was preoccupied with the future of the Italian colonies. This was a seemingly intractable question, which led to lengthy international discussions. The Ethiopian Government, for historical reasons, was particularly interested in the disposal of Eritrea. The colony, much of which prior to the late nineteenth century had formed part of Ethiopia, had been the base for two major invasions of the country, in 1895–6 and 1935–6. Acquisition of Eritrea likewise offered access to the sea, for which Ethiopian rulers had long hankered.

The future of Eritrea first came to the fore during the 1941 Ethiopian Liberation Campaign when the British had promised the colony's inhabitants freedom from Italian rule. Later, in October 1944, British Foreign Secretary Eden had declared that the Italian colonial empire in Africa was 'irretrievably lost'. Italy in the Peace Treaty with the United Nations, signed in Paris on 10 February 1947, was accordingly made to surrender its colonies. Their disposal was to be the responsibility of the then four Great Powers, i.e. the Soviet Union, Great Britain, the United States, and France. The treaty laid down, however, that, if they failed to agree within a year, the matter would be transferred to the United Nations General Assembly.

The Four Powers, as it turned out, did not agree. They despatched a joint Commission of Enquiry to the ex-Italian colonies in 1947. It found the Eritrean population divided into three main factions; pro-Ethiopian Unionists, for the most part Christians, who demanded 'reunion' with Ethiopia; adherents of a Muslim

League, strongly opposed to such union; and members of a Pro-Italia party, many of them Italian pensioners, who advocated the restoration of Italian rule. The commissioners, whose findings reflected the political biases of their respective governments, produced divided conclusions and recommendations. The question of the colony's future was then transferred to the United Nations, which, after inconclusive discussion, appointed a further commission of enquiry for Eritrea. Its members came from Burma, Guatemala, Norway, Pakistan, and South Africa. Opinion in the ex-colony had by then crystallized into two factions: the Unionists on the one side, and an Independence block, formed by a coalition of the Muslim League and pro-Italia party, on the other. The new commissioners, like their predecessors, came forward with different proposals. Guatemala, representing the pro-Italian position, then held by the Latin American countries, and Pakistan, a strong protagonist of Islam, both favoured independence for the colony; Burma and South Africa, supported its federation with Ethiopia; and Norway, outright union.

The UN General Assembly influenced by the proposals of the three latter powers, finally decided, at the end of 1950, that Eritrea should be federated with Ethiopia, under the Ethiopian Crown. The Assembly further laid down that it would appoint a commissioner for Eritrea, and that an Eritrean assembly would be democratically elected by the people. The first task of the latter body was to approve an Eritrean Constitution, to be drafted by a UN Commissioner in consultation with the then British administration of the territory as well as the Ethiopian Government. The Eritrean Assembly was duly elected, under UN auspices, and chose the Unionist leader, Tadla Bayru, as the territory's Chief Executive. This gave the federation a stamp of popular approval. The Eritrean Constitution was likewise drafted, and approved, in 1952. The text was, not surprisingly, considerably more democratic than Ethiopia's old 1931 Constitution.

Relations with Italy

The Italian Peace Treaty of 1947, which explicitly applied to the period from Mussolini's invasion of the country, on 3 October 1935, also included articles of direct relevance to Ethiopia. Provision was thus made for Italy to return all loot taken from Ethiopia.

Most of the loot was eventually returned. At least three gold crowns, which had been in Mussolini's personal possession at Dongo at the time of his attempted escape to Switzerland, in April 1944, however, mysteriously disappeared, and were not returned. Despite many Ethiopian attempts to secure its restoration a twenty-four metre high fourth-century stone obelisk, looted from the ancient Ethiopian city of Aksum, and placed by Mussolini in front of the Ministry of Italian Africa building (later the UN Food and Agriculture building) has not been repatriated at the time of our going to press in 2000.

The treaty also provided for Italy to pay Ethiopia up to 25 million US dollars as war reparations. These were largely spent in the erection, in the next few years, of a hydro-electric plant at Koka, south-east of the capital, a cotton factory at Bahr Dar, by Lake Tana, and several small ships.

The treaty likewise provided for the trial of Italians guilty of war crimes in Ethiopia. Attempts by the Ethiopian Government to prosecute Badoglio, Graziani and others whom it accused of having committed war crimes were, however, in one way or another frustrated.

Cordial diplomatic relations between the two countries were nonetheless eventually re-established in 1956. Despite much wrangling over the implementation of the Peace Treaty, and memories of fascist atrocities, the Italians were perhaps post-war Ethiopia's most favoured foreign community.

Political and Legal Reform and African Affairs

The 1950s and 1960s witnessed notable developments in the Ethiopian political, legal, and economic fields. Realization of the inadequacy of the then existing Ethiopian Constitution, and comparison with the more progressive UN Eritrean Constitution of 1952, led to the formulation in 1955 of a Revized Ethiopian Constitution. Reportedly having taken six years to draft, it was a lengthy document, which outlined in detail the respective powers of the executive, i.e. the emperor's government, the legislature, and the judiciary. The legislature was for the first time to include a fully elected Chamber of Deputies, side by side with a Senate nominated by the emperor. Provision was made for freedom of speech and of the press, in terms which were, however, to prove unenforceable. Despite the Constitution's liberal veneer the government remained essentially autocratic. Real power was retained by the emperor, whose person was, as in the previous constitution, declared 'sacred'. The Constitution's enactment was followed, in 1957, by Ethiopia's first general election, carried out on the basis of full adult suffrage.

Steps were also taken, at about this time, for codification of the law, which the emperor, thinking perhaps of the Code Napoléon, later claimed as the 'supreme accomplishment' of his life. A codification commission was appointed in 1954, after which a penal code, the first of half a dozen modern codes drawn up with the help of Swiss and other foreign experts, was promulgated in 1957. A five-year plan, formulated by Yugoslav advisors, was inaugurated in the same year.[8] A state-sponsored Confederation of Labour Unions (CELU) came into existence in 1962.

The emergence meanwhile of a succession of independent African states, in the late 1950s and early 1960s, enabled the Ethiopian Government, speaking with an authority based on the country's unique history of independence, to involve itself increasingly in the continent's affairs. Many anti-colonialist activists, among them Jomo Kenyatta and Tom Mboya, both from Kenya, visited Ethiopia, and Mau Mau freedom-fighters, also from that country, were given refuge. The emperor granted scholarships for students from parts of Africa under colonial rule to study in Ethiopia. Several dozen, from Kenya and elsewhere, attended the University which bore his name. Nelson Mandela, the future South African leader, received Ethiopian military training. Ethiopian troops played a major role in the Congo (later Zaire) during the difficulties after that country's independence in 1960. Ethiopian diplomats were active in bringing the radical and conservative African states together to found the Organization of African Unity (OAU) in 1963. The emperor used his prestige, as an older statesman, to arbitrate in several inter-African disputes, including those between Algeria and Morocco in 1963, Nigeria and Biafra in 1968–9, and the Sudan government and southern Sudanese rebels in 1972. Ethiopia was likewise responsible, with Liberia, for taking South Africa to the International Court of Justice in an unsuccessful attempt to challenge the legality of the South African occupation of Namibia. Ethiopia in this and other ways acquired

[8] On these and other developments of the period see Clapham. 1969.

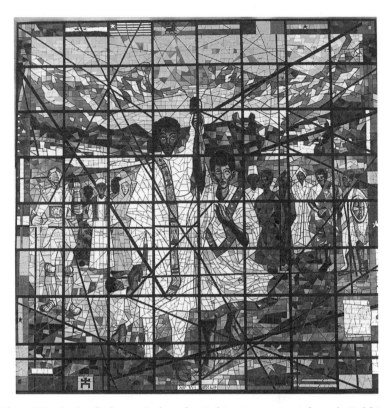

Plate 25   Stained-glass window by Ethiopian artist Afewerk Teklé, at Africa Hall, headquarters in Addis Ababa of the UN Economic Commission for Africa. The picture, entitled 'The Struggle and Aspirations of the African People', measures 150 square metres, and was completed in 1954. Photo: courtesy of the artist.

a unique status in twentieth-century African politics. This led to Addis Ababa being chosen as the permanent headquarters of the United Nations Economic Commission for Africa (ECA) in 1958, and of the Organization of African Unity (OAU) in 1963.

Notwithstanding such interest in African affairs the country's principal economic contacts were at this time with the United States. Ethiopia, in the 1950s and 1960s, was the largest recipient in Africa of American military and civilian aid. Ethiopia also had particularly close relations with Israel, which supplied security and police training, and high-level University personnel. Relations with the Jewish state were, however, reluctantly broken off by the emperor, in 1973, at the insistent behest of the OAU.

Increasing Discontent

Complaints at the slow pace of Ethiopian economic development, which was seen as comparing unfavourably with that of other African countries, and criticism of the emperor's autocratic rule, led to an escalation of political discontent in the late 1950s. During his absence on a state visit to Brazil, in December 1960, his Imperial Bodyguard staged a *coup d'état*. Its master-mind was Garmamé Neway, an American-educated radical and dedicated civil servant, whose brother, Mangestu, happened to be head of the bodyguard. The plotters arrested most of the ministers, including several of the emperor's closest confidants. The *coup* received immediate support from university college students, who demonstrated in its favour. The population as a whole, however, failed to rally behind the insurrection, as Garmamé and Mangestu had hoped. The *coup* was speedily crushed by the army and airforce. Before surrendering, however, the plotters killed most of their ministerial prisoners. The emperor, who, on hearing the news of the rebellion, had immediately decided to return, entered Addis Ababa in triumph. The *coup*'s student supporters on the other hand refused to accept defeat. In the months and years which followed they continued to agitate, and gradually succeeded in permanently politicizing the country's steadily expanding student body.

In Asmara, meanwhile, the Eritrean Assembly voted, under Ethiopian Government pressure, on 14 November 1962, for the territory's complete union with Ethiopia. Eritrea, on the following day, accordingly became an integral part of Ethiopia. The legality of this act was, however, challenged by many Eritreans. Some of them shortly afterwards founded their territory's first militant opposition organization, the Eritrean Liberation Front (ELF).

Discontent in Ethiopia itself was by then markedly on the increase. Students, particularly after 1965, demonstrated against the government more or less regularly each year, with escalating determination. They focused on the need for land reform, with the cry, 'Land to the Tiller!', as well as on the treatment of the capital's beggars, on the alleged corruption of senior officials, on the catastrophic famine of 1972–4 in Tegray and Wallo, which was comparable in intensity only to the Great Famine of the previous century, and on rising prices. Discontent also manifested itself in several small-scale peasant disturbances, mainly in the southern provinces, and in on-going agitation among the trade unions many of whose members thought that their official leadership was too subservient to the government. Many people, even within the ruling elite, were increasingly of the opinion that the mode of government was antiquated. Many were also concerned that Haile Sellassie was not apparently grooming his heir, the Crown Prince, to succeed him.

The emperor, then in his eighties, was by this time increasingly concerned with foreign rather than internal affairs, and had relaxed his previous day-to-day scrutiny and control over the administration. The government, as a whole, was moreover half-hearted in its recognition of the need for reform. It was decided in 1966 that the prime minister, Aklilu Habtawald, instead of the emperor, should chose the cabinet, but this limited constitutional reform failed to change either the composition or the spirit of the administration, and left the government's critics unsatisfied. A landlord–tenant reform bill was presented to Parliament, in 1968, but met with such strong opposition, in the landlord-dominated assembly, that it had not been passed six years later when the revolution erupted.

Despite the emperor's flair for personal diplomacy the country suffered, perhaps unavoidably, from strained relations with neighbouring Somalia. The latter country had come into existence in 1960, through a merger of the former Italian colony of Somalia (which had been for ten years under UN-sponsored Italian Trusteeship) and the former British Somaliland Protectorate. The newly established Somalia state, inspired by the earlier British idea of a Greater Somalia, from its inception claimed the Ethiopian Ogaden, northern Kenya, and the southern half of the French territory of the Afars and Issas, formerly the French Somaliland Protectorate. All three areas were inhabited by ethnic Somalis. Tension between Ethiopia and Somalia peaked in 1964, when an undeclared war broke out, and an OAU cease-fire failed to put an end to continued periodical clashes.

Ethiopian relations with neighbouring Sudan were also often tense. This was largely due to Ethiopian support for the Anya-Nya rebels in the southern Sudan, and Sudanese support for the

Eritrean Liberation Front. Refugees from both sides were placed in camps near the common frontier, thus enabling them to pursue their political agitation and other activities relatively unhampered.

The 1974 Revolution

The failure of the Ethiopian government to solve the country's pressing problems was highlighted by drought and famine in Tegray and Wallo. This had been going on for several years, when news of it broke internationally, in October 1973, and rapidly became common knowledge within the country itself. Revelation of large-scale famine was accompanied by allegations of extensive government inefficiency, and corruption. The famine also led to a considerable rise in food prices. This was followed, early in 1974, by a sharp increase in the price of imported petrol, which threatened an escalation in transport fares, and hence in urban Addis Ababa's cost of living.

This combination of events led, in February 1974, to an unprecedented wave of teacher, student, and taxi strikes. These were accompanied, for the first time in Ethiopian history, by mutinies in the armed forces. They began at Negelli in Sidamo and Asmara in Eritrea, but before long spread, as a result of improved American-supplied military radio communications, throughout the entire empire. The cabinet of Aklilu Habtawald thereupon resigned. It was the first such body ever to do so in the country's history. Members of the armed forces in Addis Ababa, acting at first more or less spontaneously, but later on orders from an elected co-ordinating committee of the armed forces, police, and territorial army, seized control of Addis Ababa radio, and began arresting former ministers. Faced with this critical situation the emperor appointed a new prime minister, Lej Endalkachaw Makonnen (son of former prime minister, Makonnen Endalkachaw). He was a young Oxford-educated aristocrat, whom Haile Sellassie was led to believe had strong support among the military. Many of the latter were reportedly still entirely loyal to the monarch, as well as to the institution of the monarchy. Endalkachaw was given a mandate to carry out far-reaching constitutional and other reforms, which the emperor by then accepted as necessary. A committee of public-spirited civil servants thereupon began the laborious work of drafting a new constitution which was in fact never promulgated. The armed forces meanwhile were given two successive salary rises.

Such measures seemed at first to have stabilized the situation, but in fact failed to satisfy an increasingly influential, and vociferous, radical group within the armed forces. Operating for the most part in great secrecy, they succeeded in gaining control of the co-ordinating committee. Insistent on achieving far-reaching reform, they soon realized that the ageing emperor, and the inexperienced government Endalkachaw had appointed, was in no position to resist their demands. They accordingly dismissed Endalkachaw, and had him replaced by Lej Mika'él Emru, the progressive son of the emperor's progressive cousin Ras Emru, who had resisted the Italian invasion almost forty years earlier. Having detained most of the former ministers, by the summer of 1974, the Committee then began arresting leading aristocrats and close confidants of the emperor, to whom they had until then ostensibly given unqualified allegiance. For the first time since his rise to power the monarch was left without supporters, and virtually helpless.

The committee, whose views were becoming increasingly radicalized, then at last felt itself strong enough to strike against Haile Sellassie himself. Using the Ethiopian media with considerable skill they began by publicizing his involvement in various local and international financial operations, which were presented as outrageous. Then, even most effectively, they showed on Ethiopian television Jonathan Dimbleby's British television film of the Wallo famine, interspersed with clips of luxurious palace banquets, and other aristocratic extravagances. The emperor, who had been ordered to watch the performance, found himself discredited almost overnight and, despite his earlier not unimpressive achievements, rejected by many of his most loyal supporters. He was deposed on the following day, 12 September, symbolically, the morrow of Ethiopian New Year. Thereafter officially referred to as the ex-king, and no more as an emperor, he was unceremoniously driven from his palace to his place of imprisonment, in a Volkswagen, and died in detention eleven months later, probably murdered. The many institutions and streets bearing his name or that of members of his family were renamed.

After seizing power the co-ordinating committee, which was deeply influenced by the country's authoritarian tradition, immediately abrogated the then existing constitution, and dissolved Parliament. In their place the committee established a provisional military government. Civilian ministers, appointed at the beginning of the revolution, were retained for the day-to-day working of the government. Real power, however, was exercized by a Provisional Military Administrative Council (PMAC), generally known as the *Derg*, the Amharic word for a committee. A far from united body, it was composed of 120 men in uniform, privates and junior officers, elected by its various units. The Derg thereupon requested the country's most popular military leader, Lieutenant-General Aman Andom, a patriotic Ethiopian of Eritrean origin, to serve as Head of State, and Chairman of the PMAC. His position was from the outset ambiguous. Some Derg members wanted him as a figure-head, but he assumed that he was to be the real ruler, in the mould perhaps of the Egyptian leader Gemal Abdul Nasser.

The Ethiopian revolution, like other such events in history, was characterized by rapidly evolving alignments, and fierce and ruthless rivalries for power among its leaders and their cohorts. The first serious struggle arose over General Aman's relationship with the Derg. After their seizure of power the Ethiopian armed forces in Eritrea had remained in their barracks, and the Eritrean Liberation Front secessionist forces, mainly based in the territory's western lowlands, had refrained from any action. This *de facto* truce was broken by the explosion of a bomb in an Asmara bar frequented by the army. Some members of the Derg, infuriated by the incident, wanted immediate retaliation, but Aman, anxious to preserve Eritrean support, insisted on a more moderate approach. Differences of opinion as to his powers *vis-à-vis* the Derg now came to the fore. Angered by a succession of slights to his authority he withdrew to his house, from which he attempted to summon supporters from army units outside the capital. He was called upon to attend a Derg meeting, but, because of a confusion, failed to do so. This angered many Derg members. Some felt themselves, and their cause, seriously threatened. They angrily decided, on 23 November, to bring Aman 'to reason', and at the same time to execute the principal ministers and other high officials then in detention. That evening Aman's house was attacked, a shoot-out followed, and a few hours later two Derg members, and fifty-seven former high-ranking civilian and military officials were executed. The Derg thereupon chose another officer, Brigadier-General Tafari Banti, as a nominal chairman and Head of State. Real power rested, however, with two vice-chairmen, Major Mangestu

Hayla Maryam, and Lieutenant-Colonel Atnafu Abata. The Death
of the Sixty, as it was called, thereafter cast a dark shadow over
what had until then proudly been referred to as Ethiopia's blood-
less revolution.

The Socialist Experiment

The aftermath of the revolution witnessed the return to Ethiopia
of many left-wing intellectuals, mainly Marxists. They grouped
themselves into two main Marxist factions, or parties. The first,
comprizing youngsters mainly from the north of the country, not
a few of whom had studied in the United States, was the Ethiopian
People's Revolutionary Party (EPRP). It accepted the principle of
Eritrean secession, was ideologically opposed to military government, and demanded an immediate return of civilian rule. The
other group, composed largely of Oromos, many of whom had
studied in Europe, and particularly France, was the All Ethiopian
Socialist Movement (AESM), better known by its Amharic ititials
MEISON. It believed that cooperation with the military, particularly in the early stages of a revolution, could advance the cause
of socialism, and therefore argued in favour of close, if qualified,
collaboration with the Derg.[9]

The PMAC, influenced largely, but not exclusively, by
MEISON, came to conceive itself, in dogmatic terms, as the van-
guard of the revolution. On 20 December 1974 it declared the
country a socialist state, and, in 1975, its first year of power,
carried out a series of revolutionary reforms, based on what it
termed the principle of *Ityopya Tikdem*, or Ethiopia First. Over a
hundred businesses, including banks, insurance companies, and
factories, were nationalized, or partly taken over by the state.
Rural and urban land, and so-called 'extra houses', i.e. any more
than one, which was alone permitted to a single family, were also
nationalized. Over 30,000 peasants' associations were set up in
rural areas, besides several hundred *kebeles*, or associations of
urban dwellers, in Addis Ababa and other towns. Both institutions, which had elected leaders, formed part of an extensive
bureaucratic hierarchy, which extended from the 'grass roots' to

[9] For an inside account of the Ethiopian student movement, and its political
ramifications, see Kiflu Tadesse, 1993.

the national level. Thousands of university and senior secondary school students were compulsorily despatched all over the country, on a national development campaign, to preach the gospel of revolution, as well as to organize health, literacy, and land reform programs. Many producers' co-operatives and a smaller number of communal farms were set up. A literacy campaign was launched. Though costly, and inefficient, particularly in the absence of sufficient reading materials, it nevertheless did much to raise the status, and self-esteem, of under-privileged members of Ethiopian society. The campaign was internationally much praised, notably by UNESCO. Such developments coincided with a steady increase in the influence of one of the two Derg vice-chairmen, Mangestu Hayla Maryam, who in 1975, began to over-shadow other PMAC members.

The revolution advanced a further stage, in April 1976, when MEISON, operating apparently in close collaboration with the Derg, launched a much publicized national democratic revolution programme. This envisaged the establishment of a Russian-style workers' party, and the introduction of scientific socialism. In the following month the MEISON leaders opened a political office, the Provisional Office for Mass Organisational Affairs (POMOA) and a political, or ideological, School. A succession of civil servants were inducted into it for socialist orientation.

Mangestu's steadily increasing influence was resented by some Derg members, who towards the end of 1976 reorganized the committee's structure in order to oust him from power. However, he staged a come-back, in February 1977. Tafari Banti and five other prominent Derg members were executed. Mangestu thereupon at last became Derg Chairman, and Head of State. Soon after this meteoric rise to power he came into conflict with MEISON, whose leaders fled the capital, in July, and were mostly killed soon afterwards. Mangestu's deputy, and former co-vice chairman, Atnafu Abata, was later executed, in November.

These struggles, and clashes of ideology, took place in an unstable, and fast changing, political and military situation. The Derg, whose army had been incapacitated by the arrest or execution of its commanding officers, by then faced two major external challenges: from Eritrean secessionists, in the north, and from a Somali Government-backed insurrection, and invasion, in the south and south-east.

The ELF, which was based in the Muslim west of Eritrea, and

a splinter, or rival, organization, the Eritrean People's Liberation Front (EPLF), centred more in the Christian highlands, collaborated in a joint attack on Asmara, which they almost captured, in January 1975. The Derg responded with a brutal counter-attack, which greatly increased popular support for secession, particularly among the Christian highlanders. The Derg thereupon raised a 20,000 strong 'people's army', which the two Eritrean Liberation Fronts easily defeated. Their armies, by the end of 1977, had taken control of virtually all Eritrea, except for five towns; Asmara, the ports of Massawa and Asab, Barentu in the far west, and Adi Qayeh in the south. Mangestu then raised a much larger militia force, of almost a third of a million men. They were trained within six months in 1977, with the help of Cubans, who had by then been persuaded to consider Ethiopia a socialist ally.

Some of the new recruits were despatched northwards to hold on to Eritrea, but the majority were rushed to the south-east, in accordance with Mangestu's slogan, 'Everything to the war front'. Several years of ethnic Somali insurgency in Ogaden, led by a Western Somalia Liberation Front (WSLF), had been followed, in July 1977, by an invasion of Ethiopia by the armed forces of neighbouring Somalia. This aggression, and skilful diplomacy on the part of the Ethiopians, caused the Soviet Union, hitherto a close ally, and military patron, of Somalia, to switch sides, in favour of Ethiopia. The United States, which had formerly supported Ethiopia, by contrast, refrained from throwing itself on the side of Somalia.

The invaders threatened both Harar and Dire Dawa, in November, but were eventually repulsed. This change in fortune owed much to Ethiopian superiority in the air, and to an improvement in Ethiopian morale, as well as to a massive, and internationally much publicized influx of Soviet weapons, tanks and aircraft. Over 15,000 Cuban and a few South Yamani troops also participated on the Ethiopian side. The forces of this grand alliance went onto the offensive, in February 1978, after which the Somalis were soon obliged to withdraw from Ethiopian territory.

This victory, which many observers had not expected, enabled the by then greatly strengthened Ethiopian army to take the offensive in Eritrea, in June. Derg forces rapidly recaptured most of the territory, except in the west where the ELF continued stubborn guerrilla resistance, and at Nacfa, in the far north, where the EPLF ensconced itself in impregnable mountains. The defenders successfully repulsed several enemy attacks. One was a much vaunted 'Red Star Operation', personally commanded by Mangestu, which suffered immense casualties.

After his victories in Ogaden and Eritrea, Mangestu, by then virtually Ethiopia's absolute ruler, and no longer beholden to MEISON, began reorganizing the country on his own state social-ist lines. Acting slowly, but methodically, he established a Com-mission for Organising the Party of the Working People of Ethiopia (COPWE) in 1979. It was based on individual members, almost three-quarters of whom were military men, chosen for their loyalty. In the following year a Revolutionary Ethiopian Women's Association (REWA), and a Revolutionary Ethiopian Youth Asso-ciation (REYA), were set up. Then, in 1982, the All Ethiopia Peasant Association (AEPA), and the All Ethiopia Trade Union (AETA), were both reorganized, on party lines. Finally, in Septem-ber 1984, a Workers' Party of Ethiopia (WPE) was inaugurated. Imposed largely from above, its leadership came mainly from the military. Members were, however, recruited from all parts of the country, including the peripheral regions. The party's ideology was largely borrowed from the Marxist intellectuals, whose own organizations had by then been destroyed in the revolutionary turmoil.[10]

The unfolding of the revolution had meanwhile led to a major switch in Ethiopia's international alignments. United States criti-cism, early in 1977, of the regime's human rights record, coupled with Ethiopian dissatisfaction at the level of American military assistance, caused Mangestu to break with Washington, and turn increasingly to Moscow. The socialist states of Eastern Europe, and North Korea, were perceived as a valuable source of economic and military assistance. Though some Ethiopian students contin-ued to go to the West for further studies the Soviet Union and its allies became the countries to which the majority were despatched. Ethiopian trade links with the United States on the other hand, continued, and Ethiopian Airlines, though pressed to adopt Soviet aircraft, continued to purchase Boeings. Mangestu's pro-Soviet position, like Lej Iyasu's pro-German stance three generations earlier, was, however, in the long run doomed on account of

[10]   On the complexities of the Ethiopian Revolution see D. and M. Ottoway, 1978; Halliday and Molyneux, 1981; Lefort, 1983; Harbeson, 1988; Clapham, 1988; Andargachew Tiruneh, 1993; and Teferra Haile-Selassie (1997).

factors entirely external to the country, in this case the world-wide fall of communism.[11]

The WPE meanwhile proceeded to draw up a socialist constitution, which was endorsed by a national referendum, in February 1987. A national Shango, or Legislature, was subsequently elected, and a People's Republic of Ethiopia was proclaimed in September. Mangestu, who by then enjoyed absolute power, perhaps reminiscent of that earlier wielded by Haile Sellassie, became President, Chief Executive, Commander-in-Chief, and Chairman of the Council of Ministers. Government, which was consistently repressive, and bureaucratic, was officially based on the principle of 'democratic centralism'. Five 'autonomous regions' were, however, devized, for Tegray, Dire Dawa, Ogaden, Asab, and Eritrea.

The last years of Mangestu's rule were from the economic point of view disastrous. Another catastrophic drought, in 1984–5, was followed by the second major famine within a generation. Despite unparalleled world media attention, assistance from abroad was tardy. Hundreds of thousands of people died.[12] The Government's over-hasty resettlement campaign to transfer 600,000 inhabitants to more fertile land in the south encountered bitter, and at times misconceived, international opposition, and was eventually abandoned. Some 200,000 refugees from Tegray were, however, conveyed to Sudan, under TPLF auspices, and 30,000 Falashas to Israel, the majority in two main aerial 'operations', named after Moses and Solomon respectively. An Ethiopian government villagization programme, designed to move inhabitants of scattered homesteads into organized villages, failed, largely because the expected health and other services were not provided. Government-sponsored communal farms proved excessively bureaucratic, and from the economic standpoint largely unviable.

Foreign aid for the Third World throughout this period came mainly from the West. Economic assistance by the ex-colonial powers, Britain and France, was largely directed towards their former dependencies, to the exclusion of Ethiopia. The latter was

[11]   Superpower rivalries in the Horn, which lie beyond the scope of the present study, are discussed in Marcus, 1983; Makinda, 1987; Hagos Mehary, 1989; Patman, 1990; and Henze, 1991.
[12]   On the phenomenon of famine in this period, see Mesfin Wolde Mariam, 1984; Janssen, Harris and Penrose, 1987; and Dawit Wolde Giorgis, 1989.

thus, so to speak, punished for the 'crime' of having maintained its age-old independence. Western aid for Ethiopia was moreover largely restricted, for political reasons, to emergency, or 'humanitarian' help. Development aid was not forthcoming, even though, by banishing poverty, it could in the long run have been perhaps even more 'humanitarian' than that so designated.

Opposition to the Derg and the Fall of Mangestu

Opposition to the Derg began early. The killing of the Ministers and others, in November 1974, was followed by several minor aristocrat-based local rebellions. These did not attract much support. A more broadly-based right of centre party, the Ethiopian Democratic Union (EDU), was more successful. Based in London, it was led by several prominent figures of the pre-revolutionary past, among them Lieutenant-General Iyasu Mangasha, an Eritrean and former Ethiopian ambassador in London, Ras Mangasha Seyum, a grandson of Emperor Yohannes IV and former governor of Tegray, and Brigadier-General Negga Tagagn, a grandson-in-law of the emperor. Their organization, which operated freely in Sudan, offered armed opposition in western Ethiopia, but was soon defeated by the Derg's much better equipped armed forces.

Opposition also came, perhaps more importantly, from the Left, i.e. from the EPRP, which attempted to organize urban guerrilla resistance to the Derg. The latter, initially supported by the EPRP's rival Marxist organization, MEISON, responded, in 1977, by arming 'revolution defence squads'. It then launched a 'Red Terror' against what it termed the 'White Terror' of the EPRP. This was the bloodiest period of the revolution, when thousands of people, including countless students were killed, and tortured in Addis Ababa, and other urban centres, and when shooting was often heard, particularly in the market area. The struggle ended with the Derg's victory over both Marxist groups, which were largely destroyed.

The collapse of the emperor's highly centralized government in 1974 had meanwhile led to the emergence of a number of ethnically based regional liberation parties, or movements. The most important spoke in the name of the Tegray, Afar, Oromo, and Somali peoples. The most active of these ethnic, or regional, organizations was the Tegray People's Liberation Front (TPLF). A Leftist organization, founded in 1975, it grew rapidly in importance. Part of its success sprang from the fact that it was able to operate fairly freely across the Sudan frontier, and received support, in training and arms, from EPLF guerrillas, in nearby Eritrea. Afar opposition began with a rebellion by the traditional Afar ruler, Sultan Ali Mirreh, and led to the foundation, in 1975, of an Afar Liberation Front (ALF), which was, however, opposed by a rival pro-Derg Afar National Liberation Front (ANLF). Oromo opposition found expression in an Oromo Liberation Front (OLF). A significantly weaker organisation than the TPLF, it drew most of its support from western Wallaga, whence its fighters could seek asylum in nearby Sudan. Somali opposition was represented by two organizations; the afore-mentioned WSLF, operating mainly in Somali-occupied Ogaden, and a Somali Abo Liberation Front (SALF), in partially Somali-inhabited Balé and Sidamo.

Though Mangestu's armies held their own against the liberation forces throughout the late 1970s and early 1980s, economic difficulties, and continuous, and seemingly endless, and often unsuccessful, fighting, led in the course of time to bitter discontent among the military. A substantial number of the country's senior officers attempted a *coup d'état*, in May 1989, against Mangestu. When it failed he ruthlessly had them executed. This intensified discontent, and outright opposition, among the soldiers, many of whom had by then lost the will to fight. The EPLF in Eritrea and the TPLF in Tegray both achieved major victories in the field.

Mangestu's government, by then facing collapse, abandoned its earlier centralizing policy, and offered a considerable measure of regional autonomy. The liberation fronts, however, found these last-minute proposals unacceptable.

The TPLF, having made itself the master of Tegray, joined with Amhara, Oromo and other opposition elements, to form an Ethiopian Peoples' Revolutionary Democratic Front (EPRDF), which toward the end of 1990 began its historic march on Addis Ababa. The EPLF meanwhile also took the offensive, and for the first time in the struggle captured Massawa, in February, thereby isolating the Ethiopian army in Eritrea. Mangestu, faced with the economic and military disintegration of his regime, and the fall of his allies in Eastern Europe, adopted a sudden change of policy. He abandoned Ethiopian socialism, took down a large Soviet-built statue of Lenin formerly erected in front of the ECA building, and announced his belated acceptance of market forces. This move was, however, too late. The armies of the liberation front accelerated their advance on the capital, whose defenders had by then largely ceased to fight. Mangestu, seeing the impossibility of his position, secretly fled the capital by 'plane, on 21 May 1991. He flew first to Nairobi, and then to Zimbabwe, where he was given asylum. Seven days later the triumphant EPRDF forces entered Addis Ababa, with the blessing of the United States.

This victory opened a new chapter in Ethiopia's age-old history.

Bibliography

Abir, M., *Ethiopia: The Era of the Princes. The Challenge of Islam and the Re-unification of the Christian Empire 1768–1855* (London, 1968).

Addis Hiwot, *Ethiopia: From Autarchy to Revolution* (London, 1974).

Aklilu Habtewold, *Aklilu Remembers, Historical Recollections from a Prison Cell* (Uppsala, 1994).

Aloisi, P., *Journal* (Paris, 1957).

Andargachew Tiruneh, *The Ethiopian Revolution* (Cambridge, 1993).

Anfray, F., *Les anciens Ethiopiens* (Paris, n.d.).

Annequin, G., De quand datent l'église actuelle de Dabra Berhan Sellasé de Gondar et son ensemble de peintures? *Annales d'Ethiopie*, 10 (1976), 215–26.

Annesley, G., Viscount Valentia, *Voyages and Travels in India, Ceylon, the Red Sea, Abyssinia and Egypt*, 3 vols (London, 1809).

Appleyard, D. L. et al., *Letters from Ethiopian Rulers (Early and Mid-Nineteenth Century)* (London, 1985).

Arnold, P., *Prelude to Magdala. Emperor Theodore of Ethiopia and British Diplomacy* (London, 1991).

Atnafu Makonnen, *Ethiopia Today* (Tokyo, 1960).

Baer, G., *The Coming of the Italian–Ethiopian War* (Cambridge, Mass., 1947).

Bahru Zewde, *A History of Modern Ethiopia 1855–1974* (London, 1991).

Bahru Zewde, R. Pankhurst and Tadaese Beyene, *Proceedings of the Eleventh International Conference of Ethiopian Studies* (Addis Ababa, 1994).

Bairu Tafla (ed.), *Aṣma Giyorgis and His Work. History of the Gāllā and the Kingdom of Šawā* (Stuttgart, 1987).

Bairu Tafla, *A Chronicle of Emperor Yoḥannes IV (1872–89)* (Wiesbaden, 1977).

Bairu Tafla, *Ethiopia and Germany. Cultural, Political and Economic Relations, 1871–1936* (Wiesbaden, 1981).

Barker, A. J., *The Civilising Mission. The Italo-Ethiopian War 1935–6* (London, 1968).

Barradas, M., *Tratatus Tres Historico-Geographici (1634)*. *A Seventeenth Century Historical and Geographical Account of Tigray, Ethiopia*, trans. E. Filleul (Wiesbaden, 1996).

Barrett, L., *The Rastafarians* (London, 1977).

Basset, R., Etudes sur l'histoire d'Ethiopie. *Journal Asiatique*, 17 (1881).

Basset, R. (trans.), *Histoire de la conquete de l'Abyssinie (XVIe siècle) par Chihab ed-din Ahmed ben 'Abd el-Qader surnommé Arab-Faqih* (Paris, 1897).

Beckingham, C. F. and Huntingford, G. W. B. (trans.), *The Prester John of the Indies*, 2 vols, Hakluyt Society (Cambridge, 1961).

Beckingham, C. F. and Huntingford, G. W. B. (ed. and trans.), *Some Records of Ethiopia, 1593–1646*, Hakluyt Society (London, 1954).

Beke, C. T., *The British Captives in Abyssinia* (London, 1867).

Berhanou Abebe, *Evolution de la propriété foncière au Choa (Ethiopie) du règne de Ménélik à la constitution de 1931* (Paris, 1971).

Berkeley, G. F.-H., *The Campaign of Adowa and the Rise of Menelik* (London, 1935).

Blanc, H., *A Narrative of Captivity in Abyssinia* (London, 1868).

Breasted, J. H., *Ancient Records of Egypt* (New York, 1962).

Breasted, J. H., *A History of Egypt* (New York, 1905).

Bruce, J., *Travels to Discover the Source of the Nile*, 5 vols (Edinburgh, 1790).

Budge, E. A. Wallis, *A History of Ethiopia. Nubia and Abyssinia*, 2 vols (London, 1928).

Budge, E. A. Wallis, *The Queen of Sheba and her Only Son Menyelek* (London, 1922).

Burgoyne, C., Lost month in Ethiopia. *Ethiopia Observer*, 11 (1967), 249–326.

Buxton, D., *The Abyssinians* (London, 1970).

Caraman, P., *The Lost Empire. The Story of the Jesuits in Ethiopia 1555–1634* (London, 1985).

Cerulli, E., *Storia della lettatura etiopica* (Rome, 1956).

Churchill, W., *The Gathering Storm* (London, 1948).

Ciano, G., *The Ciano Diaries 1939–1943* (New York, 1947).

Clapham, C., *Haile-Selassie's Government* (London, 1969).

Clapham, C., *Transformation and Continuity in Revolutionary Ethiopia* (Cambridge, 1988).

Clark, J. D., A Review of the Archaeological Evidence for the Origins of Food Production in Ethiopia. *Proceedings of the Eighth International Conference of Ethiopian Studies* (Addis Ababa, 1984), I, 55–69.

Conti Rossini, C., *Historia Regis Sarṣa Dengel*, CSCO (1907), 2 vols.

Conti Rossini, C., *Italia ed Etiopia dal trattato d'Uccialli alla battaglia di Adua* (Rome, 1935).

Conti Rossini, C., Iyāsu I re d'Etiopia e martire. *Rivista degli Studi Orientali*, 20 (1942), 65–128.

Conti Rossini, C., *Storia d'Etiopia* (Bergamo, 1928).

Conzelman, W. E., Chronique de Galāwdēwos (Claudius) roi d'Ethiopie (Paris, 1895).

Crawford, O. G. S. (ed.), Ethiopian Itineraries ca. 1400–1524, (Cambridge, 1958).

Crosskill, W. E., The Two Thousand Mile War (London, 1980).

Crummey, D., Priests and Politicians. Protestant and Catholic Missions in Orthodox Ethiopia 1830–1868 (Oxford, 1972).

Darch, C., A Soviet View of Africa. An Annotated Bibliography on Ethiopia. Somalia and Djibouti (Boston, 1980).

Davies, N. N. de G., The Egyptian Expedition of 1934–35. Bulletin of the Metropolitan Museum of Art, 30 (1935), Section II.

Davies, N. M. and N. de G., The Tomb of Amenmose. The Journal of Egyptian Archaeology, 26 (1940), 131–6.

Dawit Wolde Giorgis, Red Tears, War, Famine and Revolution in Ethiopia (Trenton, New Jersey, 1989).

De Bono, E., Anno XIIII, The Conquest of an Empire (London, 1937).

Del Boca, A., The Ethiopian War 1935–1941 (Chicago, 1965).

Del Boca, A., I gas di Mussolini. Il fascismo e la guerra d'Etiopia (Rome, 1996).

Del Boca, A., Mussolini sulla guerra di Etiopia. Il Giorno, 11–15 November 1968.

Diamantini, C. and Patassini, D., Addis Ababa, Villaggio e capitale di un continente (Milan, 1993).

Diodorus, Diodorus of Sicily, ed. G. H. Oldfather, 12 vols (London, 1917).

Donzel, E. V. van, A Yemenite Embassy to Ethiopia 1647–1648 (Stuttgart, 1986).

Dufton, H., Narrative of a Journey through Abyssinia (London, 1867).

Dye, W. McE, Moslem Egypt and Christian Abyssinia (New York, 1880).

Erlich, H., Ethiopia and the Challenge of Independence (Boulder, Colorado, 1986).

Erlich, H., Ethiopia and the Middle East (Boulder, Colorado, 1994).

Evetts, B. (ed. and trans.), The Churches and Monasteries of Egypt and Some Neighbouring Countries (Oxford, 1895).

Farago, L., Abyssinia on the Eve (London, 1935).

Fattovich, R., Remarks on the pre-Aksumite period in Northern Ethiopia. Journal of Ethiopian Studies. 23 (1990), 1–33.

Foster, W., The Red Sea and Adjacent Countries at the Close of the Seventeenth Century (London, 1949).

Funke, M., Sanktionen und Kanonen. Hitler, Mussolini und der internazionale Abessienkonflikt 1934–36 (Düsseldorff, 1970).

Fusella, L., Abissinia e Metemma in un scritto di Bĕlāttā Ḫĕruy. Rassegna di Studi Etiopici, 2 (1943), 200–13.

Gamst, F. C., The Qemant. A Pagan-Hebraic Peasantry of Ethiopia (New York, 1969).

Gaudefroy-Demombynes, M. (trans.), Ibn Fadl Allah al 'Umari, Masālik el abṣār fi mamālik el amṣār, 2 vols (Paris, 1927).

Gentizon, P., *La conquête de l'Ethiopie* (Paris, 1936).

Gerster, G., *Churches in Rock. Early Christian Art in Ethiopia* (London, 1970).

Gill, D., *The Coinage of Ethiopia, Eritrea and Italian Somalia* (New York, 1991).

Girma Bashah and Merid Wolde Aregay, *The Question of the Union of the Churches in Luso-Ethiopian Relations (1500–1632)* (Lisbon, 1964).

Glover, M., *An Improvised War. The Abyssinian Campaign of 1940–1941* (London, 1987).

Greene, D. (trans.), *The Complete Tragedies* (Chicago, 1959).

Griaule, M., Une victoire de la civilisation. *Vu* (July 1936).

Grierson, R. (ed.), *African Zion. The Sacred Art of Ethiopia* (New Haven, 1993).

Guèbrè Sellassié, *Chronique du règne de Ménélik II roi des rois d'Ethiopie*, 2 vols (Paris, 1931–2).

Guidi, I., *Annales Iohannis, 'Iyāsu I et Bakāffā*, 4 vols (CSCO, 1903).

Guidi, I., *Annales Regum 'Iyasu et 'Iyo'as*, 2 vols (CSCO, 1910–12).

Guidi, I., Le canzone geez amariñña in onore di re abissini. *Rendiconti dell Reale Accademia dei Lincei*, 5 (1889), 53–66.

Guidi, I., *Il 'Fetha Nagast' o 'Legislazione dei Re'*, 2 vols (Rome, 1897–9).

Guidi, I., *Vocabolario amarico-italiano* (Rome, 1901).

Hagos Mehary, *The Strained US–Ethiopian Relations* (Stockholm, 1989).

Haile M. Larebo, *The Building of an Empire: Italian Land Policy and Practice in Ethiopia, 1935–1941* (Cambridge, 1994).

Halliday, F. and Molyneux, M., *The Ethiopian Revolution* (London, 1981).

Hancock, G., *The Sign and the Seal. A Quest for the Lost Ark of the Covenant* (London, 1992).

Harbeson, J. W., *The Ethiopian Transformation. The Quest for the Post-Imperial State* (London, 1988).

Harris, B., *The United States and the Italo-Ethiopian Crisis* (Stanford, California, 1964).

Head, S. (ed.), *Documents on International Affairs 1935* (London, 1937).

Hecht, E.-D., Ethiopia Threatens to Block the Nile. *Azania* 23 (1988), 1–10.

Henze, P. B., *Aspects of Ethiopian Art from Ancient Axum to the 20th Century* (London, 1993).

Henze, P. B., *Ethiopian Journeys. Travels in Ethiopia 1969–72* (London, 1977).

Henze, P. B., *The Horn of Africa from War to Peace* (London, 1991).

Hertslet, E., *The Map of Africa by Treaty*, 2 vols (London, 1894).

Hitti, P. K., *History of the Arabs* (London, 1951).

HMSO, *The Abyssinian Campaigns* (London, 1941).

Holland, T. J. and Hozier, H. M., *Record of the Expedition to Abyssinia* (London, 1870).

House of Commons, *Correspondence respecting Abyssinia 1848–1868* (London, 1868).

Houtsma, M. T., *The Encyclopedia of Islam* (Leiden, 1913–38).

Huntingford, G. W. B., *The Glorious Victories of 'Amda Ṣeyon King of Ethiopia* (Oxford, 1965).
Huntingford, G. W. B., *The Historical Geography of Ethiopia From the First Century AD to 1704* (London, 1989).
Huntingford, G. W. B., *The Periplus of the Erythraean Sea* (London, 1980).
Hyatt, H. M., *The Church of Abyssinia* (London, 1928).
Ickes, H. J., *The Secret Diary of Harold J. Ickes* (London, 1955).
Isenberg, C. W. and Krapf, J. L., *Journals Detailing their Proceedings in the Kingdom of Shoa* (London, 1843).
Italy, Atti Parlamentari. *Documenti Diplomatici, Etiopia.* vols. XV, XVbis, XVII, XVII-bis, XVIII, XXVIII, XXVIII-bis (Rome, 1889–96).
Janssen, K., Harris, M. and Penrose, A., *The Ethiopian Famine* (London, 1987).
Jeffery, A., *The Foreign Vocabulary of the Qur'an* (Baroda, 1938).
Johanson, D. C. and Edey, M. A., *Lucy. The Beginnings of Mankind* (London, 1981).
Kiflu Tadesse, *The Generation* (Trenton, New Jersey, 1993).
Kitchin, K. A., Punt and How to Get There. *Orientalia*, 40 (1971), 184–207.
Korn, D. A., *Ethiopia, the United States and the Soviet Union* (London, 1986).
Labanca, N., *In marcia verso Adua* (Turin, 1993).
Lefort, R., *Ethiopia: An Heretical Revolution?* (London, 1983).
Lejean, G., *Voyage en Abyssinie* (Paris, 1872).
Levine, D. N., *Greater Ethiopia. The Evolution of a Multiethnic Society* (Chicago, 1974).
Lewis, B., *Race and Slavery in the Middle East: A Historical Enquiry* (New York, 1990).
Littmann, E., *The Legend of the Queen of Sheba in the Tradition of Axum* (Leiden, 1904).
Littmann, E. et al., *Deutsche Aksum-Expedition*, 4 vols (Berlin, 1913).
Lockot, H. W., *The Mission. The Life, Reign and Character of Haile Sellassie I* (London, 1989).
Ludolphus, J., *A New History of Ethiopia* (London, 1684).
McCall, D. F. Dragon-slayers and Kingship. *Ethiopia Observer*, 12 (1968), 34–43.
McCrindle, J. W. (trans.), *The Christian Topography of Cosmas, an Egyptian Monk* (London, 1897).
McE. Dye, W., *Moslem Egypt and Christian Abyssinia* (New York, 1880).
Makinda, S. M., *Superpower Diplomacy in the Horn of Africa* (London, 1987).
Maqrizi, *Histoire des sultans mamlouks de l'Egypte*, trans. E. Quatremère (Paris, 1840).
Marcus, H. G., *Ethiopia, Great Britain, and the United States, 1941–1974* (Berkeley, California, 1983).
Marcus, H. G., *Haile Sellassie I. The Formative Years, 1892–1936* (Berkeley, California, 1987).

Marcus, H. G. (ed. and trans.), *Haile Sellassie I. My Life and Ethiopia's Progress* (East Lansing, Michigan, 1994).

Marcus, H. G., *The Life and Times of Menelik II. Ethiopia 1844–1913* (Oxford, 1975).

Mathew, D., *Ethiopia. The Study of a Polity* (London, 1947).

Mérab, P., *Impressions d'Ethiopie* (Paris, 1922–9).

Mesfin Wolde Mariam, *Rural Vulnerability to Famine in Ethiopia 1956–1977* (New Delhi and Addis Ababa, 1984).

Mitchell, P., *African Afterthoughts* (London, 1954).

Mockler, A., *Haile Sellassie's War* (London, 1984).

Mohammed Hassen, *The Oromo of Ethiopia: A History* (Cambridge, 1990).

Molvaer, P. K. (ed. and trans.), *Prowess, Piety and Politics. The Chronicle of Abeto Iyasu and Empress Zewditu of Ethiopia (1909–1930). Recorded by Aleqa Gebre-Igzizbher Elyas* (Cologne, 1994).

Monti della Corte, A. A., *I castelli di Gondar* (Rome, 1938).

Monti della Corte, A. A., *Lalibelà* (Rome, 1940).

Moreno, M. M., La cronaca di re Teodoro attribuita al dabtarà 'Zaneb'. *Rassegna di Studi Etiopici*, 2 (1942), 143–80.

Mosley, L., *Haile Sellassie. The Conquering Lion* (London, 1964).

Muir, W., *The Life of Mahomed* (London, 1878).

Munro-Hay, S., *Aksum. An African Civilisation of Late Antiquity* (Edinburgh, 1991).

Munro-Hay, S., The Rise and Fall of Aksum: Chronological Considerations. *Journal of Ethiopian Studies*. 23 (1990), 47–53.

Munro-Hay, S. and Juel-Jensen, B., *Aksumite Coinage* (London, 1995).

Mussolini, R., *My Life with Mussolini* (London, 1959).

Naville, E., *The Temple of Deir-el-Bahari* (London, 1894).

Nelson, K. and Sullivan, A., *John Melly of Ethiopia* (London, 1937).

Nkrumah, K., *The Autobiography of Kwame Nkrumah* (London, 1957).

Olderogge, D. A., L'Arménie et l'Ethiopie au IV siècle (à propos des sources de l'alphabet arménien, Accademia Nazionale dei Lincei. *Problemi Attuali di Scienze et di Cultura*, 191, (1974), I, 295–303.

Ottoway, D. and M., *Ethiopia. Empire in Revolution* (New York, 1978).

Pakenham, T., *The Mountains of Rasselas* (London, 1959).

Pankhurst, E. S., *Ethiopia. A Cultural History* (Woodford Green, Essex, 1955).

Pankhurst, R., The Béta Esra'él (Falashas) in their Ethiopian Setting. *Israel Social Sciences Research*, 10, 2 (1995), 1–12.

Pankhurst, R., *Economic History of Ethiopia 1800–1935* (Addis Ababa, 1968).

Pankhurst, R., An eighteenth-century Ethiopian dynastic marriage contract between Empress Mentewab of Gondar and Ras Mika'el of Tegre. *Bulletin of the School of Oriental and African Studies*, 42 (1979), 457–64.

Pankhurst, R., The Emperor Theodore and the question of foreign artisans in Ethiopia. *Boston University Papers on Africa, African History*, 2 (1966), 215–35.

Pankhurst, R., Ethiopia, the Aksum Obelisk, and the Return of Africa's cultural heritage. *African Affairs, 98* (1999), 229–39.

Pankhurst, R., The Ethiopian patriots: the lone struggle 1936–1940. *Ethiopia Observer*, 13 (1970), 45–56.

Pankhurst, R., Fear God, Honor the King: The Use of Biblical Allusion in Ethiopian Historical Literature. *NorthEast African Studies* (1986), 8, 1, 11–30; 9, 1, 25–88.

Pankhurst, R., The foundations of education, printing, newspapers, book production, libraries and literacy in Ethiopia. *Ethiopia Observer*, 6 (1962), 241–90.

Pankhurst, R., *History of Ethiopian Towns from the Middle Ages to the Early Nineteenth Century* (Wiesbaden, 1982).

Pankhurst, R., *An Introduction to the Economic History of Ethiopia from Early Times to 1800* (London, 1961).

Pankhurst, R., On Two Portuguese Folios in a Medieval Ethiopic Manuscript. *The Book Collector* (Winter, 1986), 463–74.

Pankhurst, R., Reminiscences of banking in Ethiopia on the eve and beginning of the Italian fascist invasion. In Bahru et al., *Proceedings of the Eleventh International Conference of Ethiopian Studies* (Addis Ababa, 1994), I, 217–31.

Pankhurst, R., *A Social History of Ethiopia* (Addis Ababa, 1990).

Pankhurst, R., Some notes for the history of Ethiopian secular art. *Ethiopia Observer*, 10 (1966), 5–80.

Pankhurst, R., *State and Land in Ethiopian History* (Addis Ababa, 1966).

Pankhurst, R. and Germa-Selassie Asfaw, *Tax Records and Inventories of Emperor Téwodros of Ethiopia (1855–1868)* (London, 1978).

Pankhurst, R. and Ingrams, L., *Ethiopia Engraved* (London, 1988).

Paribeni, R., Richerche nel luogo dell'antica Adulis, Monumenti Antici, *Reale Accademia dei Lincei*, 18 (1907), pp. 438–202.

Parkyns, M., *Life in Abyssinia* (London, 1853).

Patman, R. G., *The Soviet Union and the Horn of Africa* (Cambridge, 1990).

Paulos Tsadua, *The Fetha Nagast. The Law of the Kings* (Addis Ababa, 1968).

Perham, M., *The Government of Ethiopia* (London, 1969).

Perruchon, J. (trans.), *Les chroniques de Zar'a Ya'eqôb et de Ba'eda Mâryâm* (Paris, 1893).

Perruchon, J., *Vie de Lalibala, roi d'Ethiopie* (Paris, 1892).

Photius, *Photius, Bibliothèque*, trans. P. Henry, 2 vols (Paris, 1959–74).

Plant, R., *The Architecture of the Tigre, Ethiopia* (Worcester, 1985).

Pliny, *Natural History*, trans. and ed. E. H. Rackham (London, 1947–56).

Portal, G. H., *My Mission to Abyssinia* (London, 1892).

Powell-Cotton, P. H. G., *A Sporting Trip through Abyssinia* (London, 1902).

P.R.O. = Public Record Office, Kew.

Prouty, C., *Empress Taytu and Menelik II. Ethiopia 1883–1910* (Trenton, New Jersey, 1986).

Quatremère, E., *Mémoires géographiques et historiques sur l'Egypte et sur quelques contrées voisines* (Paris, 1811).

Quirin, J., *The Evolution of the Ethiopian Jews. A History of the Beta Israel (Falasha) to 1920* (Philadelphia, 1992).

Rennell of Rodd, Lord, *British Military Administration of Occupied Territories in Africa* (London, 1948).

Rey, C. F., *In the Country of the Blue Nile* (London, 1927).

Rey, C. F., *Unconquered Abyssinia as it is to-day* (London, 1923).

Rinck, F. T. (trans.), *Macrizi, Historia Regum Islamiticorum in Abyssinia* (Leiden, 1790).

Rochet d'Héricourt, C. E. X., Voyage dans l'Abyssinie méridionale. *Revue des Deux Mondes*, 27 (Paris, 1841).

Rosenfeld, C. P., The medical history of Menelik II, Emperor of Ethiopia (1844–1913): A case of medical diplomacy. *Munger Africana Library Notes*, 45–6 (1978).

Rossetti, C., *Storia diplomatica dell'Etiopia durante il regno di Menelik II* (Turin, 1910).

Rostovtzeff, J. M., *The Social and Economic History of the Hellenistic World* (Oxford, 1941).

Rubenson, S. (ed.), *Acta Aethiopica I. Correspondence and Treaties 1800–1854* (Addis Ababa, 1987).

Rubenson, S. (ed.), *Acta Aethiopica II. Tewodros and His Contemporaries 1855–1868* (Addis Ababa, 1994).

Rubenson, S., *King of Kings. Tewodros of Ethiopia* (Addis Ababa, 1966).

Rubenson, S., *The Survival of Ethiopian Independence* (London, 1976).

Rubenson, S., *Wichale XVIII. The Attempt to Establish a Protectorate over Ethiopia* (Addis Ababa, 1964).

Rufinus, *Historia Ecclesiastica*, ed. J.-P. Migne (Paris, 1849).

Rüppell, W. P. S. E., *Reise in Abyssinien*, 2 vols (Frankfurt, 1838–40).

Salt, H., *A Voyage to Abyssinia* (London, 1814).

Salvemini, G., *Prelude to World War II* (London, 1953).

Sandford, C., *Ethiopia under Hailé Sellassié* (London, 1946).

Sandford, C., *The Lion of Judah hath Prevailed, being the Life of His Imperial Majesty Haile Sellassie I* (London, 1955).

Säve-Söderberg, T., The Navy of the Eighteenth Dynasty. *Uppsala Universitet Arsskrift*, 6 (1946), pp. 1–94.

Schoff, W. H. (trans.), *The Periplus of the Erythraean Sea* (London, 1912).

Sergew Hable Sellassie, *Ancient and Modern Ethiopian History to 1270* (Addis Ababa, 1972).

Shirreff, D., *Bare Feet and Bandoliers. Wingate, Sandford, the Patriots and the Part they Played in the Liberation of Ethiopia* (London, 1995).

Smith, D. Mack, *Mussolini's Roman Empire* (London, 1976).

Spencer, J. H., *Ethiopia at Bay: A Personal Account of the Haile Sellassie Years* (Algonac, Michigan, 1984).

Steer, G. L., *Caesar in Abyssinia* (London, 1936).

Steer, G. J., *Sealed and Delivered* (London, 1942).

Sykes, C., *Orde Wingate* (London, 1959).
Taddese Beyene, R. Pankhurst, Shiferaw Bekele, *Kasa and Kasa. Papers on the Lives, Times and Images of Téwodros II and Yohannes IV (1855–1889)* (Addis Ababa, 1990).
Taddesse Tamrat, *Church and State in Ethiopia 1270–1527* (Oxford, 1972).
Talbot, D. A., *Haile Sellassie I. Silver Jubilee* (Amsterdam, 1955).
Tedeschi, S., *Nuova luce sui rapporti tra Venezia e l'Etiopia (secolo XV)* (Addis Ababa, 1974).
Teferra Haile-Selassie, *The Ethiopian Revolution 1974–1991. From a Monarchical Autocracy to a Military Oligarchy* (London, 1997).
Tekeste Negash, *Italian Colonialism in Eritrea, 1882–1941: Policies, Praxis and Impact* (Uppsala, 1987).
Tekeste Negash, *No Medicine for the Bite of a White Snake. Notes on Nationalism and resistance in Eritrea, 1890–1940* (Uppsala, 1987).
Tellez, B., *The Travels of the Jesuits in Ethiopia* (London, 1710).
Tomasselli, C., *Con le colone celeri dal Mareb allo Scioa* (Milan, 1936).
Toy, B., *In Search of Sheba* (London, 1961).
Trimingham, J. S., *Islam in Ethiopia* (London, 1952).
Ullendorff, E. (trans.), *The Autobiography of Emperor Haile Sellassie I. 'My Life and Ethiopia's Progress' 1892–1937* (London, 1976).
Ullendorff, E., *Ethiopia and the Bible* (London, 1968).
Ullendorff, E., *The Ethiopians. An Introduction to Country and People* (London, 1973).
Ullendorff, E. and Beckingham, C. F., *The Hebrew Letters of Prester John* (London, 1982).
Vychill, W., Notes on the Story of the Shipwrecked Sailor. *Kush*, 5 (1957), 183–4.
Waldmeier, T., *Erlebnisse in Abessinien* (Basle, 1896).
Walker, C. H., *The Abyssinian at Home* (London, 1933).
Watt, W. M., *Muhammad at Mecca* (London, 1953).
Waugh, E., *Remote People* (London, 1931).
Weld Blundell, W., *The Royal Chronicle of Abyssinia 1769–1840* (Cambridge, 1922).
Whiteway, R. S., *The Portuguese Expedition to Abyssinia in 1541–1543* (London, 1902).
Wilson, H. R., *Diplomat between Wars* (London, 1941).
Work, E., *Ethiopia. A Pawn in European Diplomacy* (New York, 1936).
Wright, W., *Catalogue of the Ethiopic Manuscripts in the British Museum acquired since the Year 1847* (London, 1872).
Wylde, A. B., *Modern Abyssinia* (London, 1901).
Zervos, A., *L'empire d'Ethiopie. Le miroir de l'Ethiopie moderne 1906–1936* (Alexandria, 1936).
Zewde Gabre-Sellassie, *Yohannes IV of Ethiopia. A Political Biography* (Oxford, 1975).

Index